OneStream Fundamentals

Ricky Parkash

OneStream Press

Published in 2026 by OneStream Press.

Copyright (c) 2026 OneStream Software LLC, Ricky Parkash

OneStream and the OneStream logo are trademarks of OneStream Software LLC, www.OneStream.com, and used with permission.

ISBN: 978-1-0683338-1-1

OneStream Press has endeavored to provide trademark information about all the companies and products mentioned in this book by the appropriate use of capitals. However, OneStream Press cannot guarantee the accuracy of this information. OneStream Press is an imprint of Play Technologies (England) Limited. 6 Woodside, Churnet View Road, Oakamoor, ST10 3AE, United Kingdom.

www.OneStreamPress.com

Disclaimer

While the advice and information in this book is believed to be true and accurate at the date of publication, OneStream Press, the authors, and OneStream Software LLC do not guarantee the accuracy, adequacy, or completeness of any information, and are not responsible for any errors or omissions or the results obtained from the use of such information.

OneStream Press, the authors, and OneStream Software LLC make no warranty, express or implied, with respect to the material contained herein, and hereby disclaim any liability to any party for any loss, damage, or disruption caused by errors or omissions, whether such errors or omissions result from negligence, accident, or any other cause.

The example organization – Top Training Inc. – used in this book is fictitious. Any resemblance to similarly named businesses or business matters is purely coincidental.

About the Author

Ricky Parkash FCCA is a Senior Instructor in the OneStream global education team. A qualified accountant, he worked in financial and management accounting for both the public and private sectors early in his career. He then became a development accountant, implementing SAP globally for Nestle, and taught business and finance part-time at a local college whilst authoring business and accounting books. Ricky has been a consultant and trainer for various IBM corporate performance management platforms, achieving top talent status and multiple recognition awards, and also authoring two IBM corporate performance management books. He later led the enablement team for an Anaplan partner. Ricky's experience includes consolidation and planning projects, and he now teaches OneStream to corporations worldwide.

Acknowledgements

I would like to extend my gratitude to the immediate team who have supported me throughout the writing of this book. I am thankful to James Lumsden-Cook for presenting the idea, and to Amanda, the publishing manager at OneStream, for offering a clear roadmap. My appreciation goes to Peter Fugere for inspiring me to become a published author with OneStream after just one meeting. I also wish to thank Eric Hanson, Nick Bolinger, and Chul Smith for their insightful reviews and profound expertise in the OneStream domain; my managers Nick Redford and Craig Cason for their support, encouragement, and providing me with the time to write; and my OneStream mentors – Matt Grundey, Carlo Testoni, and Tom Linton – and the rest of the training team.

I also want to acknowledge my wife, Meera, for her support during the writing of this book and throughout my career in performance management, which required frequent travel away from home. Her companionship has been invaluable.

Technical Reviewers

Nick Bolinger is a Distinguished Architect on the OneStream services team with an MBA and 15 years of experience in the corporate finance space. Joining OneStream in 2016, his entire tenure has been dedicated to designing and developing solutions for companies of all sizes and complexities. Nick is an active member in the OneStream community and has been featured on Tech Talks, Podcasts, Webinars, and publishes articles in his spare time. His goal is to help empower OneStream users everywhere to gain efficiencies and unlock their full potential with the platform.

As a Senior Field Product Manager at OneStream, **Eric Hanson** brings hands-on implementation experience and strategic product insight. Since joining OneStream in 2021 as a Senior Consultant, he has played a pivotal role in delivering innovative solutions for some of the company's largest and most complex customers. With a deep understanding of the platform – first as a customer and then as a consultant – Eric became a Director in 2024 and led a high-performing implementation team, known for executing some of OneStream's most successful projects.

In 2025, Eric transitioned into the product space to help shape the future of the platform, leveraging years of field experience to inform product strategy and development. As a certified Lead Architect (OSP), he brings technical depth and a customer-first mindset to every initiative. Passionate about solving real-world challenges and driving innovation, Eric continues to bridge the gap between customer needs and product vision, ensuring OneStream evolves in ways that truly empower its users.

Chul Smith has over 25 years of accounting, finance and IT experience using, maintaining, implementing and supporting consolidation and finance systems as both client and consultant. In 2006, he moved from corporate consolidations in Minneapolis, MN, to HFM consulting in Paris, France. In 2007, he relocated to London, England where he spent the next four years consulting with a small Swedish IBM Cognos Controller consultancy. The use of Controller across Europe expanded his work experience to nine countries in multiple industries.

His 2012 United States homecoming triggered his return to HFM & FDM as a freelance consultant with projects in New York City, Montreal, and Sherbrooke, Quebec. He began working with OneStream in 2013 and a year later, was hired to join their services team. Today, he's a Distinguished Architect within OneStream's Strategic Customer Advisory team.

Chul holds a Bachelor of Science in Accounting from the University of Minnesota – Carlson School of Management and a non-practicing CPA license in the state of Minnesota.

Errata

Despite best efforts, mistakes can sometimes creep into books. If you spot a mistake, please feel free to email us at **errata@OneStreamPress.com** (with the book title in the subject line).

The errata page for this book is hosted at
www.OneStreamPress.com/Fundamentals

Version Updates

The OneStream platform is constantly evolving, with each release bringing new features and capabilities. The majority of the material in this book covers the OneStream Platform Version of at least 8.4.

25% OFF VOUCHER

Certification

Validate your technical competence and gain industry recognition with OneStream Software.

In purchasing this book, you are eligible to claim a 25% discount on any OneStream Certification Exam.

To request your voucher, open a case with Credentialing via the ServiceNow Support Portal (https://onestreamsoftware.service-now.com/).
Include proof of purchase that contains your name and address, the book title, date of purchase, and proof of payment.

onestream

Contents

Chapter 1: Become One with OneStream   1

Why Learn OneStream?   1

What is Corporate Performance Management?   1

OneStream and the Office of Finance   2

Where Does OneStream Knowledge Come From?   3

What Role Should Do Which Course?   4

    Project Manager   5

    Developer   5

    Administrator   6

    Report Writer   7

    Subject Matter Expert (SME)   7

Other OneStream Resources to Extend Your Knowledge   8

OneStream Artifacts   8

    Dimensions   9

    Cube   10

    FX Rates   10

    Import   10

    Forms   10

    Journals   11

    Transformation Rules   11

    Confirmation Rules   11

    Certification Questions   11

    Cube Views   11

    Dashboards   11

    Spreadsheets   11

    Report Books   11

    Extensible Documents   11

    Workflow   11

    Security   11

Other OneStream Components to Understand Before We Dive In   12

  OneStream and Consolidation   12

  OneStream and Planning   12

  OneStream's Extensibility Feature Used in Planning   13

    Extended Capabilities   14

Let's Look Ahead in This Book   15

Conclusion   16

Chapter 2: The Learning Begins: Fasten Your Seatbelt   **17**

OneStream's High-Level Learning Road Map   17

User Interface   18

  Creating a New Application   19

Let's Talk About Dimensions and Members   20

  Members Hierarchies   21

    Parent Member   22

    Child Member   22

    Base Member   22

    Sibling Member   22

    Ancestors   23

    Descendants   23

Dimensions Make a Cube   24

  Cube Point of View (POV)   26

Working Through a Workflow   27

  Typical Workflow Tasks   30

  Lowest (Base) Level Tasks   30

    Import   30

    Validate   30

    Load   30

    Forms   30

    Pre-Process   30

    Journal Input   31

Next Level Up Tasks   31

    Process   31

    Confirm   32

    Workspace   32

    Certify   32

  Highest Level Tasks: Multi-Period Processing   33

  Corporate Only Workflow Requirement Option   33

Reporting Overview   34

  Cube Views   34

  Dashboards   34

  Extensible Documents   35

  Spreadsheets   36

  Report Books   37

Application Properties and FX Rates   37

  Foreign Exchange Currencies   39

Security   40

  User   40

  Group   40

  Role   41

  Object   41

  Piecing Security Together   41

Conclusion   43

Chapter 3: Dimensions, Dimensions and More Dimensions   **45**

Designing Dimensions   45

Members and None Member   47

The Dimension Library And Configurable Dimensions   48

  Entity Dimension   49

    Entity And Consolidation Process   50

    Entity Business Areas and Alternate Hierarchies 50

  Scenario Dimension   52

Account Dimension   56

Flow Dimension   59

User Defined (UD) Dimensions   59

Configurable Dimensions Outside the Dimension Library   60

Parent Dimension   60

Intercompany Dimension   60

Time Dimension   61

Consolidation Dimension   62

Top   62

Currencies   63

Analysis   63

System-Defined Dimensions   63

Origin Dimension   63

View Dimension   64

Building Dimensions   66

Naming Conventions and Creating Dimensions and Members   66

Using The Grid View for Multiple Configurations   70

Importing Dimension And Members   71

Member Properties   72

Constraints Member Property   72

Conclusion   73

Chapter 4: Cubes (Hexahedrons Sounds Smarter)   **75**

Let's Make Cubes   75

Super Cube Linked to Detail Cubes   76

Exclusive Cube   76

Monolithic and Specialty Cubes   76

Building a Cube   77

Don't Forget Your Cube Properties Tab   77

Pick Your Dimensions Carefully in the Cube Dimensions Tab   80

Cubes References Tab   81

Data Access Tab 82

Integration Tab 82

Did Someone Mention Data Units? 84

Let's Fall in Love with Extensibility 85

Vertical Extensibility 86

Horizontal Extensibility 88

Existing OR New Cube? That is the Question! 88

Conclusion 89

Chapter 5: Importing That All-Important Data **91**

Data Import Preparation 91

Knowing Your Data Source Types 92

Fixed Files 92

Delimited Files 92

Connectors 92

Data Management Export Sequences 92

Creating a Data Source 93

Creating a Delimited File Data Source 93

Assigning Dimensions To Source File 94

Creating a Fixed File Data Source 99

Matrix Data Source 100

Transformation Rules 101

Types of Transformation Rules 102

One-To-One 102

Composite Mapping 103

Range 103

List 103

Mask 104

Creating Transformation Rules in OneStream – Groups and Profiles 104

Preview Of When The Import Setup Is Used 105

Summary of Data Source and Transformation Rule Process 106

Conclusion   106

Chapter 6: Figuring Out Calculations   109

What is a Calculation in OneStream   109

  Stored Calculations   110

  Dynamic Calculations   111

What Are Rule Types And Expressions   112

Business Rules   112

Member Formulas   113

Cube View Calculations   114

  GetDataCell Expression   115

    Divide Function   116

    Variance Function   116

    VariancePercent Function   116

  api.data.calculate Expression   116

  Column / Row Expressions   117

Understanding The Syntax and Functions   118

Other Areas Using Calculations   119

  The View Dimension   119

  Account Type and Aggregation Weight   120

  Calculation, Translation, Elimination, Consolidation 121

    Calculate   121

    Translate   121

    Consolidate   121

  Calculation Status   123

How Calculations Are Run   123

  Cube View Icons   124

  Data Management Job   125

    Workflow Profiles – Calculation Definitions 127

  Other Options Where A Calculation Can Be Run From   127

    Dashboard Button   127

Data Unit Calculation Sequence (DUCS) 128

Handling All The Calculations 128

    Calculation Documentation Matrix 128

    Application Reports And Administrator Solution Tool 129

Conclusion 129

Chapter 7: Let Your Workflow **131**

How a Workflow Helps Bring It Together 131

    The Purpose of Workflow 131

    Workflow Profile Types 131

        Base Input Profiles 132

        Parent Input Profiles 132

        Review Profiles 133

Constructing The Workflow 134

    Profile Properties 137

        Security 137

        Workflow Name 137

        Profile Active 139

        Data Source and Transformation Profile Name 139

        Input Forms Profile Name 140

        Journal Template Profile Name 141

        Confirmation Profile Name 142

        Certification Profile Name 144

        Intercompany Matching Settings 146

    Calculation Definitions 148

    Entity Assignment 149

        Workflow Suffix 150

Keep A Workflow Template Handy 151

Conclusion 153

Chapter 8: Reporting Part 1 – Show Me The Data!   155

Report Types   155

    Cube Views   156

Building a Cube View for Top Training Inc.   158

    POV Slider   160

    General Settings Slider   161

    Report Header   162

    Rows and Columns Slider   162

        Overrides   163

    Report Footer   164

Copying a Cube View   164

Running The Cube View   165

    Data Cell Values   166

Calculations In Cube Views   167

Data Spreading Options   169

    Even Distribution   169

    Fill   170

    445 or 454 or 544 Distribution   170

    Factor   171

    Accumulate   171

    Proportional Distribution   171

Substitution Variables and Parameters   172

    Substitution Variables   172

    Parameters   173

        Member List   174

        Member Dialog   174

        Delimited List   174

        Input Value   174

        Literal Value   174

        Bound List   174

Formatting The Cube View   175

Formatting Using a Literal Parameter   177

Conditional Formatting   178

Suppression Formatting   179

Spreadsheet   180

OneStream Login   180

Refresh and Submit Sections   180

Calculation Section   180

Explore and Analysis Sections   180

Spreading   180

Quick Views In Spreadsheets   181

Cube Views In Spreadsheets   182

Which Spreadsheet Option To Use?   184

Report Books   184

Best Place To Store Data For Reporting   186

Conclusion   188

Chapter 9: Reporting Part 2 – Show Me Even More Data!   **189**

Dashboards   189

The Power of Dashboards and Introducing Genesis   189

The Genius of Genesis   190

Installing Genesis Could Not Be Easier   190

The Genesis Framework   191

Application Groups   192

Navigation Groups   193

Pages   193

Content Blocks   194

Showcasing Genesis   195

Home Page   196

Cube View Advanced   197

Cube View Charts   198

Cube View Spreadsheet   199

Dashboard Layouts	199
KPI Tile	201
Pivot Grid	201
Spreadsheet Tree	202
Link an Existing Content item from a Shared Workspace	202
Colors and Styles	203
Genesis Can Make You a Star	203
Dashboard Overview in Workspaces	204
Here are the main pieces now laid out on the table	205
Logo	205
Label	205
Combo Box	205
Button	206
Chart (Advanced)	206
BI Viewer	206
Image	207
Data Adapter	207
Three Ways To Get To One Dashboard	208
Designing A Dashboard	208
Dashboard Layout	209
Grid	209
Tabs	209
Uniform	210
Horizontal Stack Panel	210
Vertical Stack Panel	210
Constructing A Dashboard	210
Workspaces	210
Maintenance Unit	211
Dashboard Groups	211
Cube View Groups	212
Components	213

Data Adapters   213

Parameters   213

Piecing It All Together   214

Conclusion   218

Chapter 10: OneStream in The Real World and Troubleshooting   **219**

OneStream Project Implementation   219

Analyze   219

Design   220

Build   221

Test   221

Unit and Integration Testing   222

Data Integrity and Data Validation Testing   222

User Acceptance Testing (UAT)   222

Performance Testing   222

Rollout   223

Roles and Responsibilities   223

Governance   223

Central Repository   224

Improvement and Innovation   224

Troubleshooting – You've Got This!   224

Roll-up of Data   224

Aggregation Weight   225

Aggregation Property Configuration   227

Account Dimension Type – Allow Input configuration   228

Missing Currency Code   229

Preventing Import Errors   229

Source Dimension for Data Source   230

Data Load Errors   230

Cube View Errors   231

Cannot Modify Data   231

Rows and Columns Dimension Type Selection Required   232

Cube View Cell POV   233

Drill Down   233

Audit History   235

Workflow Profile   235

Task Activity and Processing Log   236

Dashboard Issues   237

Carry On Learning   237

Conclusion   238

Index   **239**

Introduction
Become One with OneStream

Why Learn OneStream?

Why should you learn OneStream? Well, as a corporate performance management solution (CPM), also known as an enterprise performance management (EPM) solution, incorporating consolidation, planning, and reporting, used by more than 1,500 organizations (and counting) and top-rated by technology research companies... why wouldn't you?

At the time of writing, your author had embarked on the OneStream learning journey just six months previously and already feels confident enough to write a book about it. That's got to be a testament to the platform and how easy upskilling is, right? (Or you're thinking, wow, that must be some clever author... hey, no argument here!) But seriously, the founders set out to encapsulate disparate CPM products and create a world-beating all-in-one platform. Now the vision and knowledge started by them is spreading globally.

Learning OneStream involves understanding its terminology, architecture, use cases, and intelligence. This will be part of a new learner's roadmap.

If you are new to corporate performance management, then let's begin here.

What is Corporate Performance Management?

All organizations have goals (e.g., revenue, profits, customer numbers, etc.), and getting there takes hundreds if not thousands of transactions on a weekly, monthly, or longer basis. This amounts to a lot of data consisting of manual (e.g., spreadsheet or text) files, possibly databases, and – for larger organizations – enterprise resource planning (ERP) solutions. This data then needs to be collated and turned into information for various teams to use and make decisions on, and this is where OneStream steps in.

Corporate performance management has become an integral part of the Office of Finance and beyond in an organization, where everyone from the operational teams right up to the C-suite relies on up-to-date real-time information to know what's happened in the past, work efficiently in the present, and plan with ease for the future.

The OneStream platform handles the organization's evolving requirements and is often the single source of truth for finance and operations. Its capabilities extend to being able to add additional use case functions and build new solutions directly on the platform.

Introduction

For an end-user, a workflow (a sequence of processes through which work passes) acts as the platform's backbone. The workflow brings together all the built artifacts in a user-friendly manner, tailoring each user's role and tasks. These tasks might include importing, entering, adjusting, and reviewing data, and the results might be presented in bespoke reports and dashboards.

Dashboards can also quite easily be designed to be the user's home page. This will then be the front-end portal that is set up to guide them through a workflow or other dashboard reports.

OneStream and the Office of Finance

The Office of Finance, which consists of financial and management accounting, is responsible for the organization's statutory and management reporting. For a group, this could be a consolidation of all its entities (foreign exchange translations, ownership and minority interest calculations, intercompany eliminations, group currency reporting, and more).

Other aspects could be the monthly cadence of various reporting needs, as well as monthly and quarterly close activities. This entails collating reliable information from around the organization's functional or budget managers.

The Office of Finance also sets the yearly budgets, plus long-term plans that are monitored and reported for any deviations.

The output to a lot of this is financial statements, (income statement, balance sheet, cash flow), supplemental accounts (which provide context to the statements), and supporting commentary.

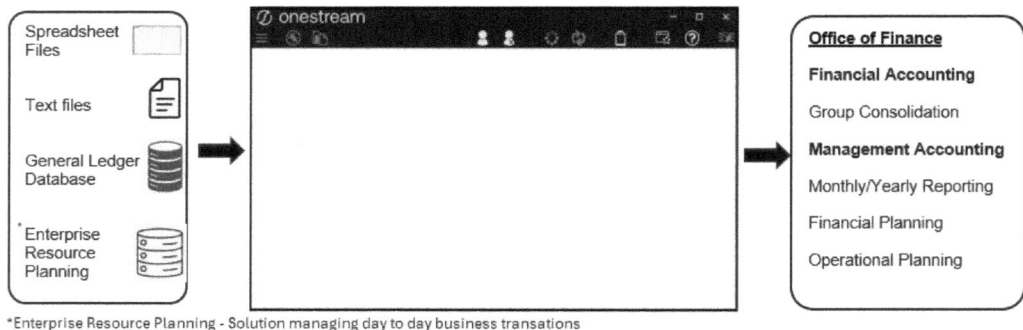

*Enterprise Resource Planning - Solution managing day to day business transactions

Figure 1.1

OneStream can be the driving force for all this and, after being implemented, could be owned by the Office of Finance, or by a Systems support function in the organization. The platform will play its part in various roles and be managed by a dedicated administrator.

The administrator will support the ongoing business changes required in OneStream, understand the processes (from data integration input to end user output), and collaborate with key stakeholders such as the financial controller, tax and treasury professionals, and auditors.

The skillset of a OneStream administrator can be varied but will center around an interest in systems, a basic understanding of accounting concepts and project management, a fondness for troubleshooting, and an understanding of the evolving business.

For an implementer of OneStream, the skillsets are similar to those of an administrator, with a further emphasis on what each project phase entails. Broadly speaking, they must have the acumen to be able to:

- **Analyze** the organization's current eco-system and requirements
- **Translate** findings and **Design** structures for the eventual **Build** into OneStream
- Be part of the **Test** team to get to the sign-off stage
- **Roll out** a version of OneStream that the administrator within the organization takes over and maintains

Where Does OneStream Knowledge Come From?

At OneStream, there has been a lot of investment to form a best-in-class Global Education Services (GES) team with the skills to turn product development and ongoing work into quality learning and training material. The courses created range from complete beginner to skilled OneStream user, and can delve into specialized topics.

The OneStream product development group will initially have a team working on technical education writing, which will be the basis of a course. Then the global education services content developers and learning experience designers create world-class training that can be taken on-demand or delivered by one of the expert instructors in a classroom or virtually. There are also micro-courses, podcasts, and published books.

There are many resources available, so where's the best place to start learning about OneStream?

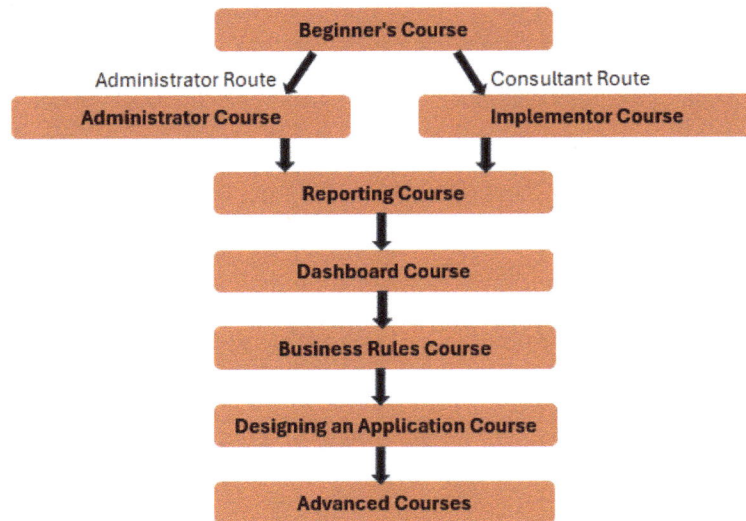

```
                        ┌──────────────────┐
                        │ Beginner's Course │
                        └──────────────────┘
     Administrator Route  ↙            ↘  Consultant Route
┌──────────────────────┐        ┌──────────────────────┐
│ Administrator Course │        │  Implementor Course  │
└──────────────────────┘        └──────────────────────┘
            ↓                               ↓
            ┌──────────────────────────────────┐
            │         Reporting Course         │
            └──────────────────────────────────┘
                            ↓
            ┌──────────────────────────────────┐
            │        Dashboard Course          │
            └──────────────────────────────────┘
                            ↓
            ┌──────────────────────────────────┐
            │      Business Rules Course       │
            └──────────────────────────────────┘
                            ↓
            ┌──────────────────────────────────┐
            │  Designing an Application Course │
            └──────────────────────────────────┘
                            ↓
            ┌──────────────────────────────────┐
            │        Advanced Courses          │
            └──────────────────────────────────┘
```

Figure 1.2

As a starting point, the OneStream website training page has a good roadmap of which courses build upon each other, as well as the process of signing up for a classroom or buying an on-demand course.

The learning management system (LMS), known as **Navigator**, is the one-stop-shop training portal. It contains premium and micro courses, quick tips, videos, tech talks and podcasts, and platform release notes.

For the 'go-getters', OneStream has official certification exams to test your knowledge and obtain credentials in different areas of expertise. There are various exams targeting administrators, implementers, lead architects, and end-users. Guidance and preparation for these can also be found on Navigator.

OneStream's dedicated forum site, **OneStream Community**, has a network of experts keen to interact. The forums are categorized by knowledge area, together with blogs, technical documents, and user groups. You're never alone while learning!

What Role Should Do Which Course?

The following chapters will discuss various components of OneStream (commonly known as artifacts) that are put together to form tasks for various team members in an organization. Each team member has a generic role related to OneStream (their actual job titles may be organization-specific) and takes the form of:

- In-house Project Manager
- In-house Developer
- Administrator

- Report Writer (can also be referred to as a Super User)
- Subject Matter Expert (SME)

Let's look at each role and the tasks the role performs to determine which type of course is suitable.

Project Manager

As part of the OneStream implementation project, the project manager (also possibly known as the Scrum master) will be responsible for:

- Keeping in line with the statement of work (SOW)
- Assisting with organizational requirements
- Resourcing the project
- Organizing the sprints of the project phases
- Managing daily and monthly project team meetings
- Project troubleshooting/escalation management

The OneStream knowledge required at this level would consist of an understanding of terminology and concepts used, OneStream's high-level functionality, extended use cases with which the OneStream project team can enhance the platform, and an understanding of courses available for future team members to attend.

The courses suitable for the project manager would be:

- OneStream Beginners course
- Additional self-service micro courses, such as tech talks or quick tips, platform release videos, and OneStream community forums.

Developer

Developers can be seen as product owners who are responsible for making sure the OneStream application performs optimally. They focus on the design and build of a OneStream application. Tasks include, but are not limited to:

- Understanding the organization's requirements
- Comprehending OneStream's data integration inputs
- Metadata build
- Rule writing
- Applying security settings
- Working with administrator(s) on enhancements and platform updates, with the ability to foresee any impacts on performance

Introduction

The OneStream knowledge required focuses on understanding how source systems can be integrated with OneStream, building artifacts, writing business rules, and testing the application.

The courses suitable for the developer would be:

- Implementer course
- Business Rules course
- Security micro course
- Reporting course
- Dashboard course
- Further micro courses on specific use cases are also applicable, such as Account Reconciliations and Integrator Connector.

After the courses, implementation certification can be taken.

Administrator

As the day-to-day overseer of OneStream, the administrator's role will have a lot of overlap with the developer's role and will also be responsible for:

- Maintenance
- End-user training
- Collaborating with the developer on enhancements
- Data integration
- Data quality control and application integrity
- Process checks and improvements
- Auditor requirements gathering
- Report writing

The OneStream knowledge required is quite extensive and administrators are considered experts or go-tos for all things OneStream.

The courses suitable for the administrator would be:

- Beginners course
- Administrator course
- Security micro course
- Reporting course
- Dashboard course
- Advanced courses on BI Blend, connectors, and application design

After the courses, administration certification can be taken.

Report Writer

The report writer (or super user if the role is not just limited to writing reports) manages the user base and executive board pack and is responsible for:

- Building and maintaining reports
- Data analysis
- Workflow updates
- Internal reporting
- External reporting
- Verification of data

The OneStream knowledge required is an overview of terminology and concepts and a detailed understanding of OneStream report outputs.

The courses suitable for a report writer would be:

- Beginners course
- Reporting course
- Dashboard course
- Advanced dashboard course

Subject Matter Expert (SME)

The SME is knowledgeable about the organization's business processes and works closely with all the above roles regarding requirements. SMEs are responsible for:

- Assisting with the design requirements for OneStream
- OneStream troubleshooting
- Assisting with OneStream user training
- May have an input concerning any business needs that require a change in OneStream

The OneStream knowledge required will consist of terminology and concepts as well as ad hoc topics (as and when required).

The courses suitable for the SME would be:

- Beginners course
- Reporting course
- OneStream podcasts

Introduction

- OneStream community
- Micro courses

The roles above, and the numbers of people in each role, depend on the size of the organization. The administrator can be one team member, but for some organizations (e.g., those that insist on the segregation of duties) with SaaS offerings, this can be split into two; one being the **application administrator** responsible for the OneStream Application use case (as much of the OneStream environment is required for their role); and the other being the **system administrator,** responsible for other OneStream Environment jobs where security tasks could be a large part of their daily activities.

Other OneStream Resources to Extend Your Knowledge

OneStream regularly updates the platform. To keep up with the changes, and add to your knowledge, there are **platform release micro courses** nicely laid out to work through the added features.

There is also a **Design and Reference Guide** as OneStream's main help resource. It has detailed explanations about the platform's features.

Solution Exchange is the go-to for OneStream platform expansion. Containing many solutions and blueprints created by OneStream, partners of OneStream, or the open community, it consists of downloadable applications and templates that can be easily uploaded onto the OneStream platform.

OneStream's **support** site has a large knowledge base where users can browse and search various articles and guides.

OneStream Artifacts

As mentioned earlier, there is a logic and flow to learning OneStream, and one perspective is that of a jigsaw puzzle. The box cover has the whole picture so you can see the result then, once opened, you can lay out all the pieces on the table and study each individual tile to understand where that piece fits in the bigger picture.

Here is OneStream's front cover of some of the artifacts:

OneStream Artifacts		Report Types
Dimensions	Masterdata: FX Rates	Cube Views
Entity	**Data Sources**	Dashboards
Scenario	Import	Spreadsheets
Account	Forms	Extensible Documents
Flow	Journal Adjustments	Report Books
User Defined 1-8	Transformation Rules	
Parent	Confirmation Rules	
Intercompany	Certification Questions	
Time		
Consolidation		
Origin		
View		
Cubes		
Extensibility		
Workflow		
Security		

Figure 1.3

Here are the main pieces now laid out on the table:

Dimensions

Classed as metadata, these are a set of related members. Each member in a dimension is an item name that labels, so to speak, the data it represents. So, if our dimension has been called Fruit, the members inside it could be named Oranges, Apples, Grapes, and Peaches, and the data for each item could point to unit sales. Dimensions are built per dimension type as follows:

Entity Dimension

The organization's business areas used for statutory or management reporting.

Scenario Dimension

A version of data that can reflect various Scenario Types such as Actual, Budget, or Forecast.

Account Dimension

The structure representing the organization's chart of accounts, both financial and non-financial members.

Flow Dimension

Set up to provide the movements and details on how account values change over time.

User Defined (UD) Dimension

The ability to create hierarchies that can be used to analyze a report further, such as products, regions, or cost centers.

Parent

Resides within the Entity dimension and provides the mechanism to further break down an entity's business area.

Intercompany

Determines which entities within the Entity dimension trade in the group and are involved with intercompany activity.

Time Dimension

Data can be stored and reported at weekly, monthly, quarterly, half-yearly, and yearly levels.

Consolidation Dimension

Provides the analysis of rolled-up data from its local currency to translation, share, elimination, adjustments, and final value in the parent entity's member.

Origin Dimension

Identifies the data's origin with an import, form entry, or journal adjustment.

View Dimension

Shows the data from different perspectives, for example, year-to-date, month-to-date, or quarter-to-date.

Cube

A collection of relevant dimensions to form a multi-dimensional financial model that has data for analyzing and reporting.

FX Rates

The currency codes used for currency exchange rates.

Import

A mapping setup of the source file to the target cube for the purpose of loading data.

Forms

A manual (or import option if required) way of entering data into sheets for the purpose of collating values. For example, headcount.

Journals

Adjustments to the loaded data, providing governance of when and who performed the adjustment. As well as manually creating the journal, there is also an import feature that is able to create the journal using an Excel or Comma Separated Values file.

Transformation Rules

The rules behind which source items map to which target items.

Confirmation Rules

A developer-built data quality check feature to prevent continuation of the workflow, if needs be, until all is acceptable. For example, the balancing of a balance sheet.

Certification Questions

Use of a questionnaire to sign off on data as acceptable.

Cube Views

The main building blocks for reports and dashboards, used to display and/or enter cube data.

Dashboards

Developers design dashboards to display data in a user-friendly manner and can set them to be an end-user's landing page, Workspace in a workflow, or a series of guided reporting selections.

Spreadsheets

A spreadsheet workbook directly connected to OneStream data that can be displayed and updated in real time.

Report Books

A combination of different report types to form a report pack that can be distributed to stakeholders.

Extensible Documents

A blend of OneStream content with Microsoft content that references OneStream data.

Workflow

A guided approach for users to complete specific assigned tasks at specific times.

Security

A way to permit users to only access objects relevant to their tasks in OneStream.

Other OneStream Components to Understand Before We Dive In

When learning the OneStream platform, it is useful to read how existing organizations have implemented it (customer stories on the OneStream website). They might have done so primarily for consolidation or planning (or both) and then extended its capabilities to other functional requirements. This section wants to bring OneStream's use cases to the surface. Artifact (a built component such as a dimension, cube, or rules) terminology will be discussed in more detail later.

OneStream and Consolidation

OneStream's consolidation algorithm engine can be triggered to work through an organization's entities and detect whether translations, calculations, and consolidations are needed after any data or metadata changes.

The algorithm rolls up data from a child member to the immediate parent. The child-level entity's local currency is translated to the parent-level's currency. Then, any adjustments can be applied at this parent level, and a share of ownership and any eliminations can be calculated. Post adjustments are applied, if needed, and the final value is stored at the top of the hierarchy for statutory reporting.

Driving the consolidation (behind the scenes) is the loading of foreign currency exchange rates, the intercompany entity setup for the eliminations, and the Consolidation dimension showing the analysis.

OneStream and Planning

Along with all the other artifacts required for planning (for example, entities, accounts, cubes), OneStream has Scenario dimensions with embedded Scenario Type label options ranging from Actual, Budget, and Forecast, to Long Term. Further additional labels can also be used. Each Scenario Type is a new collection of data.

Then, as well as Scenario Types, User Defined dimensions can further break down planning by whatever the organization's requirements are (for example, products, regions, and cost centers), and can be built in by the developer.

OneStream's planning capabilities – for example, a possible planning scenario for an organization – can start off with the user having historic and/or actual data (collated using a task – via a workflow – such as an import or form data entry). Various seeding rules (a process that sets a baseline) can then be created to uplift by a percentage input. Next, the new uplifted values can be allocated to various business units over a period, according to agreed drivers.

There are also built-in spreading methods (the ability to populate cells over several columns or rows without having to type in each cell, discussed later), with a selection of driver options – such as equal spread or 4, 4, 5 – that an end-user can execute from menu options to allocate future periods.

Planning capabilities in OneStream can extend to many use cases; examples can be People, Sales, Cash, and Capital Planning to name a few, and not forgetting the nicely-named Thing Planning which is open to any type of planning.

OneStream's Extensibility Feature Used in Planning

A key component of OneStream is the use of extensibility (worth a more extensive discussion later), which provides a fantastic way to build one hierarchy through connected extended dimensions. Each lower level of the extended dimension contains further detailed members.

Once the extended dimensions have been built then – at the cube creation stage – we slot in the dimension level best suited for that business area cube.

Let's use the Account dimension, for example. Corporate will just be interested in seeing the operating sales account value for the group, as per figure 1.4.

Manufacturing will want to be able to input values that make up part of that operating sales account at a lower level, and therefore in their cube could see account members named third party sales, part sales, and subassembly.

Services, by comparison, may have account members called services revenue and event revenue under operating sales in their cube.

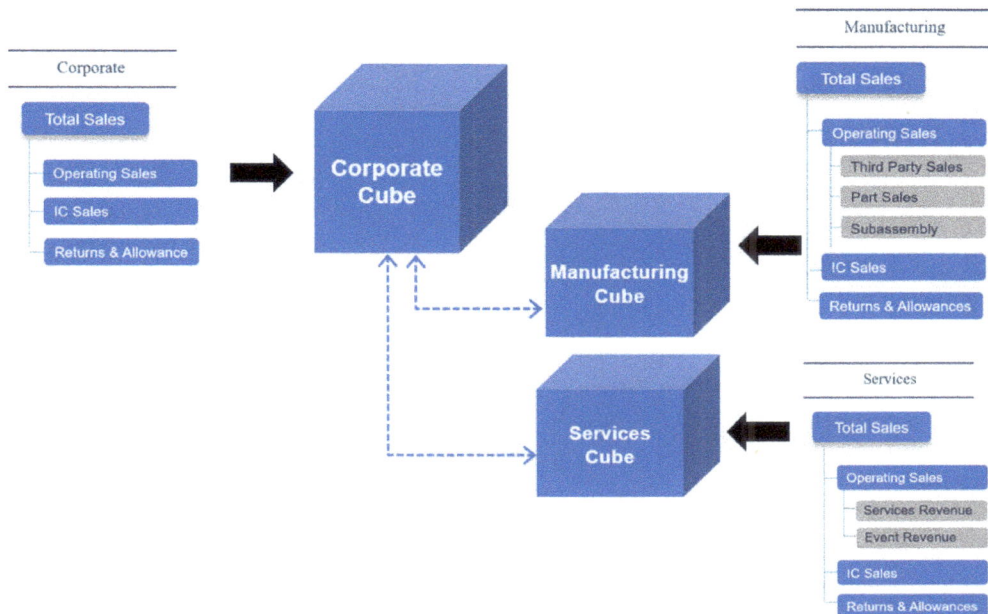

Figure 1.4

Hierarchy terminology is best left as a topic to discuss when we talk about dimensions later.

A final word on planning for now. When planning for a group (where all the child entities are rolling up to the final parent), OneStream's consolidation engine – which is used for statutory reporting – can be switched to using an aggregated feature when it comes to planning. This will bypass a lot of the algorithm's processing on some of the unrequired consolidation options and, therefore, collate values much faster.

Extended Capabilities

Solution Exchange (mentioned earlier) provides the option to select additional capabilities to extend OneStream's platform. Here is a brief explanation of some use cases:

Task Manager

Governs the process of what needs to be done – for example, the entire end-to-end monthly or yearly closing activities. Task Manager provides easy-to-use menu options and visual aids to assess status.

Account Reconciliations

Allows, for example, individual entities to reconcile intercompany trading, chart of accounts activity, and reported data. Capabilities such as auto reconciliation rules, balance checks, and materiality level can be embedded, either as single or multiple currencies.

Transaction Matching

Provides the mechanism to bring points of data that enable the process to perform transactional reconciliation, for example general ledger source to bank statements. It has useful features, such as automated, suggested, or manual matching, alongside capabilities to embed rules-driven drivers for matching transactional-level data.

> **Note:** both Account Reconciliations and Transaction Matching have been combined with the Journal Entry Manager solution to now form OneStream Financial Close from the Solution Exchange.

Enterprise Tax Reporting

Enhances tax provisioning and consolidation, and provides the mechanism to split this by each country's tax rules.

Incentive Compensation Management

Able to calculate sales commissions and bonuses.

Lease Accounting

Lease Accounting manages lease contracts, performing the necessary accounting standards for compliant calculations.

Dynamic Cash Flow

With Dynamic Cash Flow, users can work on the cash flow process as it interacts with the balance sheet and income statement, with drill-down capabilities to understand account activity.

Let's Look Ahead in This Book

This book is focused on being a great springboard as you start your OneStream learning journey. It aims to provide the initial onboarding knowledge of OneStream's components, how they fit together, and how they are used.

To aid our progress, the book will use a fictitious organization known as **Top Training Incorporation** – a global training company selling soft skill classroom or online courses, training materials, and subscriptions to resources and podcasts.

Initially, we'll look at the platform components at a high level before the main deep dive. This entails an overview of dimensions, cubes, workflow, reporting, application properties, and security.

Then, taking the dimension concept further, it is all about naming and building dimensions and the members they contain. We shall explore hierarchy build and terminology, which is key to what is considered a good metadata design.

Cubes will then make an appearance in the book. By this point, we will have covered dimensions enough to be able to build cubes, understand some of their key properties, and comprehend what is meant by a Data Unit when it comes to measuring performance.

With the cubes now in place, it is all about getting the data from the source files into the cubes and the tools used to do this efficiently and effectively.

Workflow is an important aspect of OneStream and should be on every beginner's to-do list. We shall look at how they can be used to provide guided end-user tasks and what more can be done to protect data quality and provide the governance needed for any audit. This nicely flows into reporting and a further explanation of reporting types with a detailed emphasis on Cube Views and dashboards.

Finally, even with the best designs, there are always problems that need to be addressed. We all become more savvy over time in spotting where issues lie and how to address them, but this book will hopefully provide the training ground for good old-fashioned OneStream troubleshooting detective work.

Conclusion

This first chapter was to provide an understanding of what learning OneStream entails, together with an initial breakdown of platform components. As mentioned, components are like jigsaw pieces that can fit together to form a much bigger picture.

There should also now be an understanding of what is meant by corporate performance management and how the Office of Finance can save time when it comes to reporting cycles. Also, how it is able to handle large volumes of data to form one version of the truth.

Are you now ready to really dig into OneStream? Then let's do this!

2

The Learning Begins
Fasten Your Seatbelt!

OneStream's High-Level Learning Road Map

This chapter is all about understanding the high-level end-to-end of OneStream. The rest of the book will then break it down into manageable modules. We will do a first pass on *how* OneStream works and then – from the next chapter onwards – learn *why* it works.

Here is this chapter's learning journey:

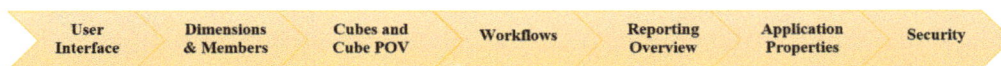

| User Interface | Dimensions & Members | Cubes and Cube POV | Workflows | Reporting Overview | Application Properties | Security |

Figure 2.1

As we progress, it will be easier to relate our understanding of OneStream concepts to a working organization. As mentioned in the first chapter, we shall be using **Top Training Inc.**, a world-class training company that has implemented OneStream as part of its core financial operations of planning and consolidation, making extensive use of workflow and reporting in OneStream.

Top Training offers soft skills classroom and online courses, training materials, and subscriptions to resources and podcasts. Their headquarters are based in the US, with satellite offices globally, working mainly on a business-to-business model that serves clients in the Americas, Europe, and Asia Pacific.

There are 500 employees, comprised of executives, instructors, and support staff, working in finance, product development, operations, and human resources.

As you work through the book, consider yourself the new Top Training OneStream administrator (congrats on your new role!), and your author will be a OneStream consultant beside you. Let me start by introducing you to the user interface.

User Interface

The platform's Graphical User Interface (GUI) is logged into by selecting an application. Then, the panes, tabs, menu selections and icons are seen. A user's interface view and selection options will depend on the user's role, with features that may or may not be available (as determined by security and/or configuration settings).

The left navigation pane has three tabs: OnePlace, Application, and System. Access to a particular tab is through security settings, driven by the user's login and their OneStream role within the organization. For example, an end-user might only be able to see the OnePlace tab, a power-user role might only be able to see the OnePlace and Application tabs, and an administrator will be able to see all three.

Further, certain menu options in each tab may or may not be visible to the end-user or power-user. The administrator will generally see everything, unless it is decided that admin tasks should be split between two team members, one being the application administrator (seeing the OnePlace and Application tabs) and the other a system administrator (only seeing the System tab).

The pane on the right side holds the Point Of View (POV) settings that can be unique to each user. The Cube POV within the POV pane will contain the default settings that could be applied when, for example, running reports. For a first-time login, some of the POV dimensions could show just a question mark (instead of a selected member), and this indicates that a selection needs to be made (as mentioned later in this chapter).

Both the Navigation pane and the Cube POV pane can be expanded or collapsed (shown or hidden) by clicking the three horizontal lines icon on the far left (fondly referred to as the hamburger menu) for the Navigation pane, or clicking the cube (with a three horizontal-line backdrop) on the far right for the Cube POV pane. These panes can be pinned to keep them expanded permanently.

On occasion, after logging in, both panes may be hidden automatically. This will then lead to a blank white screen (with the OneStream black banner and icons on top).

In between both panes is a series of icons providing the user with features such as the ability to select different applications, task activity logs, refresh, and accessible help documentation.

The File Explorer is a useful option for saving OneStream-formatted files as well as other formats such as PDF outputs, spreadsheets, and text documents. Figure 2.2 shows the login to the OneStream Windows app.

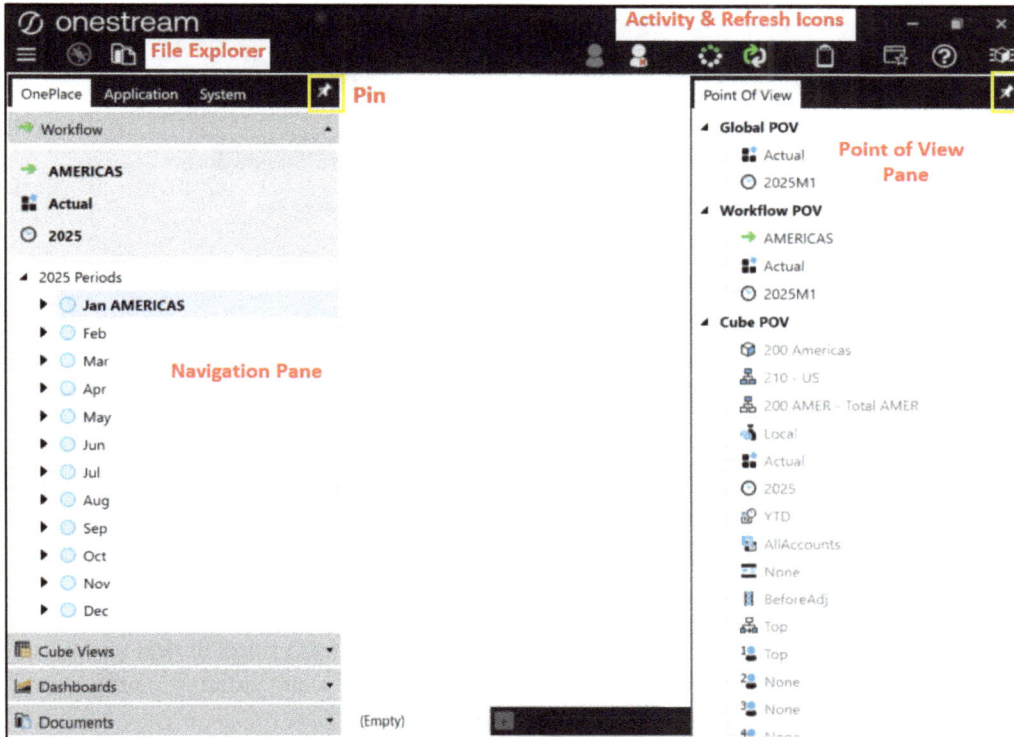

Figure 2.2

An end-user may have the option to login from OneStream's **Modern Browser Experience (MBE)**.

Creating a New Application

An application is the OneStream database containing all the objects for a particular use case. In a OneStream environment, there can be many applications.

For a new blank application database to be created, this is done in the System tab from the Applications menu.

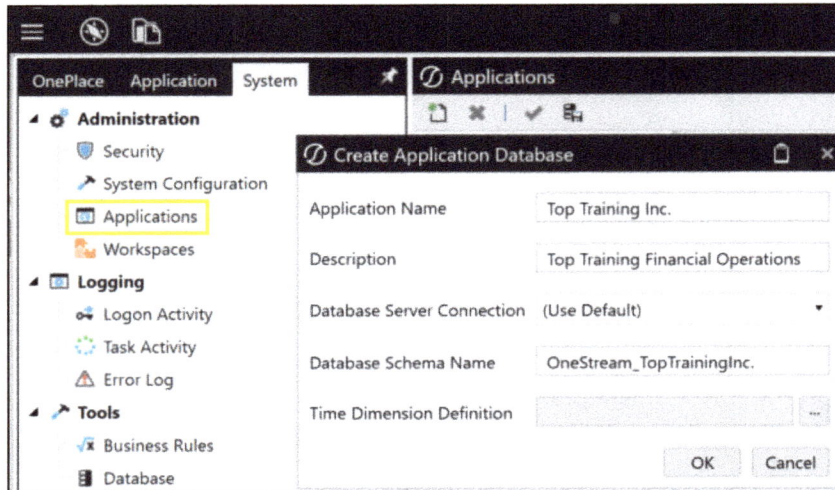

Figure 2.3

For Software as a Service (SaaS) customers, copying applications can be done using the **Cloud Administration Tool** that can be downloaded from the Solution Exchange. The creation of a new application and the database behind the application will require the assistance of OneStream support.

With a brief overview of the GUI discussed, let us now talk about dimensions and members, then cubes, workflows, reporting, and security, together with some background properties.

Let's Talk About Dimensions and Members

Dimensions are the foundation of platform design. Commonly known as metadata (data of data), they each contain a set of related members. These dimensions will eventually be part of a selection process to build our cubes.

If we take our organization's setup, for example, we know Top Training is based in various locations, sells training products, and does this over a period of time. These can all be represented by building dimensions called Location, Products, and using the Time dimension that has been created by OneStream (simple!).

Members are items *within* a dimension that will point to data in a Cube View, which will then be used for reporting. For our example, the members will be:

- New York (residing in the Location dimension)

- Software course (residing in the Products dimension)

- 2025M1 - Jan 2025 (residing in the Time dimension)

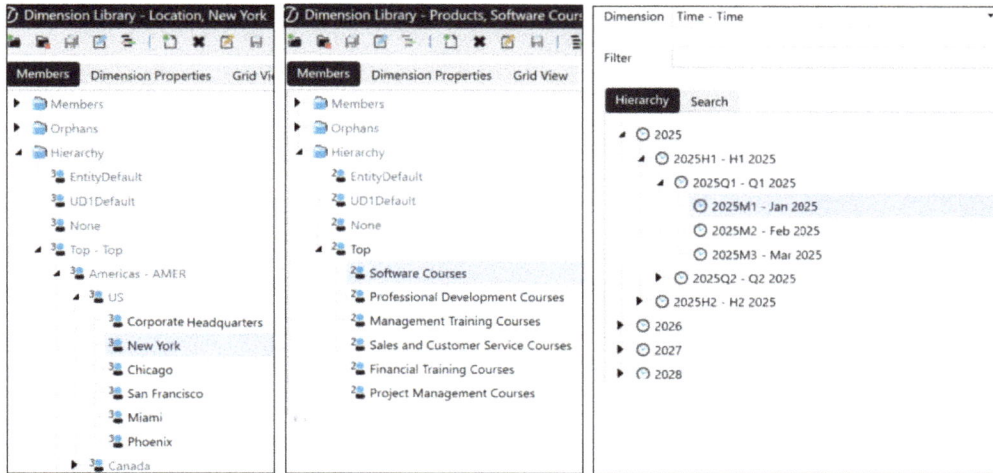

Figure 2.4

To make building even easier, OneStream has a genius way of categorizing dimensions, called **dimension types**. Each one has its own setup, and in the next chapter, we will be taking a deep dive into dimension types and creating dimensions and their members.

Members Hierarchies

As mentioned, a member is an item within a dimension, and this is where data is loaded. Later, when we discuss cubes, we'll identify that each data cell point in our cube will be represented by one member from each of the dimensions that make up that cube.

There are going to be many members in a dimension, some racking up to thousands. The typical setup of all these members is hierarchies (ordered by levels). Hierarchy terminology is key to determining the relationship between the members, especially for reporting purposes.

Using Figure 2.5, below, we can identify the hierarchy relationship terminology of **parent** and **child**, **base members**, and **siblings**.

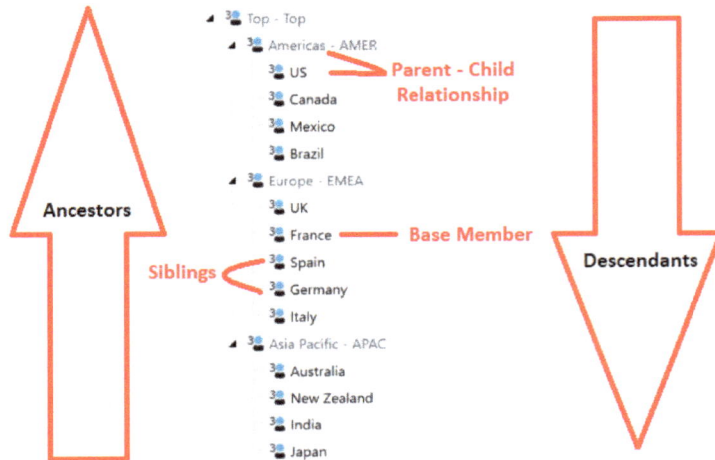

Figure 2.5

Digging deeper…

Parent Member

A parent member is the main and the top member of the group, overseeing a common grouping known as the 'child' members. Americas – AMER is an example of the parent-level member, with US, Canada, Mexico and Brazil as the child members.

Child Member

A child member sits below a parent member and may or may not inherit certain properties from the parent, such as currency or security settings. US is an example of a child member situated directly below the parent member. In this example, it is also a base member.

Base Member

A base member is at the bottom or lowest level of a hierarchy. For OneStream dimensions, data is only entered at the base level (with an exception for the Origin dimension discussed later).

France is an example of the lowest level member – a base member.

Data can be entered for France, and the country is also a child member for Europe – EMEA.

Sibling Member

Sibling members in a hierarchy are members that share the same parent.

Spain and Germany are examples of sibling members to France as they share the same parent, called Europe – EMEA.

Ancestors

Ancestors is the grouping structure that builds up through all the levels to the Top member. It can typically start from the base member and include all levels of parents; for example, Mexico's ancestors will be Americas – AMER and Top – Top.

Descendants

Descendants work in the opposite direction to ancestors. From the Top member downwards, moving through all levels to the bottom Japan member.

The hierarchy in Figure 2.5 shows an **even level hierarchy** relationship, where every child has a parent level above.

Hierarchies can be varied in structure. A **ragged hierarchy**, could be utilized where a base member may have a parent directly one level above, and another base member's parent is three levels above.

For example, in Figure 2.6, 431- Support Center South and 432 – Support Center North report to parent 430 – India, but support center 433 – Support Center Central reports to a higher-level parent… 400 APAC – Total APAC.

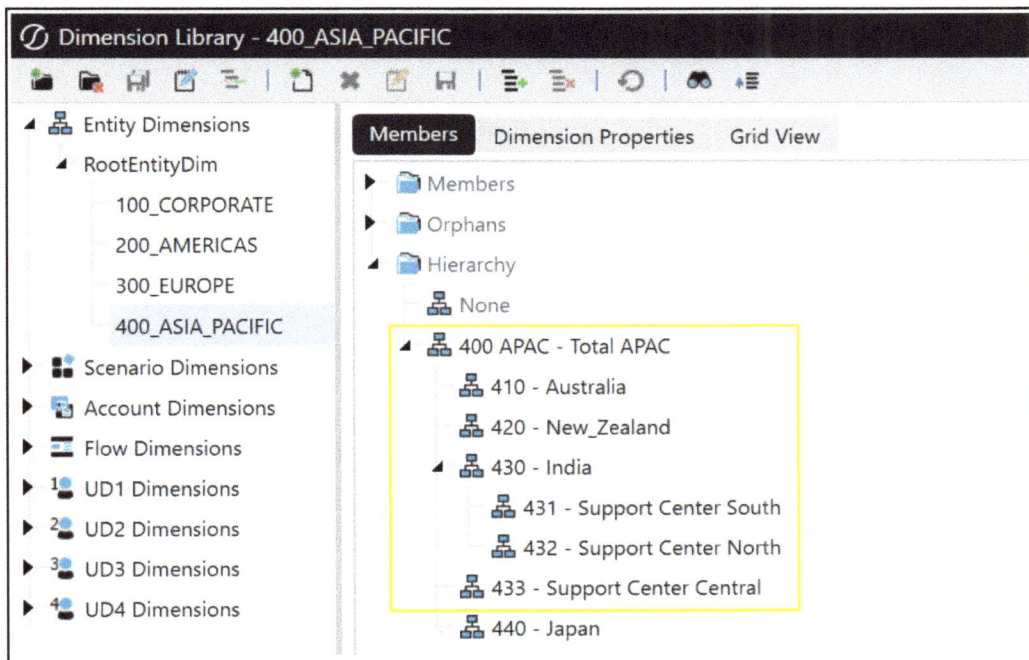

Figure 2.6

In turn, an **alternate hierarchy** is a variation of the main statutory hierarchy for internal management reporting purposes where the children are reporting to a different set of parents. This can be constructed within an existing Entity dimension, copying the main statutory hierarchy members to regroup under a new hierarchy structure.

Dimensions Make a Cube

Cubes are formed by selecting the relevant dimensions. They are designed with business areas in mind and which members those areas will be using. A cube is considered a multidimensional structure that controls how data is stored, calculated, translated and consolidated, as well as how it will be used for analyzing and finally reporting.

The multidimensional setup will provide the flexibility to rotate members between **rows**, **columns** and **pages** with the option to nest dimensions together. Where members intersect is known as a **data point**. All of this will be discussed in the reporting section of the book when we look at Cube Views.

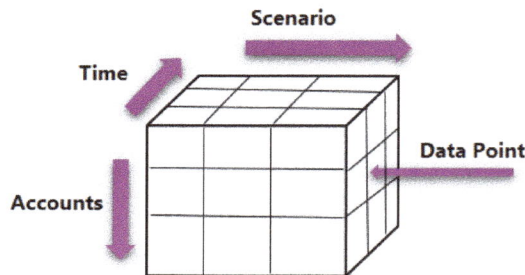

Figure 2.7

A small number of applications contain just one cube, but it is common to have applications with multiple cubes. Some will be linked together to provide the extensibility feature we will be discussing further in the cubes chapter, and some will be stand-alone (also known as monolithic). In OneStream, once a cube is created and data loaded, a Cube View is built where the data is then viewed, analyzed, and pivoted between rows, columns, and pages.

The formation of a cube is created in the cube's menu using the Cube properties and Cube dimension tabs.

In the Cube properties tab (as shown in Figure 2.8), the Time dimension is selected, security settings are configured, any business rules are applied for calculations, and the currency code and rates for translations are chosen, alongside how the cube will be used within the workflow settings.

If the cube is for consolidating business areas, then it will be considered the top level (or super cube), to which other cubes are linked.

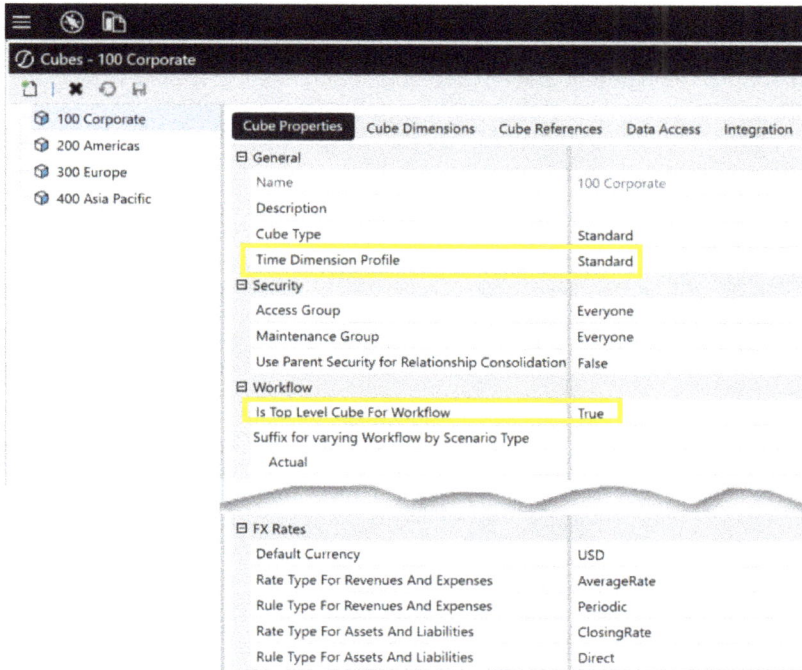

Figure 2.8

The Cube dimensions tab has the facility to choose which dimensions can be selected by Scenario Type. Each Scenario Type can have a different selection of dimensions.

In Figure 2.9, we are able to see the 200 Americas cube for Top Training. It requires an initial entity and Scenario dimension selection for the default setting, and these two selections will then be shared across *all* Scenario Types. Additional dimension default types can continue to be selected, or selected instead by Scenario Type as we have done for the Budget, where the selections have been made from the Account dimension to the final User Defined dimension.

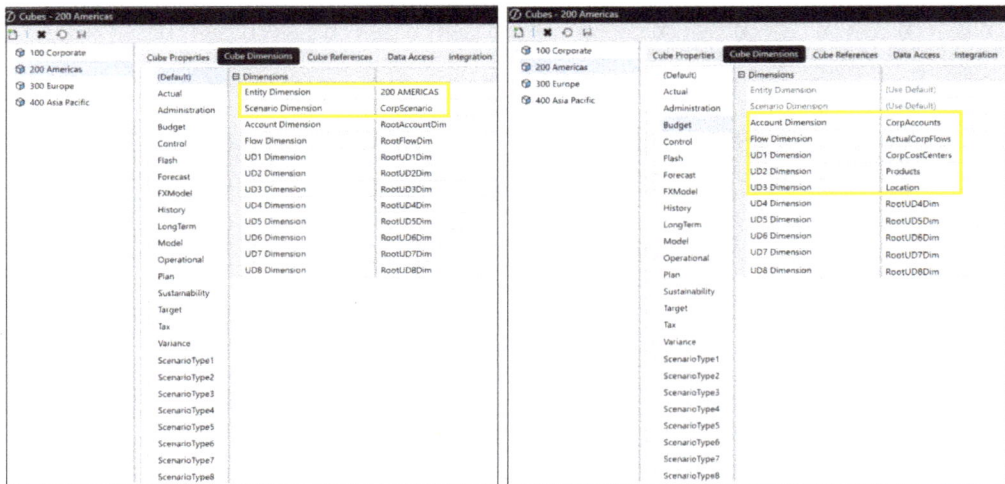

Figure 2.9

Cube Point of View (POV)

Figure 2.10, below, shows a cube's point of view (POV). These are a user's default members, used in, for example, a Cube View report if the Cube View POV has no selected members.

The Cube POV in the right-hand pane represents a chosen cube, alongside the selection of dimension members from each of the cube's dimension types.

All users can have Cube POVs that are unique to them and their reporting needs, and can be focused on their business areas. For example, US users will set their Cube POV to the 200 Americas cube, and possibly a particular user-defined location such as New York, whereas in the UK, a user will have the 300 Europe cube and user-defined location London.

Note the distinction between a Cube POV and the Cube View POV, which are the local settings within a Cube View. The reports generated by the user will initially use the member selection within the Cube View POV, but – where no selection has been made – the Cube POV setting will act as the next option. Therefore, the Cube POV could end up controlling the data reported in many Cube Views, dashboards, and – for Spreadsheet users – the Cube POV will set the default selections when creating reports called **QuickViews** (discussed in the reporting chapters).

The Cube POV can be saved to favorites in the File Explorer and reinstated back to the original setting if required. Other options available are setting the Cube POV for new users or copying the current setting directly into a Cube View POV selection (we will cover this later).

If a question mark appears in any of the dimensions because of a member change, it represents an invalid intersection, and a new selection is required for each question mark.

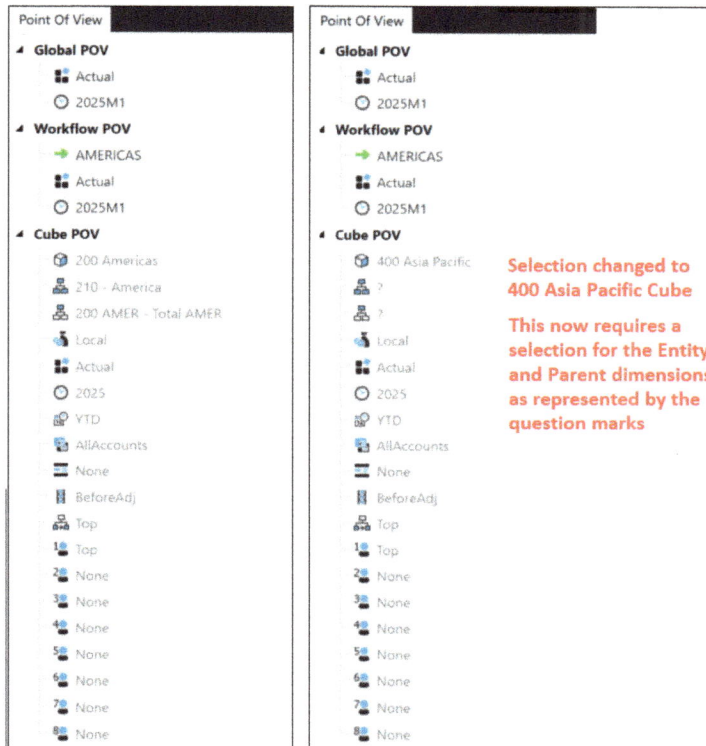

Figure 2.10

Working Through a Workflow

Workflows are constructed to guide users through specific tasks they need to perform at specific times of the reporting cycle. For example, as well as loading monthly values, there may be tasks to enter the month end closing headcount, or to reconcile intercompany balances. All tasks can be coordinated and monitored at a corporate level to eventually have the results consolidated and reported for the whole group.

Tasks such as loading data, data entry, and adjustments can be set either monthly, quarterly, half-yearly, or yearly. The workflow is able to control and organize the tasks and can be customized to the user's roles and business processes to increase efficiency.

The workflow is constructed within the Application tab and executed by the end-user in the OnePlace tab. The user will initially select their Workflow Point of View (POV), which consists of the Workflow Profile, scenario and year. This selection will then also be reflected in the Workflow POV on the right-hand side.

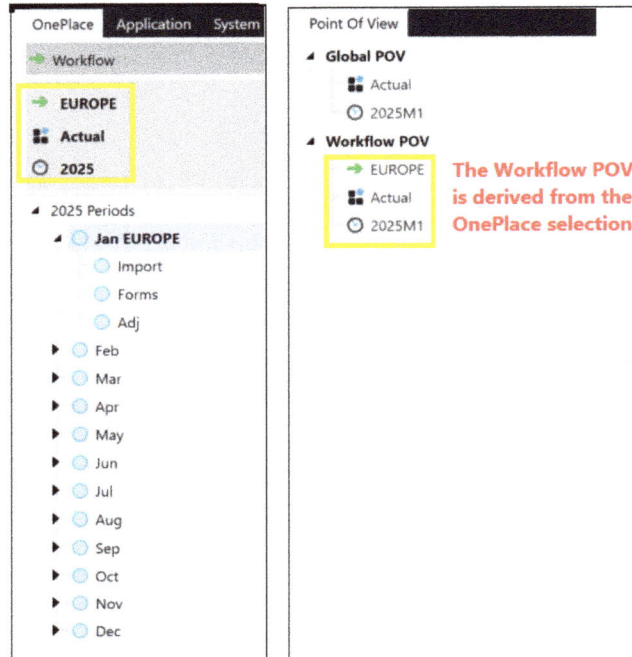

Figure 2.11

The Workflow Profile type depends on the user's role in the organization and consists of selecting either a **base input** where tasks will comprise of importing data, entering data in forms and (if required) making account adjustments using journal templates, or a **parent input**. Parent input consists of only entering data in forms and the ability to make account changes using journal templates. The third option is **review**, where no data entry can be made, just the ability to confirm data quality and certify the governance of the data.

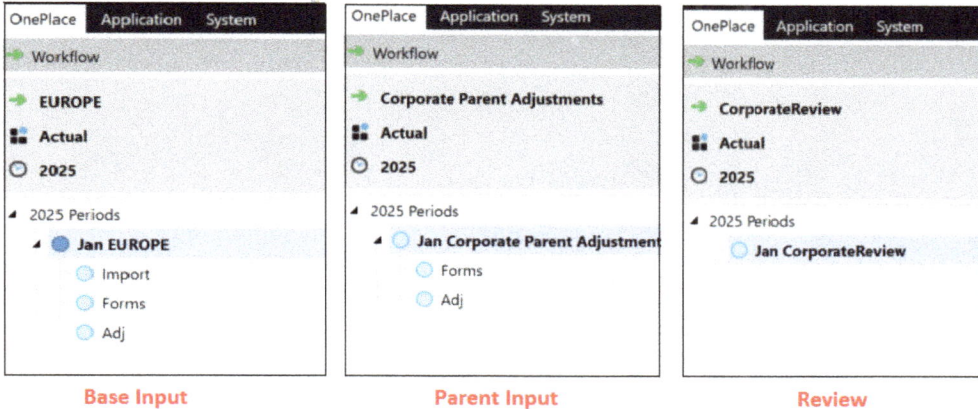

Figure 2.12

Task options – based on workflow requirements – can be renamed, or additional ones added. Administrators are also able to disable a task from the Application tab. This is then not seen in the OnePlace tab.

Figure 2.13 shows the renaming of the base input profile tasks that are applicable to Top Training, but the names can be changed to cater for any organization's requirements. Note how the 'Adj' task (for journal adjustments) that was seen in Figure 2.12 is not showing in Top Training's base input profile below. This is to do with a task configuration in the Application tab that can be turned off if a task is not required.

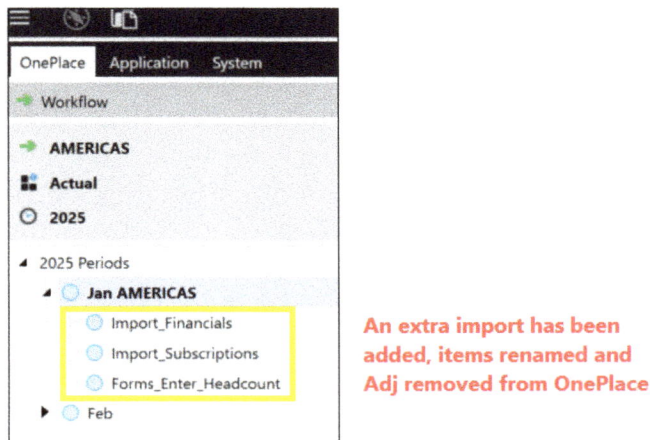

Figure 2.13

Typical Workflow Tasks

The administrator can set up many combinations of tasks. The below covers quite a few, and broadly represents what a user will be facing.

Lowest (Base) Level Tasks

Import

Consists of uploading a file or direct connection to a source system for data to first be imported to a staging area.

Validate

Data is transformed and checked for omitted mappings and any invalid intersections that must be corrected before the final load to the cube.

Load

Once validation has passed, this is the point where data is then loaded to the cube.

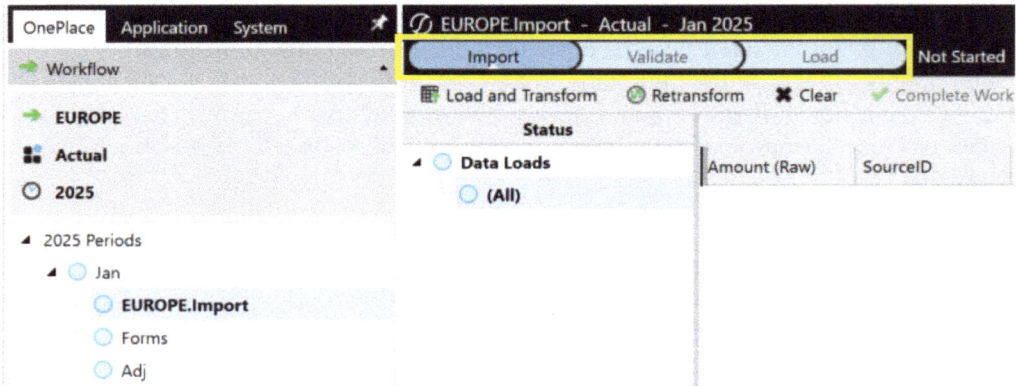

Figure 2.14

Forms

Forms can be a required or an optional part of the process for data to be manually entered or loaded. Form data can be key metrics such as headcount, or product managers entering unit forecasts.

Pre-Process

Pre-Process can be a useful task for running some preliminary calculations before any manual data entry or adjustments in forms.

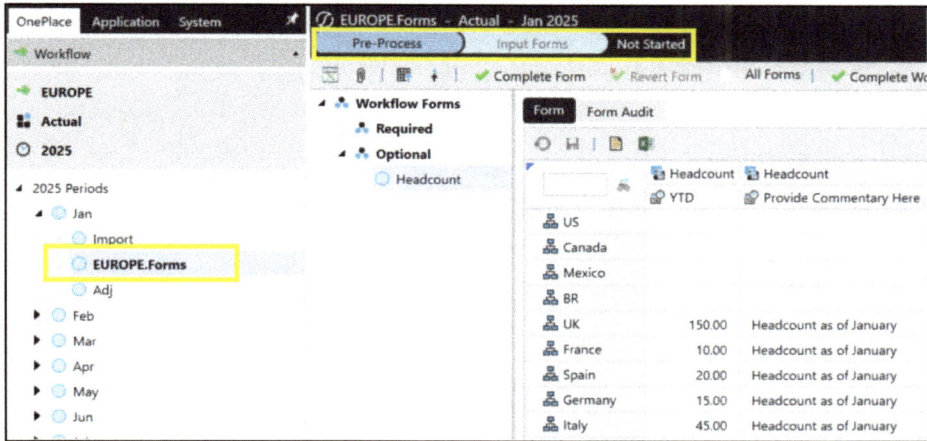

Figure 2.15

Journal Input

Sometimes, users need to be able to adjust data. To allow this, the administrator will have created permissions for a **journal template** to be used in the OnePlace tab.

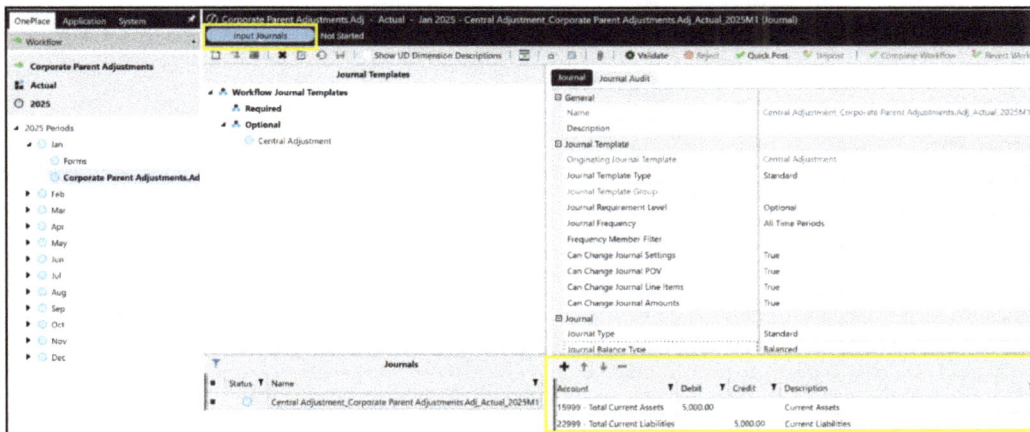

Figure 2.16

Next Level Up Tasks

Process

At this stage, any calculation definitions (set on the workflow, as explained later in the book) embedded for the cube (calculate, translate, consolidate) will be executed when Process Cube is selected.

Confirm

For the confirm workflow task, data can typically be checked for its validity. This might entail balance sheets balancing and/or annotation being added.

Workspace

This is the most commonly used workflow task in Planning. This task is used to define specific steps that involve user interactions with dashboards or other Workspace-related tasks.

Certify

Certify is considered the final step of the workflow. Here, a series of questions may be embedded into the administrator's process to verify that data governance requirements have been achieved. Once answered satisfactorily, the sign-off process can begin.

If there are no questions to be assigned, the administrator can select **quick certify**, which is an out-of-the-box option that requires the user to certify the workflow is complete.

Figure 2.17

Task status is colored. **Blue** means it has not started; **red** means there is an error that needs fixing; **green** means the task has been completed.

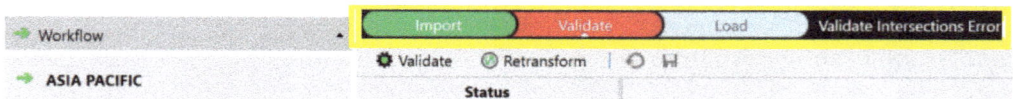

Figure 2.18

Highest Level Tasks: Multi-Period Processing

Multi-period processing allows a number of workflow steps to be completed for one or more periods in one executed batch run. These can consist of locking (as well as unlocking) to protect data or other options such as running the cube calculations or certifying the workflow.

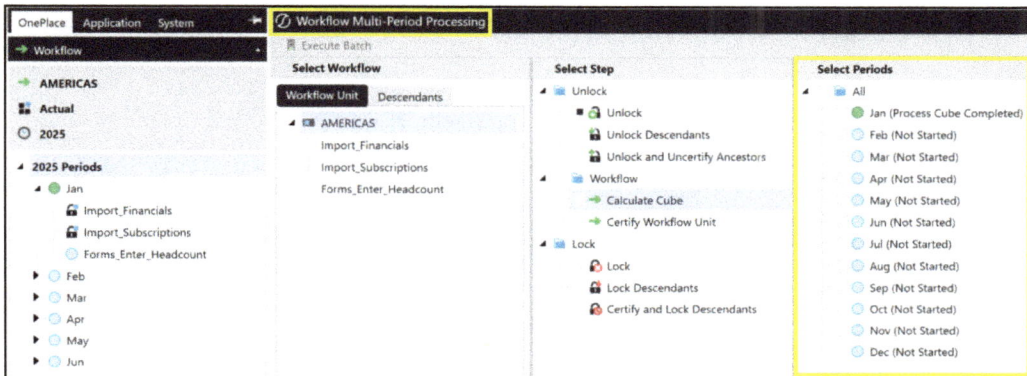

Figure 2.19

Corporate Only Workflow Requirement Option

Where Top Training has a centralized requirement, especially when controlling import data, the administrator of the OneStream platform can set up the import to only be performed by corporate. This can be on behalf of all entities and is known as a central import. Doing this prevents individual entities from loading data, and their facility is greyed out (indicating a central load setup). Other tasks, like data entry forms and journal adjustments, can still be carried out if activated.

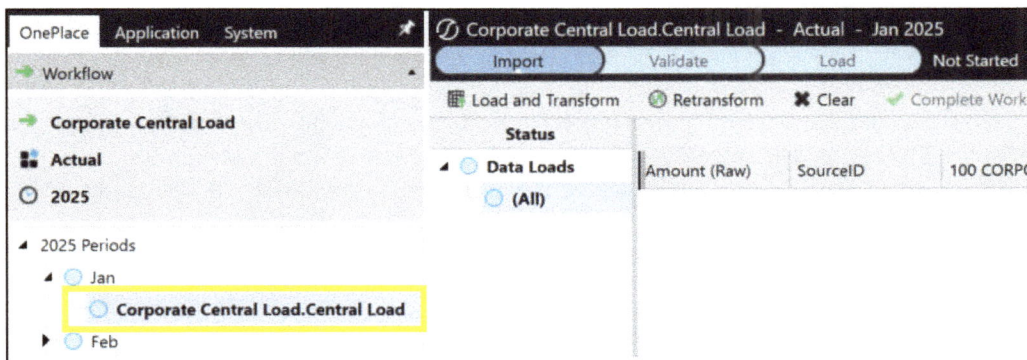

Figure 2.20

Reporting Overview

With OneStream's seamless input functionality bringing in data from various external sources, it also has an extraordinary ability to deliver many options for data output. Data outputs can be used for querying, adjusting, analyzing, and then finally reporting to stakeholders. At this stage of the book, we shall explore these options then go into more detail in the reporting chapters.

Cube Views

Simple to create and maintain, and considered the main building blocks of reports, Cube Views can be used as a stand-alone reporting tool or embedded in dashboards, spreadsheets, report books, and extensible documents.

Cube Views display cube data that can be queried or additional data added. There is also the ability for the user (if granted permission by the administrator) to run calculations, translations, and consolidations directly from the Cube View. Cube Views can be converted to a **report viewer** format or exported to **Spreadsheets**.

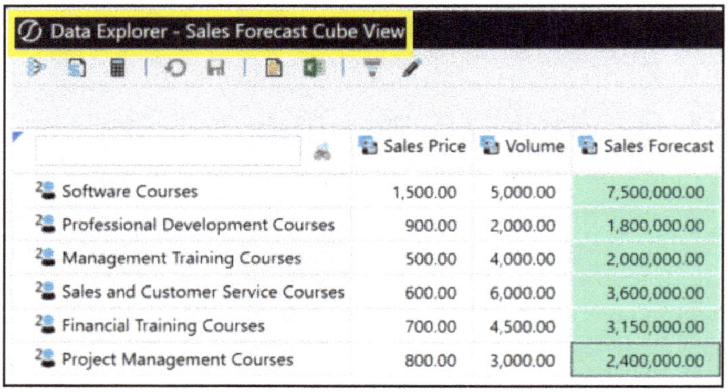

Figure 2.21

Dashboards

These are customer-designed and used to query data from the cube (and possibly data from outside, too; for example, from the staging area or external databases). Dashboards can display other dashboards within themselves, and can also contain Cube Views, spreadsheets, report books and extensible documents.

When used for the purpose of executive reporting, dashboards can display key performance indicators (KPIs), charts, tables, and commentary. They provide the data snapshots that an organization needs. Dashboards can also be used for the purpose of functional interaction and analysis, working on a series of tasks, and can be used to modify or calculate data.

Finally, end-users can be set up to interact with dashboards. This can be by clicking specific cells on interactive charts to then view a change in a table. Or the dashboard can be used as read-only to view the KPIs in real time.

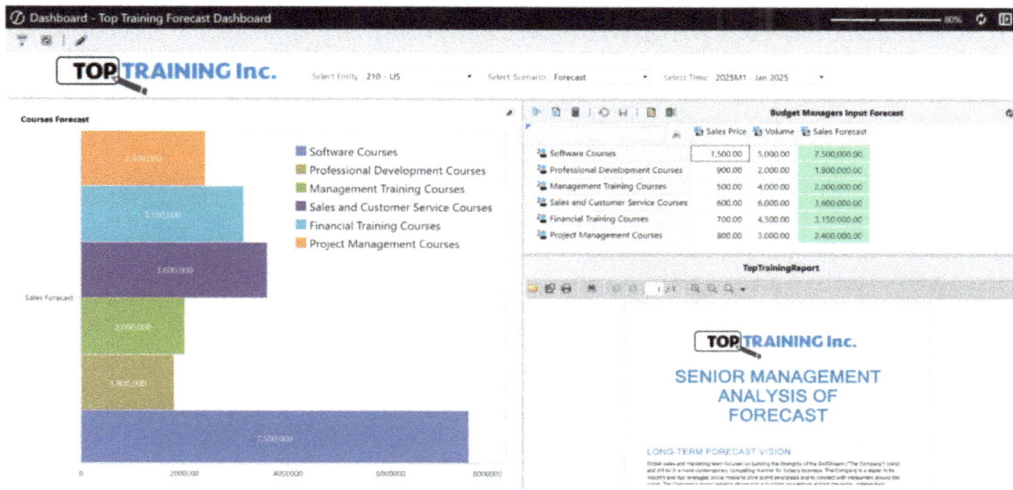

Figure 2.22

Extensible Documents

The idea of extensible documents is to embed OneStream parameters (variables used as placeholders that are executed at report run time, replacing the parameter setting with actual OneStream data and metadata) in Word, PowerPoint, Excel or text files. Extensible documents are low maintenance for the report author as the specifics of reports are automatically updated each month (e.g., time periods and various KPIs).

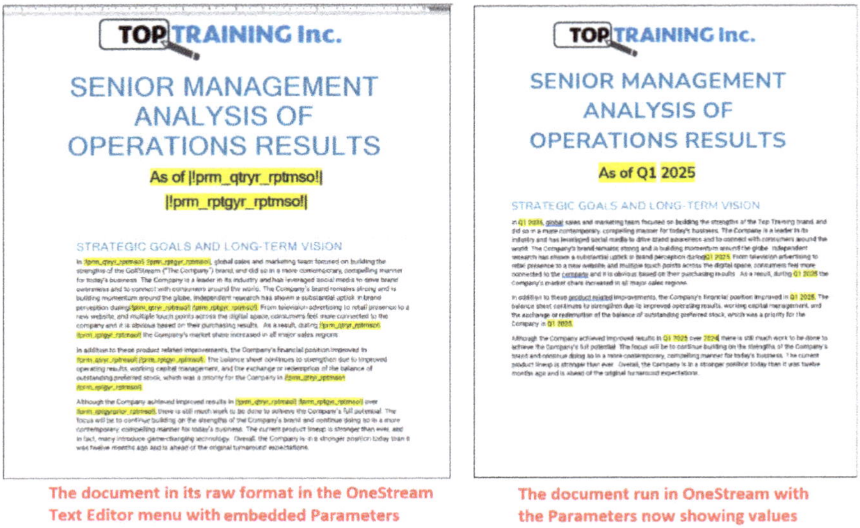

The document in its raw format in the OneStream
Text Editor menu with embedded Parameters

The document run in OneStream with
the Parameters now showing values

Figure 2.23

Spreadsheets

OneStream has two choices when it comes to spreadsheets. A built-in Spreadsheet tool within the platform which comprises most Excel functionality, or an Excel Add-In which can be installed in the Excel application.

The options are to bring a Cube View into the Spreadsheet or create Quick Views. These provide OneStream metadata connections to manipulate the data and make use of the Quick View POV, which also acts as a pivot table.

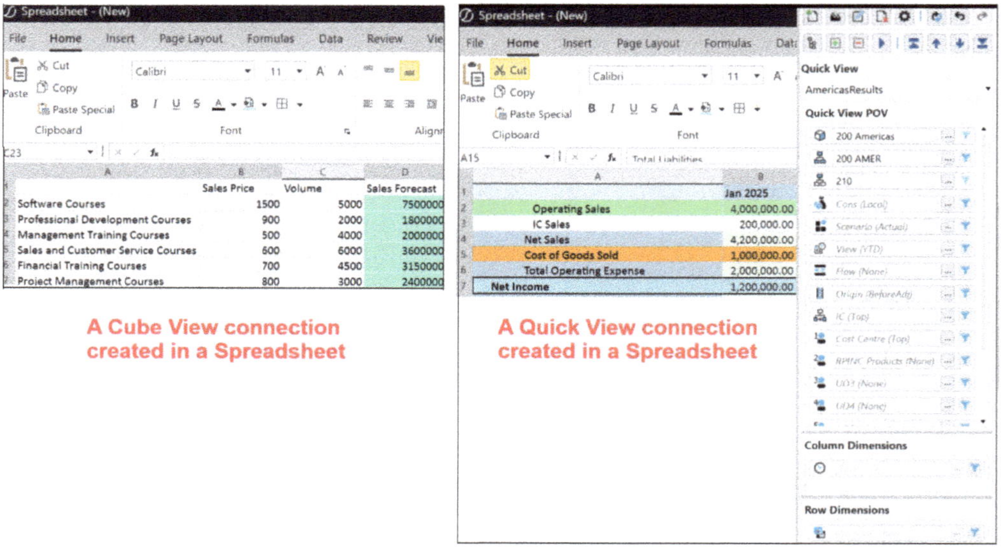

A Cube View connection
created in a Spreadsheet

A Quick View connection
created in a Spreadsheet

Figure 2.24

Creating Table Views is another option in Spreadsheets, allowing users to interact with data in a tabular format. Data can be retrieved from OneStream using a business rule to populate the Table View.

Report Books

Report books are a combination of various report types run as one report, and are made up of Cube Views, spreadsheets, dashboard charts, and extensible documents. Report books can be shared as PDFs, spreadsheets, or zip files.

Ultimately, the use of this feature will be to automate the generation of multiple reports, and be able to adjust which POVs the reports are using. For example, being able to run a report book which is made up of Cube View reports, extensible documents, and a dashboard chart, repeated for as many entities required, and all in one final preview.

Application Properties and FX Rates

Some platform settings are applied soon after the creation of the application and are located within Application Properties (under the Tools section in the left-hand navigation pane). These will be the default property settings of the application and are made up of three tabs:

The General tab has the Global Point of View settings that apply to all Scenario Types and must be set for users to be able to load data as part of their workflow in OnePlace. As we will be looking at troubleshooting issues towards the end of the book, checking if the Global Point of View has been configured as one option – when an import error occurs – is something to bear in mind.

Other key settings include the addition of Top Training's name and logo, which will then feature on reports by default. Also, we can set the decimal number format for reports here.

The Currency Filter provides the ability to select a range of currency codes used by the organization; the currency codes that are set in Application Properties will then be the only selection codes available when entering FX rates, for example.

Finally, take a look at Lock After Certify, which we'll revisit when we dive into Workflows. This relates to automatically padlocking the workflow once data certification has been completed.

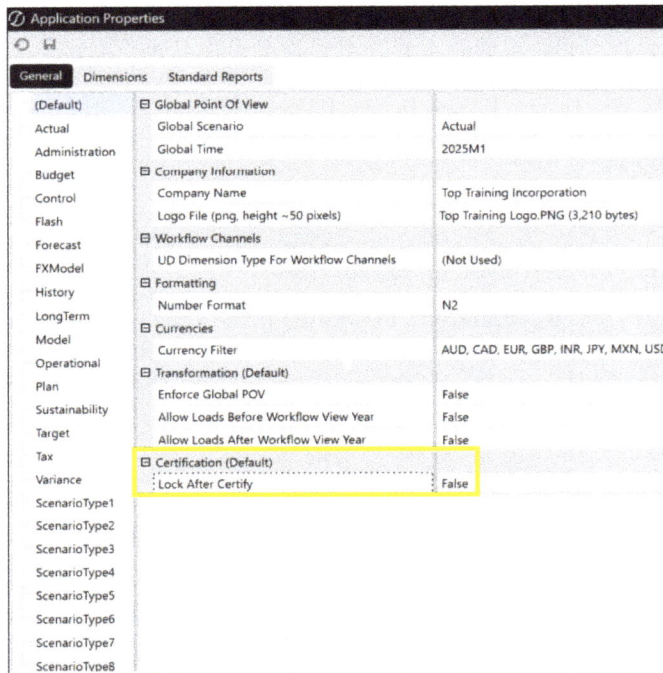

Figure 2.25

The Dimensions tab is a straightforward time and user-defined description setting. When selecting a year option, this tab allows the setting of the start year and end year, then limits the selection to this setting in other parts of the application where time is applicable.

User Defined Description(s) enable names to be entered that will, for example, be reflected in the tooltip when hovering over the dimension in the Cube POV.

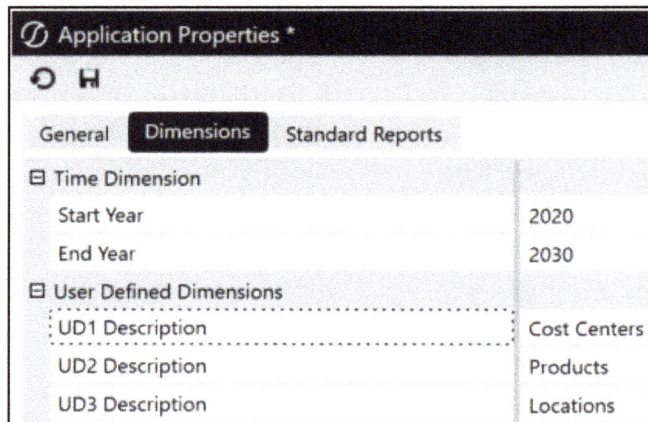

Figure 2.26

The Standard Reports tab allows for formatting of the logo, title, header and footer in the reports. Some settings can be overwritten in specific reports if needed.

Foreign Exchange Currencies

When OneStream has its consolidation hat on for a global group – such as Top Training Inc. – it will inevitably deal with a range of foreign currencies that will eventually need translation to the group currency.

A starting point for FX rates is the selection of currency codes (as mentioned in the Application Properties above). Once these have been established and various entities have been set up with their specific default currency codes, the rates will then be loaded into OneStream.

The rates sit under the Cube section in the left-hand navigation pane and can be manually entered or imported. They are viewed by FX rate type, where the application has predefined selections that cannot be deleted. These are **average**, **opening**, **closing** and **historical rates**, although further specific rates and rate types can be added if required.

The setup is straightforward. Start by selecting the rate type, then the Time dimension member for which the rate is being stored, the source currency as the starting currency, and the destination currency as the translated one.

The FX rate is read as one unit of the source currency to the value of the destination currency. At the time of writing, this would equate to 1 GBP source being 1.24 USD destination.

Once rates are in OneStream, there is the option to get the values locked by time. A padlock symbol represents this and further changes are no longer possible.

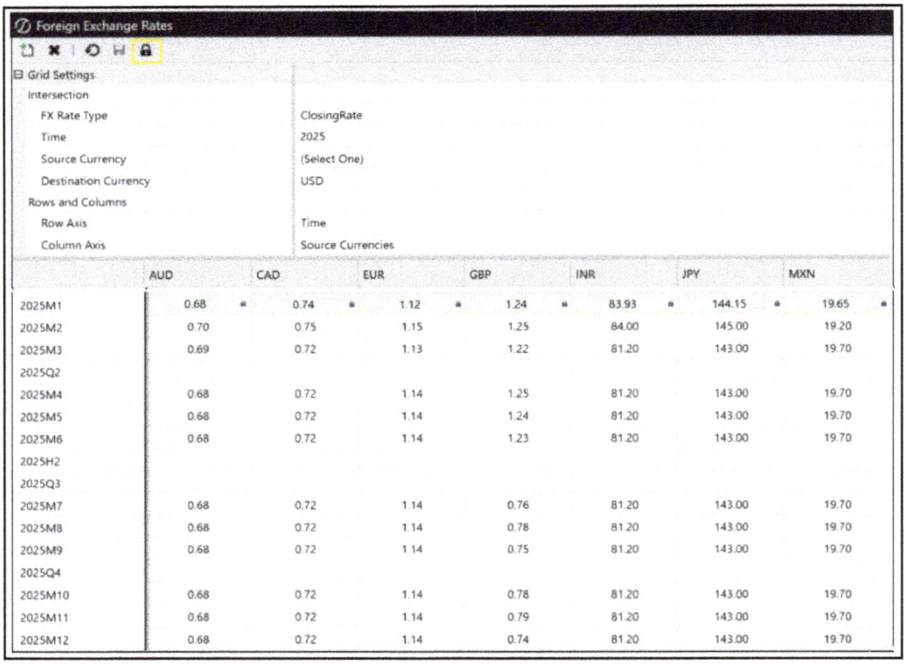

	AUD	CAD	EUR	GBP	INR	JPY	MXN
2025M1	0.68	0.74	1.12	1.24	83.93	144.15	19.65
2025M2	0.70	0.75	1.15	1.25	84.00	145.00	19.20
2025M3	0.69	0.72	1.13	1.22	81.20	143.00	19.70
2025Q2							
2025M4	0.68	0.72	1.14	1.25	81.20	143.00	19.70
2025M5	0.68	0.72	1.14	1.24	81.20	143.00	19.70
2025M6	0.68	0.72	1.14	1.23	81.20	143.00	19.70
2025H2							
2025Q3							
2025M7	0.68	0.72	1.14	0.76	81.20	143.00	19.70
2025M8	0.68	0.72	1.14	0.78	81.20	143.00	19.70
2025M9	0.68	0.72	1.14	0.75	81.20	143.00	19.70
2025Q4							
2025M10	0.68	0.72	1.14	0.78	81.20	143.00	19.70
2025M11	0.68	0.72	1.14	0.79	81.20	143.00	19.70
2025M12	0.68	0.72	1.14	0.74	81.20	143.00	19.70

Figure 2.27

Security

Top Training's data in the OneStream platform is sensitive and requires each user only to see what is relevant to their role. The requirements for security would have been discussed in the analysis and design phases of the project implementation, with the setup and execution implemented during the rollout phase.

Using the jigsaw analogy from the first chapter, it is easier to see the individual tiles that make up security in OneStream first, before we see how they correctly join to provide the bigger picture.

User

A team member in OneStream who was added by the administrator.

Group

Groups are considered **objects** (see below) in OneStream and can be named to represent a department, location, or team name, or a group can be created for a particular tab in OneStream, for example, a group that only has access to the OnePlace tab.

Each group has relevant users assigned to it. For example, for a group called OnePlace, we will assign all the end-users who should only see the OnePlace tab in the Navigation pane.

Role

Roles have already been predefined within OneStream and provide the user with access to specific actions or pages. For example, Top Training's power users will have access to building Cube Views and will be assigned the CubeViewPage role. Other users that update the FX Rates will be assigned the FxRatesPage role.

Object

Objects (which can also be referred to as artifacts as these two terms can be used interchangeably) are created items, such as dimensions, Cube Views, dashboards and groups.

Piecing Security Together

OneStream security enables us to create a user, add the user to a group that may contain existing users, and assign the group to an object such as a dimension, cube, or dashboard. This then provides the user with access.

Most objects have a security option – **Access Group** – which provides view-only access to the users in the group. By comparison, there is also **Maintenance Group**, which will provide maintenance access such as create new objects, edit, and delete. For example, maintaining Cube Views in Cube View Groups.

Taking it further, there are also predefined **application security roles** that are only related to the application in question. Here, groups can be slotted in for certain tasks, such as locking or unlocking FX rates in the FX rates page, or disabling the viewing of the FX rates page itself.

In Figure 2.28, below, we have created a user called EndUser who slots into a group called OnePlace Tab Only Group. That group slots into the Top Training Application and OnePlace tab role.

The result: the end user can only access the OnePlace tab in the Navigation pane, and cannot see the Application or System tabs.

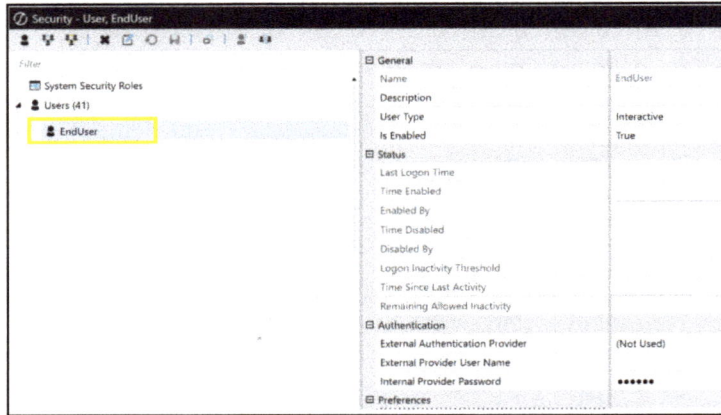

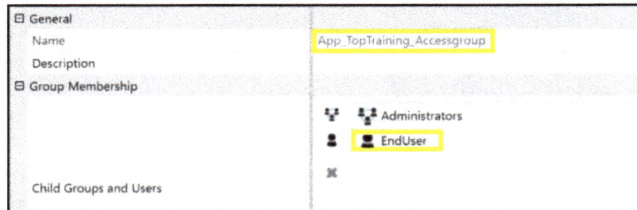

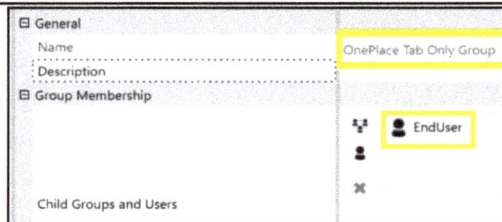

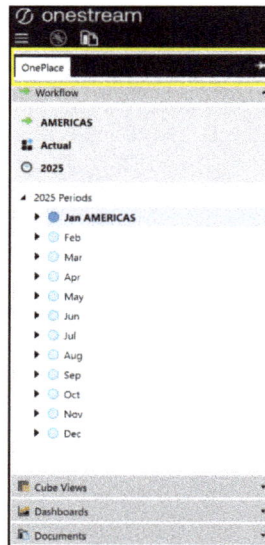

Figure 2.28

Other roles are **system security roles** that are related to user access for *all* applications in the environment where groups can be added, for example, in the ViewAllTaskActivity role. Access can also be revoked, so users can be omitted from the task activity page in their user interface login.

It is worth noting that groups can be assigned to other groups, which – in turn – are assigned to objects. Therefore, it is important to keep track of how users have access to objects. As part of the initial design of groups, a naming convention should be used to provide clarity on a user's level of access. For example, using prefixes such as E_View or E_Write signify if these groups can view the entity only, or write to it.

For a deep dive into security, please see the *OneStream Security Essentials* book.

Conclusion

To accelerate our understanding of the OneStream platform, we have learned that dimensions are the foundational component. Required to be designed and correctly built (so other components work well), they can always be revisited to add further members when needed.

Also, cubes built with efficiency in mind, alongside well-thought-out workflow designs with the right security settings, will deliver good reporting with Cube Views, dashboards, and spreadsheets presenting the right data to the right team members.

Now, let's take a deeper dive into what we've grasped in this chapter!

3

Dimensions, Dimensions and More Dimensions

Designing Dimensions

As mentioned in the previous chapter, good dimension design and build is a crucial part of any implementation and will provide a solid foundation for the remaining OneStream artifacts.

So, in this chapter, our learning journey will take us *end-to-end* in terms of dimensions:

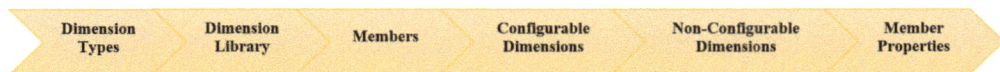

Figure 3.1

The scoping session in our Top Training organization example will determine which dimensions are required. Generally, there is a similar set between most organizations; these being the Entity, Time, Scenario, and Account dimensions. It will be the members in each that will be specific to the organization's requirements.

Dimensions are designed and created by **Dimension Type**. Dimension types are used to organize data into similar categories. Let us revisit the dimension types in the OneStream platform before we work on each one.

The following are found in the dimension library and are all configurable:

- **Entity:** The organization's business areas, set up for statutory and management reporting.

- **Scenario:** A version of data that can reflect, for example, Actuals, Budgets, and Forecasts.

- **Account:** The organization's financial and non-financial values.

- **Flow:** Set up to provide the movements and details on how account values change over time.

- **User Defined (UD):** Eight types of dimension used for further analysis and reporting.

The following are not in the dimension library but are still indirectly configurable:

- **Parent:** Provides the mechanism to see the entities in their parent grouping. Automatically configured when a parent member is added in the Entity dimension.

- **Intercompany:** Determines which entities within the group trade together. Automatically configured when the setting Is IC Entity is set to True.

- **Time:** Data reported weekly, monthly, half-yearly, and yearly. The descriptions for each have been set by the administrator in the Time Profile.

- **Consolidation:** The various stages of data rolling up to the top for a final group report. Showing only the currencies that have been specifically enabled.

The remaining are system dimension types that are not in the dimension library and are not configurable.

- **Origin:** Identifies the data entry method, such as import, forms, or adjustments.

- **View:** Able to show the data from different reporting perspectives, such as year-to-date or monthly.

Some dimension types can have multiple dimensions. These can be created as levels, with each one inheriting the dimension above. The goal of this is to form extended dimensions, with each level catering to different business area members and business processes.

For example, in Top Training, the country managers will require management reports relating to their country, but the regional executives at corporate level will only want a summary by region (with the option to drill down to lower levels if required).

In this case, we can create a User Defined Region dimension that then extends by Country (see below). This is an example of OneStream's Extensible Dimensionality, providing great flexibility for choosing dimensions when building cubes.

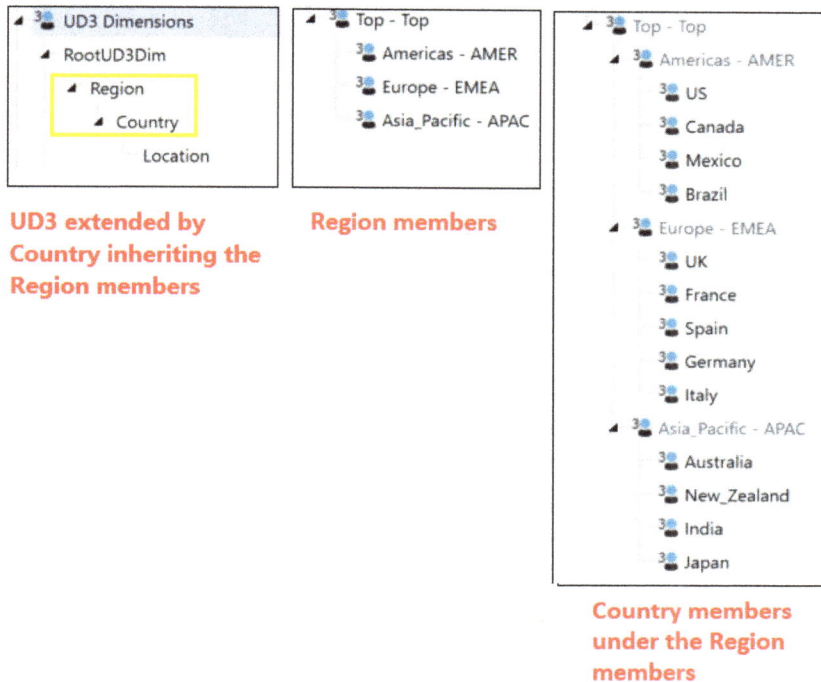

UD3 extended by
Country inheriting the
Region members

Region members

Country members
under the Region
members

Figure 3.2

Members and None Member

As discussed, dimensions are made up of members. These members store data and can be laid out in a hierarchical formation if required. Depending on where they sit in the hierarchy, members can be base level, children, parents, descendants, ancestors, siblings, or orphans.

In our User Defined Cost Center detail dimension, shown in Figure 3.3, examples of members are CC_120 Course Support, CC_310 Finance, and CC_330 Marketing.

Most dimension types also have a None member. These are there by default and cannot be deleted or edited. The None member can be an orphan or added as part of the hierarchy to roll up into a parent member we can name Top.

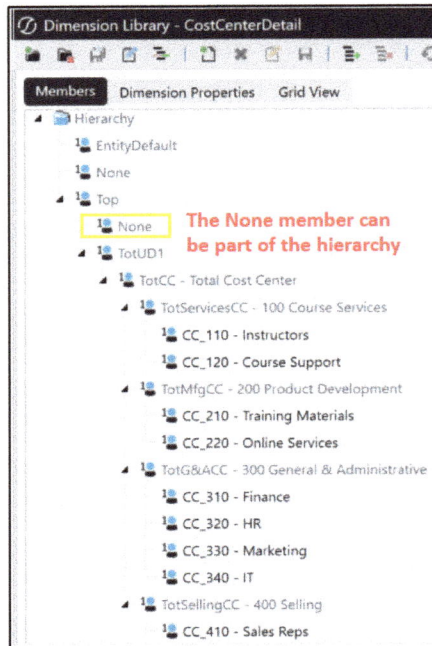

Figure 3.3

Note: For some dimensions, such as Scenario, it is advisable not to use the None member, as a Scenario selection will be required; for example, in the Workflow POV.

What is the purpose of the None member? In a Cube View, data points are represented by every dimension type and their respective members. When a dimension is not used in the cube formation, a member must still be selected. In this case, the None member is chosen for the unused dimension. This is where the data for the dimension resides.

The Dimension Library And Configurable Dimensions

Only the dimension types of Entity, Scenario, Account, Flow, and User-Defined are created and maintained in the dimension library, which is accessed from the Dimension menu, situated in the Application tab of the Navigation pane.

Administrators are the most likely team members who will maintain these dimensions, but some organizations may delegate this task to power users or end-users who become responsible for adding additional members in these dimension types.

The Dimension menu is where dimensions are created, deleted, renamed, or moved (the Entity dimension type cannot be moved), as well as where members are created, deleted, renamed, or their relationships altered if required. The members in these dimensions can be unique to each application.

Entity Dimension

The Entity dimension's makeup – relating to certain aspects of its build – makes it different from the other dimension library dimensions. Firstly, created Entity dimensions cannot be extended; secondly, the hierarchy structure build can flow upwards (compared to the Account, Flow, and User Defined dimensions where the creation of the hierarchy flows downwards as we extend the dimensions… bear with me!).

In Top Training, the Entity members are the countries where the organization's training offices are based around the world. In the design phase, geographical locations were decided upon. In Figure 3.4, compare how Entity dimensions (that cannot inherit other Entity dimensions) are set up to the other library dimensions (where inheriting dimensions is possible). In this example, we have the 100_CORPORATE Entity dimension on the left, and the CostCenterDetail UD1 dimension on the right.

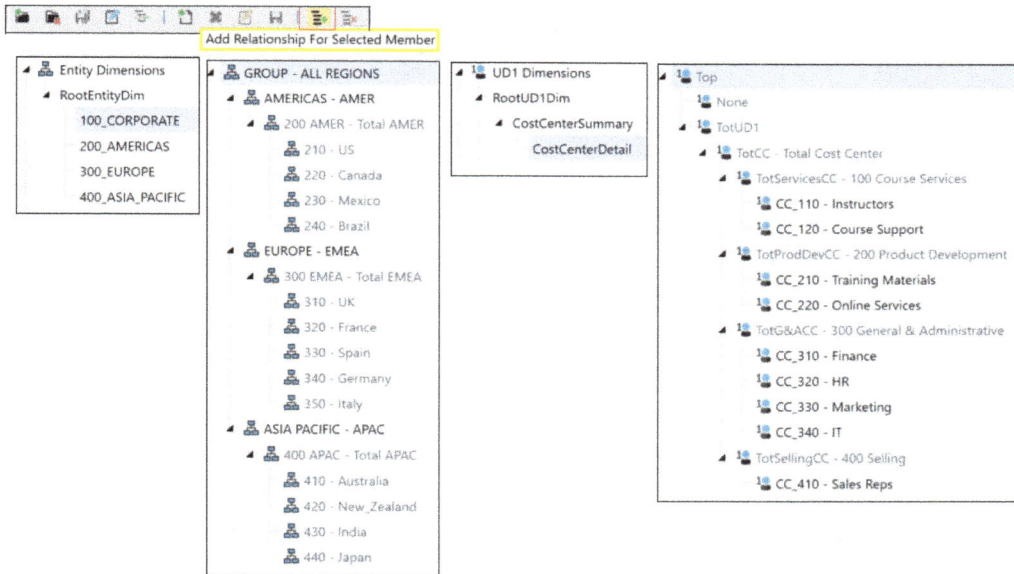

Figure 3.4

In 100_CORPORATE, the black-colored members signify they were created in this dimension, whereas the gray members have been pulled from 200_AMERICAS, 300_EUROPE, and 400_ASIA_PACIFIC using the **Add Relationship For Selected**

Member feature, shown in Figure 3.4. This would have been done by selecting the `100_CORPORATE` dimension then (within it) the `EUROPE - EMEA` member, and creating a relationship by selecting the members from the `300_EUROPE` dimension. This is then repeated for the `AMERICAS - AMER` (selecting `200_AMERICAS` members), and `ASIA PACIFIC - APAC` (selecting `400_ASIA_PACIFIC` members).

But `CostCenterDetail`, on the other hand would have started by inheriting the `CostCenterSummary` dimension and its members. Then (for example) in the gray-colored `TotServicesCC - 100 Course Services` member, we would have created the children `CC_110 - Instructors` and `CC_120 - Course Support`.

Entity And Consolidation Process

The Entity dimension type uses the consolidation process (see also Consolidation dimension, below) to roll data up to the parent-level members. The data at the parent level is populated by running the consolidation, which also includes translation, share ownership, intercompany eliminations, and adjustments. An Entity's share of roll up to its parent is determined by the Percent Consolidation value in the properties, as shown in Figure 3.5.

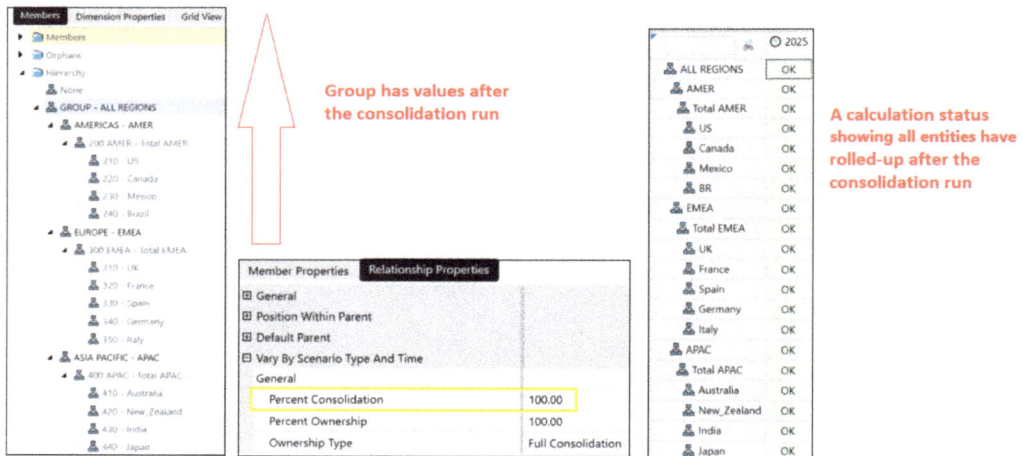

Figure 3.5

Entity Business Areas and Alternate Hierarchies

For other organizations, entity selection is not limited to just location. It is what an organization considers its business areas. Entities can be tangible items, such as the names of shops, warehouses, factories, or intangible items, like profit or even cost centers.

Our initial and main entity set-up would be considered the legal entity hierarchy, wherein all reports using this structure are for **statutory** or external purposes. (They can be internal, too.)

An alternate entity hierarchy will be a duplicate of the same base-level Entity members as the statutory structure but under different parent members – commonly known as a **management structure**. In practice, the management structure can be set up in a User Defined dimension, to avoid creating unnecessary hierarchies in the Entity dimension.

For Top Training, general managers are responsible for certain countries, and each one would like to see reports and data that are only under their remit.

Both statutory and management reporting hierarchies should reconcile because – even though child members are seen as reporting to different parents in the two structures – the data rolling up to each parent is the same.

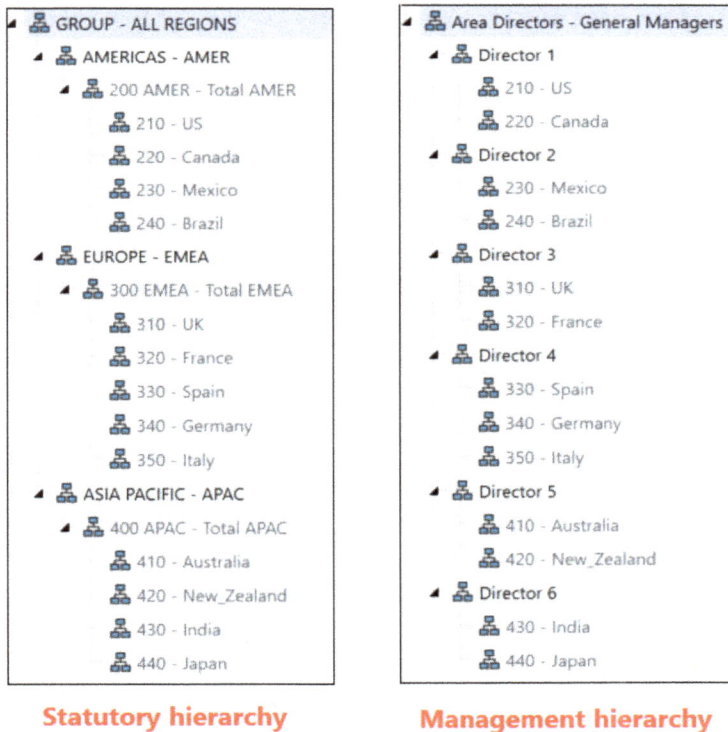

Statutory hierarchy   **Management hierarchy**

Figure 3.6

Other properties that must be considered for the Entity dimension include intercompany trading (Is IC Entity), as well as consolidation (Is Consolidated), and what currency setting is going to be defined, as shown in Figure 3.7.

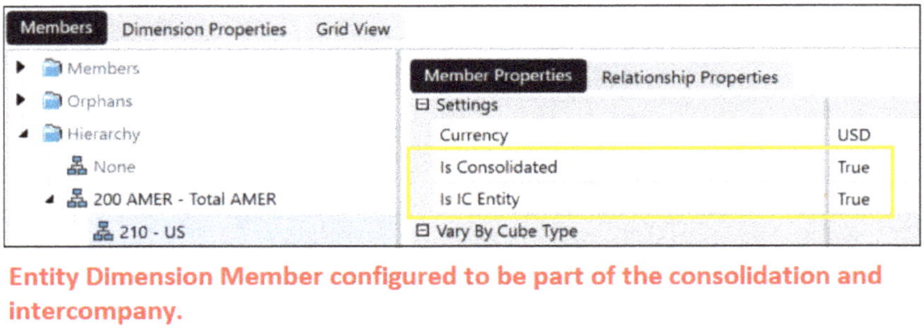

Entity Dimension Member configured to be part of the consolidation and intercompany.

Figure 3.7

Scenario Dimension

Scenario's members represent the type of data we are looking at in OneStream. When we load or enter data in OneStream, we must question what the values represent for decision-making. For example, in Top Training, the executives want to know if the data is what *has* been achieved in terms of sales over the last five years, or what we will achieve over the *next five years*.

Historic or Actuals are member names for financial and non-financial values that have already happened. The future is what we are predicting, though, and can have a member name of Forecast. This is what the Scenario dimension does; it identifies the type of data: Actuals, Forecast, Budget, and so on.

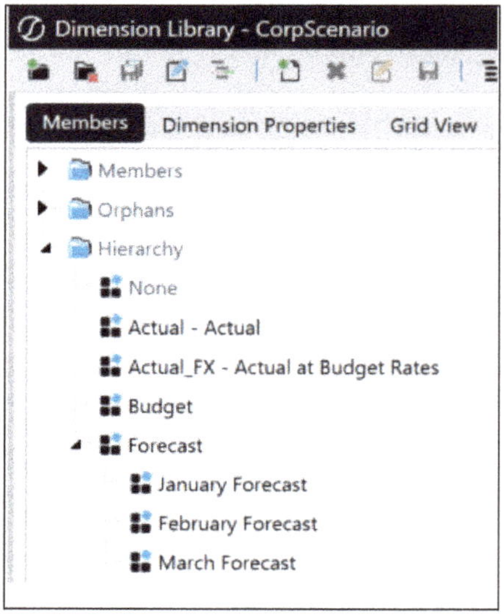

Figure 3.8

As well as creating a Scenario member, we then have the option to select a **Scenario Type** (if enabled to be selected). It is good practice to select a Scenario Type as this will further group our Scenario and allow application properties in other parts of the platform to be configured by Scenario Type, which exponentially increases flexibility.

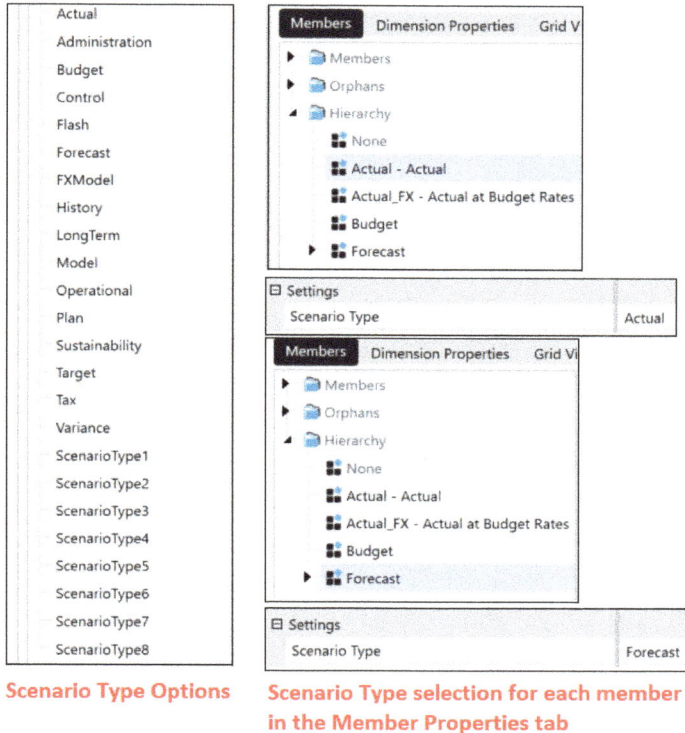

Scenario Type Options   **Scenario Type selection for each member in the Member Properties tab**

Figure 3.9

For example, when adding a Member Formula to, say, a particular account member, we can select the Scenario Type and Time that the formula will apply to, leaving other Scenario Types unaffected. This could mean that – *for the same account member* – we could apply a formula to its Actual Scenario Type and not to its Forecast Scenario Type.

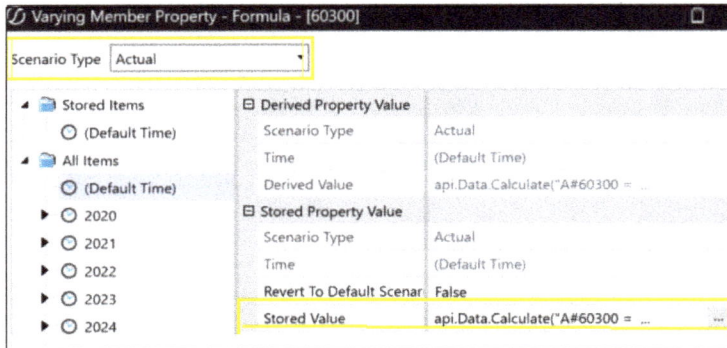

Scenario Type Actual has a formula in Stored Value for account 60300

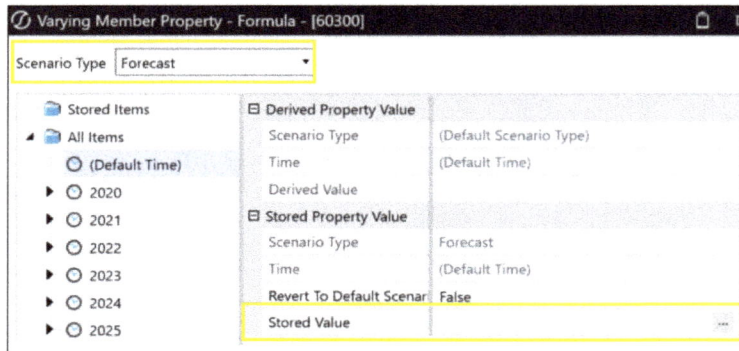

Scenario Type Forecast does not have a formula in Stored Value for account 60300

Figure 3.10

> **Note:** The Member Formula can also be written for the Default Scenario and Time, if required, to apply to all Scenario Types.

Each Scenario member has a setting to establish the frequency of use. For example, Actual data loads are a monthly or weekly occurrence, and Budget can be a yearly one.

Other property configuration options for scenario members, such as Use in Workflow can be set to False if not required.

The option not to use the cube's FX settings (but instead use a specific rate and rule type for a scenario member) is useful if – for example – the Budget scenario is required to use a specific budget rate type set, instead of the rate types in the cube.

Also, the Data Binding Type property. This feature controls how data can be linked between scenario members such as Budget and Forecast. You can:

- **Copy data:** The members remain independent. Changes to one do not affect the other.

- **Share data:** The members stay synchronized. Changes in one (i.e., Budget) automatically update the other (i.e., Forecast).

Use case examples can be requiring Forecast to always reflect the latest Budget data, or when smaller data sets require further analysis from large cubes, the scenario being copied for specific Accounts or User Defined dimension members such as cost centers.

Finally, it is possible to add a parent in a Scenario dimension, but this is for grouping purposes only (like creating separate buckets), which visually helps too, but no data is rolling up into this parent member; it simply acts as the placeholder for the grouping. For example, Figure 3.11 shows the various Forecast scenario iterations separated from Actual and Budget by creating a parent member placeholder. Further groupings have been created for Constant Currency Collections and Budgets.

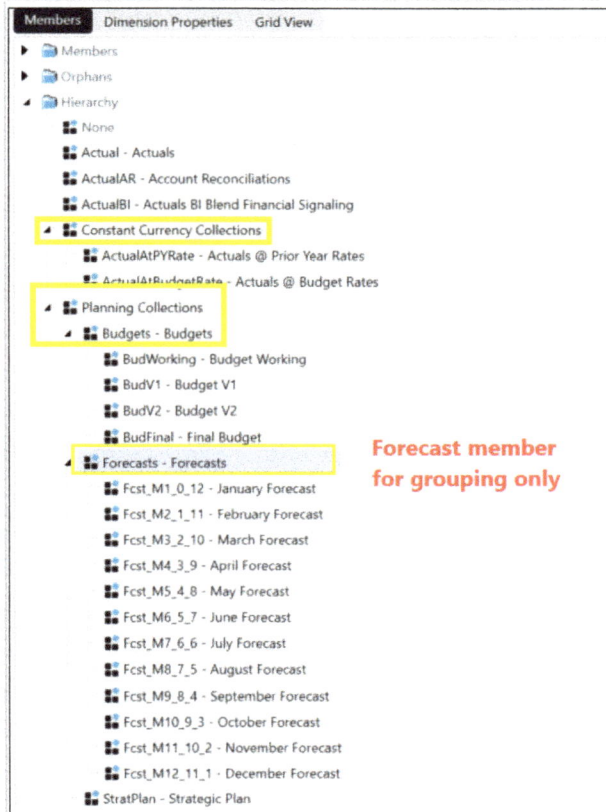

Figure 3.11

Account Dimension

Account members are the very items that represent financial and non-financial values. They can be for 'pens purchased' with the transaction recorded in the stationery account, or a bank deposit amount updated in the cash account.

The creation of all the account members is known as a chart of accounts.

In OneStream, the Account dimension stores financial and non-financial data (headcount or calculated accounts, for example) and is represented as hierarchies, with each account member having a configured **account type**, which is situated in the Member Properties tab.

An account type provides financial intelligence within the platform, and its selection will determine how the value in the account member will roll up. For example, in Figure 3.12, Operating Sales has a revenue account type, and Operating Cost of Goods Sold has an expense account type. With this in place, the roll up to Net Sales will be the Operating Sales amount less the Operating Cost of Goods Sold amount. This is done automatically, and the term used in OneStream is *dynamically*.

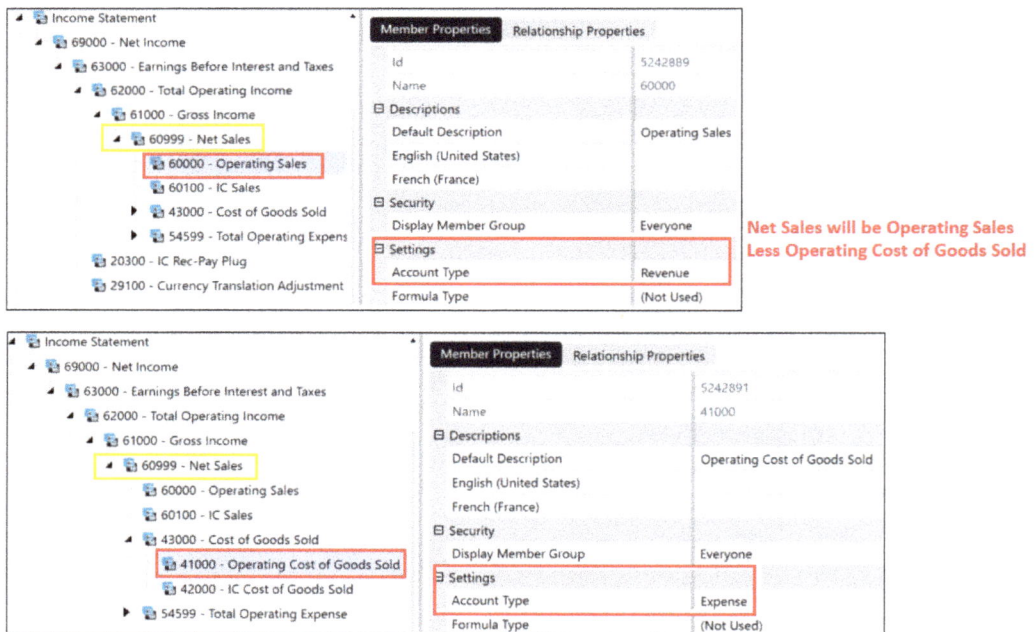

Figure 3.12

As well as the account type being used as the roll up, there is also the use of the Aggregation Weight property in the Relationship tab that is also in Flow and User

Defined dimensions. The input of 1 will provide a positive roll up, with -1 a negative, and 0 no roll up at all.

In Figure 3.13, the weight determines how the finance cost center will roll up to TotG&Acc – 300 General & Administrative. In this case, the 1.00 signifies a positive roll up.

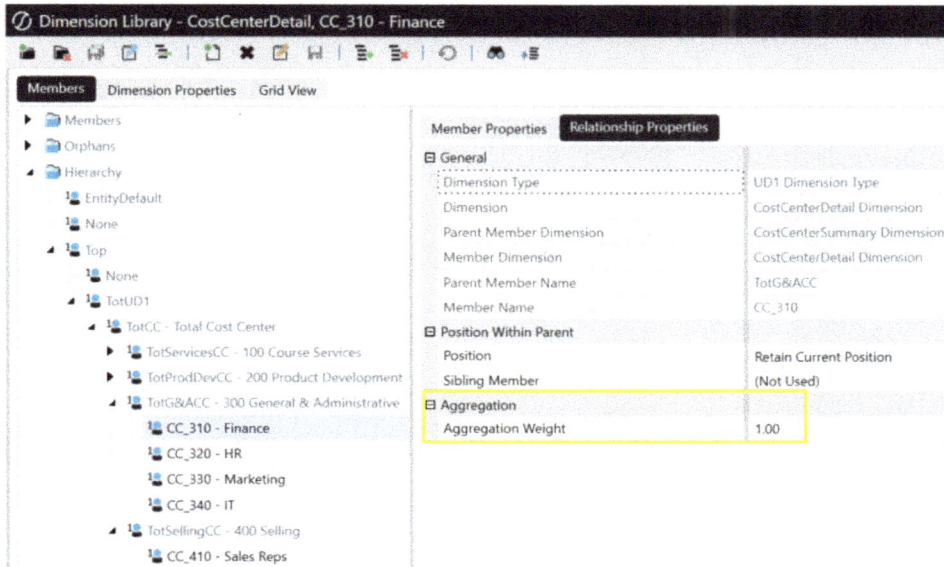

Figure 3.13

Many reports are driven by the chart of accounts and its hierarchies, and provide information such as income statement, balance sheet, or cash flow.

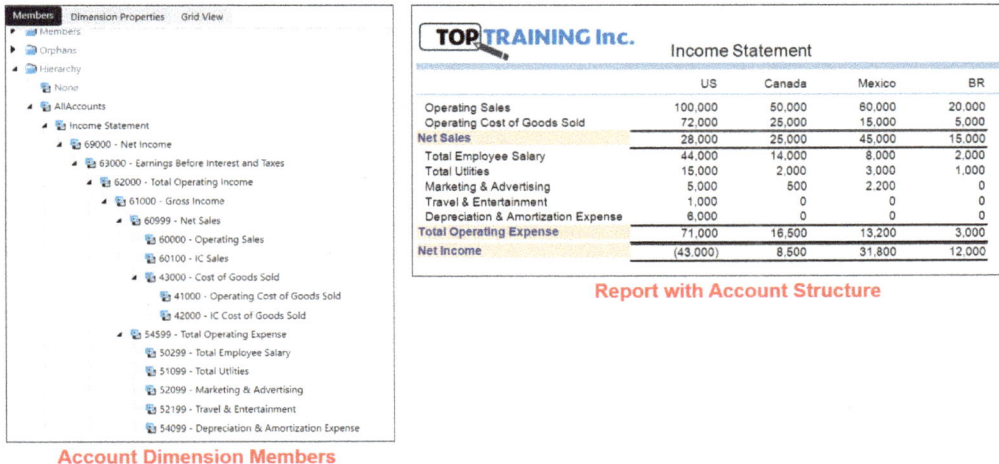

Account Dimension Members

Report with Account Structure

Figure 3.14

Another key member property for the Account dimension is the intercompany trading setting. Through this property setting, we can make another account member deal with any transactional differences between selected intercompany accounts by configuring it to be the Plug Account.

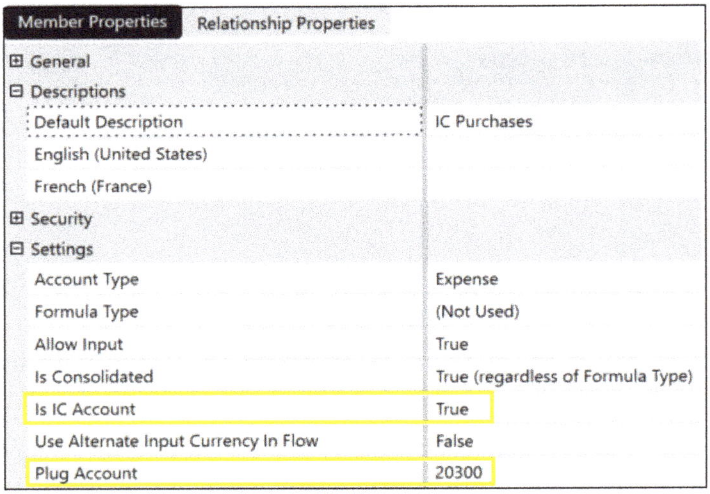

Member Properties	Relationship Properties
⊞ General	
⊟ Descriptions	
Default Description	IC Purchases
English (United States)	
French (France)	
⊞ Security	
⊟ Settings	
Account Type	Expense
Formula Type	(Not Used)
Allow Input	True
Is Consolidated	True (regardless of Formula Type)
Is IC Account	True
Use Alternate Input Currency In Flow	False
Plug Account	20300

Figure 3.15

The Aggregation property prevents a particular Account member – when intersected with other dimension types – from rolling the data to parent members. For example, as Figure 3.16 shows, a Unit Price account's Aggregation property of Enable UD2 Aggregation set to False, will prevent the Unit Price values for each product in UD2 from aggregating to the UD2's Top parent member. This saves processing data that is unnecessary and never reported on.

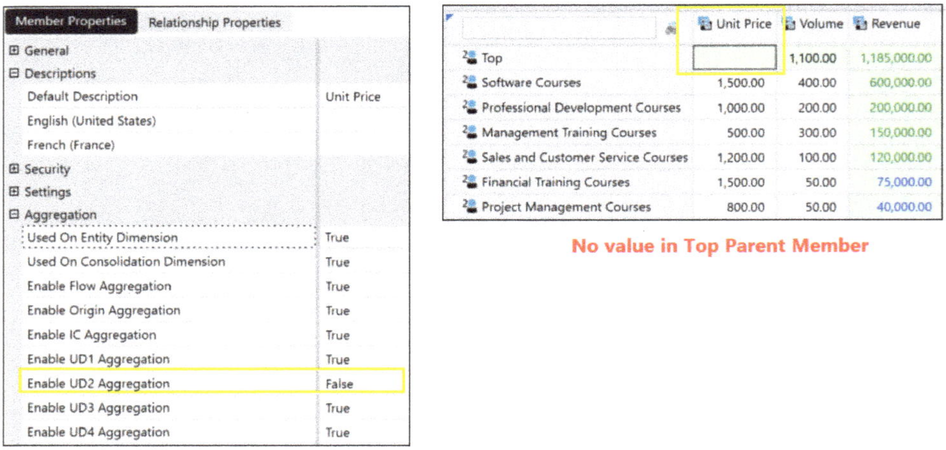

Member Properties	Relationship Properties
⊞ General	
⊟ Descriptions	
Default Description	Unit Price
English (United States)	
French (France)	
⊞ Security	
⊞ Settings	
⊟ Aggregation	
Used On Entity Dimension	True
Used On Consolidation Dimension	True
Enable Flow Aggregation	True
Enable Origin Aggregation	True
Enable IC Aggregation	True
Enable UD1 Aggregation	True
Enable UD2 Aggregation	False
Enable UD3 Aggregation	True
Enable UD4 Aggregation	True

	Unit Price	Volume	Revenue
Top		1,100.00	1,185,000.00
Software Courses	1,500.00	400.00	600,000.00
Professional Development Courses	1,000.00	200.00	200,000.00
Management Training Courses	500.00	300.00	150,000.00
Sales and Customer Service Courses	1,200.00	100.00	120,000.00
Financial Training Courses	1,500.00	50.00	75,000.00
Project Management Courses	800.00	50.00	40,000.00

No value in Top Parent Member

Figure 3.16

Flow Dimension

As we now understand the Account dimension, it is worth extending our knowledge on how further detail can be provided – if required – that shows how values have changed. This is commonly known as **movements** on the account. For example, at the start of a particular year, Top Training had 280 staff members globally. A growth strategy meant 235 new hires were employed during the year, with 25 leaving the organization, ending in 490 staff members by the end of the year.

The Flow dimension is where all these movements can be recorded, with its simplest setup (for, say, Top Training's headcount example) as member names: Beginning Headcount, New Hires, Leavers, Closing Headcount; to more complex scenarios such as Top Training's Cash Flow movements.

	Beginning Headcount	New Hires	Leavers	Closing Headcount
US	20	50	(5)	65
Canada	15	-	-	15
Mexico	40	20	(2)	58
BR	20	30	(3)	47
UK	30	40	-	70
France	20	30	(5)	45
Spain	10	-	-	10
Germany	20	-	-	20
Italy	10	30	(2)	38
Australia	20	10	(3)	27
New_Zealand	40	5	(5)	40
India	10	10	-	20
Japan	25	10	-	35
ALL REGIONS	280	235	(25)	490

Figure 3.17

Once again, the Aggregate Weight property will dynamically roll up the values in Flow dimension members as either a positive or negative.

The Flow dimension allows users to view balances; for example, asset or liability account balances on a periodic basis when used with the View dimension. It can also extend to other use cases, such as currency movement, roll forwards, beginning balance, and ending balance load.

User Defined (UD) Dimensions

When organizations such as Top Training report on information, reports can be displayed at either a very high level (showing a few key account values) or a very detailed low level (which can be the whole account structure for every course in every location). It is at this point in the analyze and design phase of the OneStream project implementation that we would know if any of the User Defined dimensions are required and what the members will represent.

The User Defined dimension is organization-specific and is used to create custom member hierarchies that provide additional detail for data load, entry, and reporting.

Typically, they span a common theme of cost centers (a way of defining, say, each department in Top Training to ascertain costs attributable to it), regions, products, or even customers; but other reporting metrics or some critical data component (that needs to be seen) can be created.

Configurable Dimensions Outside the Dimension Library

There are additional dimension types with configurable properties sitting outside the dimension library, that will have a selection requirement at certain points around the platform, for example, in the Cube POV, or when creating reports.

Parent Dimension

A requirement in the Cube POV is to select the parent member (on selection of the Entity member, its parent is automatically selected). The parent member is sitting in the Entity dimension and forms part of the hierarchy. It is the entity's parent-level member. So, for Top Training, we've established the reporting entities are the countries such as France, Germany, and Italy, and the parent for each of these European countries, and the Parent dimension selection in the Cube POV, will therefore be 300 EMEA.

Intercompany Dimension

Intercompany, as the word suggests, is trading within the group structure. An individual business unit can report their sale to another business unit in isolation for their financial statements, but when it's the group consolidating total sales, Corporate will need to eliminate intercompany selling and intercompany purchasing to avoid double counting sales and purchases made to (or with) businesses trading within the group.

The Intercompany (IC) dimension is created by configuring an entity as Is IC Entity is True and will then be marked as an entity that is involved in intercompany activity within the group. This is only required for base-level entities. Once done, this is reflected in the IC dimension, which can be accessed from the Cube POV and is a flat list of intercompany entities.

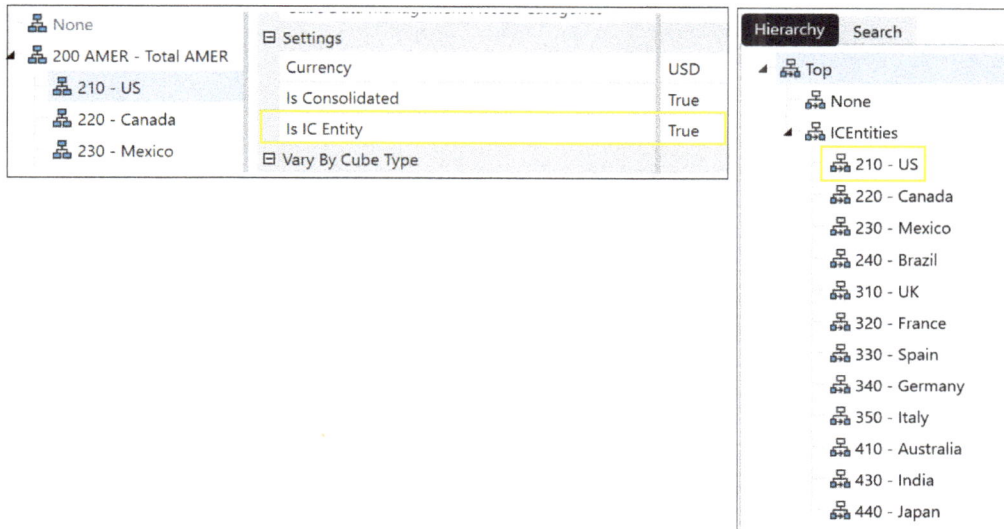

Figure 3.18

> **Note:** Where no intercompany is present, then the None member can be used; for example, when data loading or for report member selection.

Time Dimension

Time is considered a key component when reporting. In OneStream, the formation of the Time dimension can either be by OneStream's default offering of months, quarters, half-year, or year, which is the **Standard Time** dimension, or a bespoke setup utilizing further granularity, such as weekly. OneStream also has the capability to extend the timeline for adjustment periods.

The selection of Time is required in the cube for workflows, Cube POV, Cube View POV, various reporting options, and within referencing formulas and business rules. Therefore, it is imperative the setup is correct, with minimal changes once data has been loaded into the application.

As a reminder, Time is within the Application properties menu, where the start year and end year have been set. This acts as a filter to only show these years when a user is selecting a particular year.

The Time Profiles menu is a separate setting and menu option to the Time dimension. It is used to configure the Time dimension, mainly adding a description to the generic member names such as M1, Q1, and H1. Top Training's financial year is January to December; therefore, M1 will be assigned January as the description. However, some organizations – where the financial year is April to March – can assign M1 as April.

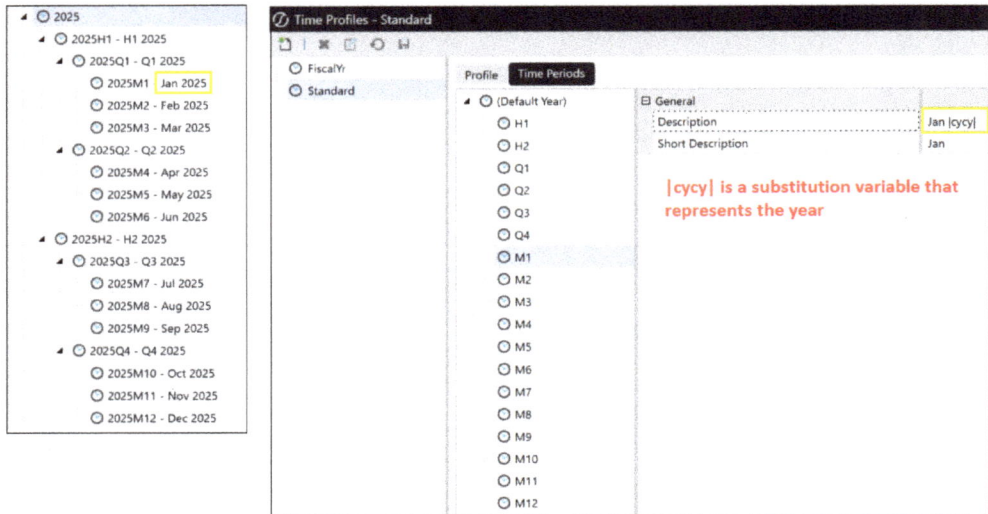

Figure 3.19

An organization can have many time profiles set up (if required) for a calendar year and various fiscal years, but the formation of a cube only has the option to select one. Therefore, a situation may arise if a number of cubes are created for different business areas and they have different time profiles.

Consolidation Dimension

OneStream's consolidation calculation will require members to derive values from low-level child Entity members to high-level top group members. Consolidation members have already been pre-defined by the platform and are part of the Cube POV selection and also Cube View POV selection.

The Consolidation dimension shows the translation, share of equity, and any eliminations due to intercompany activity, together with adjustments and currencies assigned to the application. The dimension has been divided into three groups:

Top

This contains the members that show the translation, share of equity, and any eliminations due to intercompany activity, together with adjustments. In Figure 3.20, the left box shows the Consolidation dimension with members. The right box shows examples for Canada, Mexico and Brazil. Starting at the bottom in their local currency values, we work upwards, first translating each to USD, next applying the group's share of equity, then taking into account any intercompany eliminations, and finally making any group adjustments. The top value then being reported is in the group financial statements.

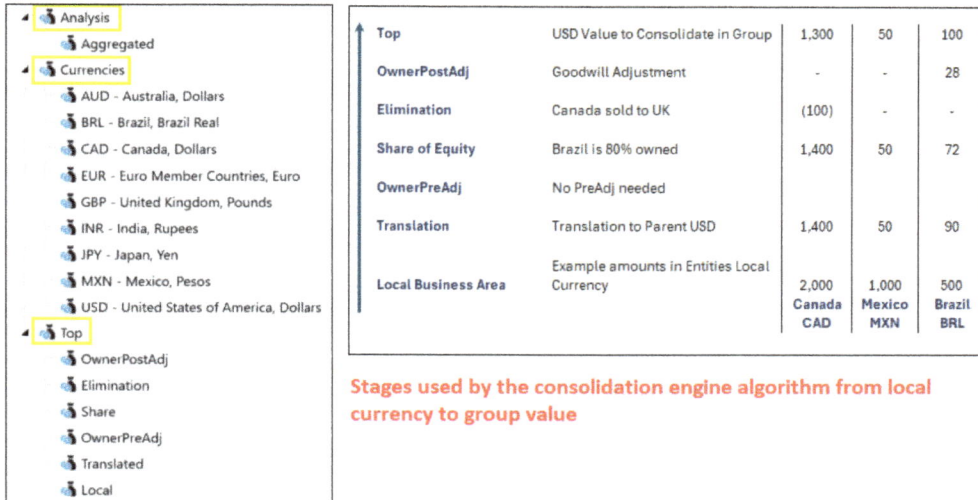

Top	USD Value to Consolidate in Group	1,300	50	100
OwnerPostAdj	Goodwill Adjustment	-	-	28
Elimination	Canada sold to UK	(100)	-	-
Share of Equity	Brazil is 80% owned	1,400	50	72
OwnerPreAdj	No PreAdj needed			
Translation	Translation to Parent USD	1,400	50	90
Local Business Area	Example amounts in Entities Local Currency	2,000 Canada CAD	1,000 Mexico MXN	500 Brazil BRL

Stages used by the consolidation engine algorithm from local currency to group value

Consolidation Dimension Members

Figure 3.20

Currencies

These are the currencies assigned and used in the specific application. Initiated by the Application Properties selection, we can either select 'Local' or the currency the entity uses when it comes to selecting the Consolidation dimension in a report. The currency type is assigned at the entity level and drives the local currency.

Analysis

This has the option for aggregation, providing a mechanism to roll up data a lot quicker. This excludes the Data Unit Calculation Sequence (DUCS), and instead calculates mathematically from bottom to top. The engine bypasses some aspects of consolidation. This is useful for planning purposes or real-time report views where only translation and share of equity are required.

System-Defined Dimensions

Origin and View are the final two dimensions, both of which are non-configurable and outside the dimension library. As per all the other dimensions, member selection is required for data to be included in a report.

Origin Dimension

When analyzing in OneStream, we might sometimes wonder if the values are a consequence of data entry input or adjustments made, or part of a larger data load, and the Origin dimension can help us here. The dimension differentiates between the data origin and has predefined members called Import, Forms, and Adjustments. (There is also an Elimination member.)

When the workflow tasks of Import and Forms are executed in OnePlace by the user, this will populate the Import Origin and Form Origin members in the Origin dimension. Figure 3.21 shows the workflow tasks matching their counterpart in the Origin dimension.

The `AdjInput` member will reflect the individual child-level entities' journal adjustments also carried out from the workflow task. Once a consolidation is run, these all consolidate into the `AdjConsolidated` members in the parent-level entity.

The Origin's elimination member will be populated when the Consolidation dimension's elimination member has been posted because of intercompany activity. Also, for information purposes only, there is a `DirectElim` member (eliminations at the first common parent) and an `IndirectElim` member (parent showing an elimination that is due to entities lower down the hierarchy).

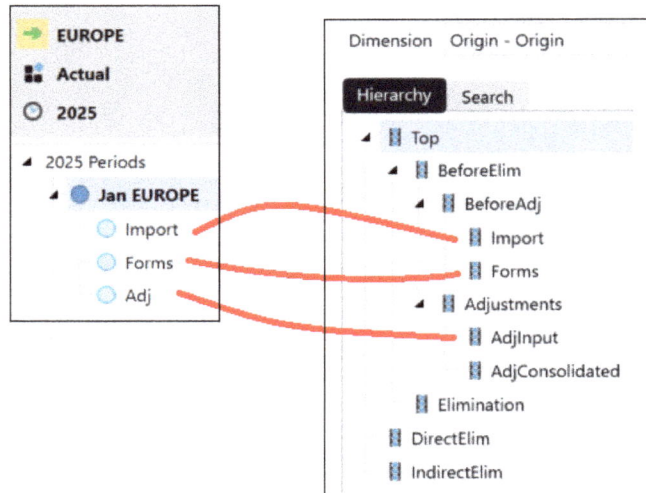

Figure 3.21

View Dimension

As the name of the dimension suggests, even though data is stored year-to-date, it can be viewed dynamically as month-to-date or quarter-to-date, for example (as well as common calculations like averages and trailing totals). The view members are common in all applications, and there are no hierarchies.

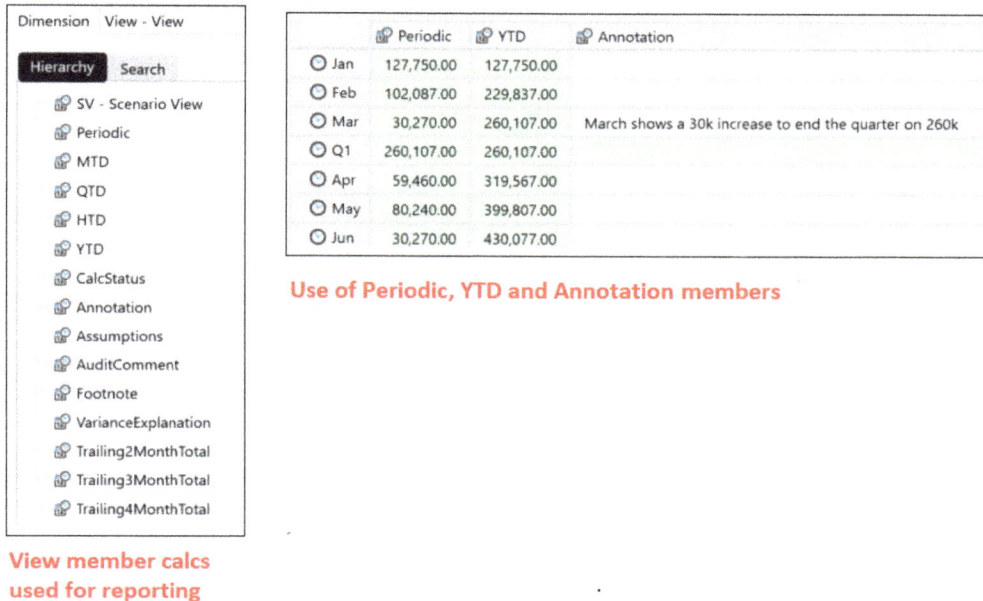

View member calcs used for reporting

Use of Periodic, YTD and Annotation members

Figure 3.22

Features such as comments in annotation cells (V#Annotation, V#VarianceExplanation) and attachments in data cells provide audit trails if required.

The calculation status member in the View Dimension – CalcStatus – displays a status code that indicates if a calculation needs to be run. This is a very prominent feature and will be discussed later on in your learning journey.

After absorbing a topic, your author always makes a point of trying to see the bigger picture. In the case of the dimensions, it is worth summarizing key aspects in one snapshot, as shown in Figure 3.23.

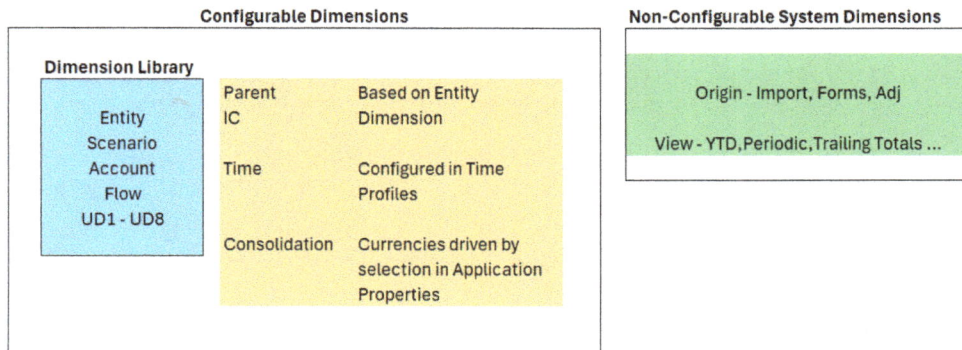

Figure 3.23

65

As a reminder, dimensions are the metadata structures required to build cubes. With many cubes built in the application, we can use the same dimensions over and over again. If we do not use a dimension when creating a cube, then – for most dimensions – when it comes to selecting members for a report, the None member is chosen. This doesn't apply to the Time, View, or Origin dimensions, where core members are required to be selected for data to be seen.

For me, grasping the concept of having to select a None member – when, clearly, we are saying the dimension is not being used – was a moment to pause to understand the concept fully. If we revisit the cube and data point discussion from the last chapter, a cube's frame is made up of the 18 dimensions discussed above, and we are selecting which of the 18 are relevant to the Cube. *But the remainder are still part of the build.*

When data is loaded into the cube, all 18 dimensions are still part of that load. A member selection is required from *all the dimensions* to provide the data point, and None is, therefore, the option for the unused dimensions.

Building Dimensions

Dimensions can be created manually, one by one, along with their members. From a learning point of view, this is good to see. Then, once we understand how dimensions are built (and extended, if required) and how members are then created inside dimensions, we can move forward to dimensions and members being uploaded from a recognized OneStream file in bulk (such as through the Metadata Builder Utility tool provided by OneStream in the Solution Exchange. See further down in the Importing Dimension and Members section). The file still needs to be created by the administrator, but this is a speedy way to load hundreds, if not thousands, of members.

Naming Conventions and Creating Dimensions and Members

As part of the design, dimension names should be relevant to the members inside it, and the member names should be consistent throughout the hierarchy. The reasons for a proper naming convention include a good standard kept by all team members, dimension names that flow through other parts of the application can be recognized easily, and requirements for renaming are kept to a minimum (otherwise, a name change may need manual updates in other places where the dimension is being used).

It is considered easier to have names without spaces, using underscores instead. This makes rule-building conventions easier to apply, as brackets will not be required. All members have a default description property option; this is an alias for the member name and can be displayed in the end-user reports if Description is the chosen option during the report build rather than Name.

In the dimension library, there are dimension groups. Inside each group, dimensions are created under the predefined **RootDim**. For Top Training, the UD3 dimension (for example) has been created to represent its geographical setup.

Under RootUD3Dim, the Region dimension is first created with three region members.

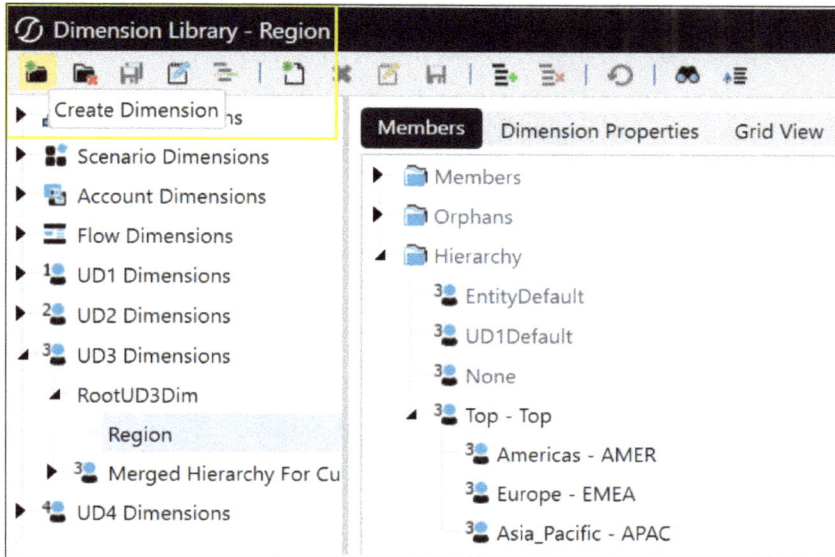

Figure 3.24

Then the Country dimension extends below, with the Region as the Inherited Dimension, and the country members in it.

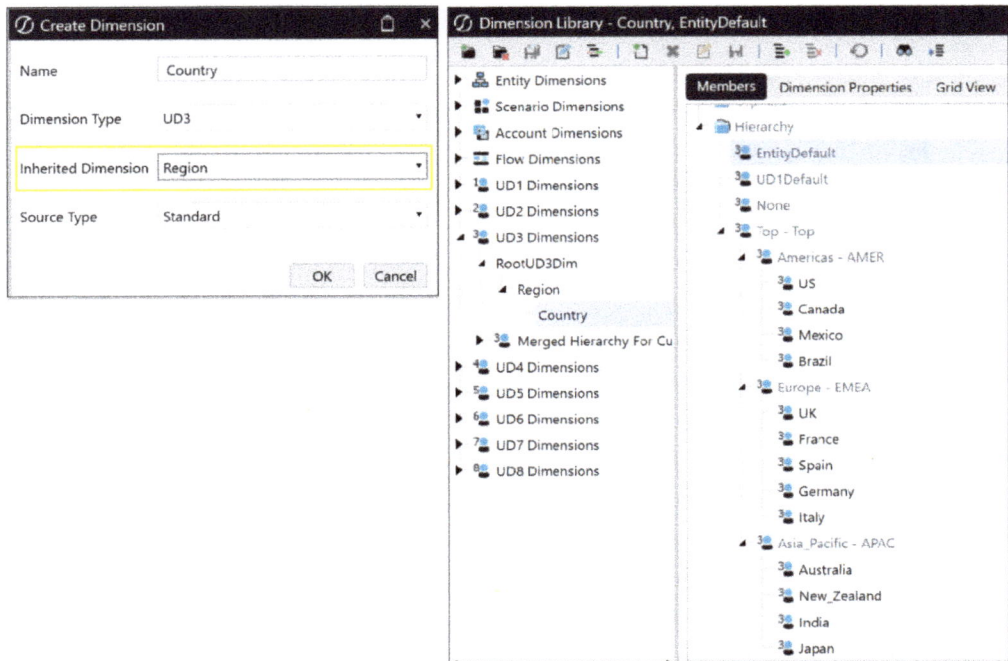

Figure 3.25

Then, finally, the Location dimension is below the Country dimension, with the location members.

Members can be created from the Create Member icon or by using the Clone Member menu option (a right-click activity). Figure 3.26 shows the creation of a new member by cloning an existing one. Settings are copied, except for the formula types and formulas, which do not copy to the new member.

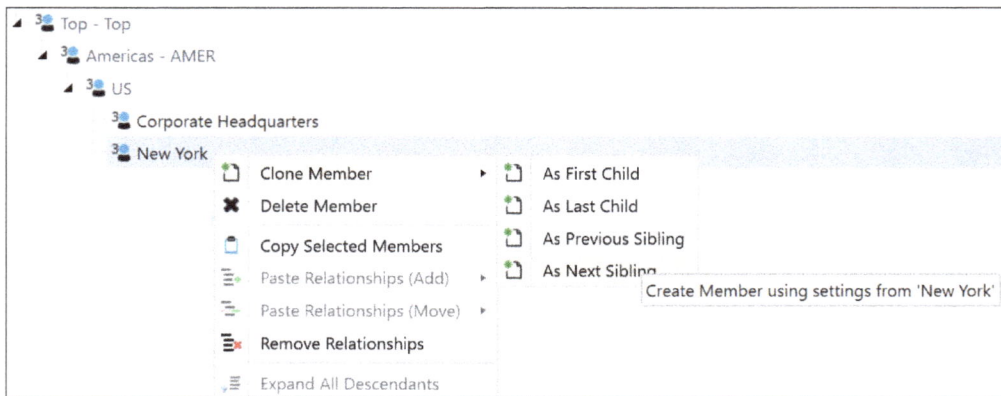

Figure 3.26

There are also options to copy and paste a member. Once copied, the member can be shifted somewhere else in the hierarchy by selecting Paste Relationships(Move) or duplicated somewhere else by selecting Paste Relationships(Add).

A relationship can also be broken if required. This takes the member out of the hierarchy and places it in the Orphans folder of the dimension. Figure 3.27 shows Phoenix in the Orphans folder after the relationship has been broken with the US parent member.

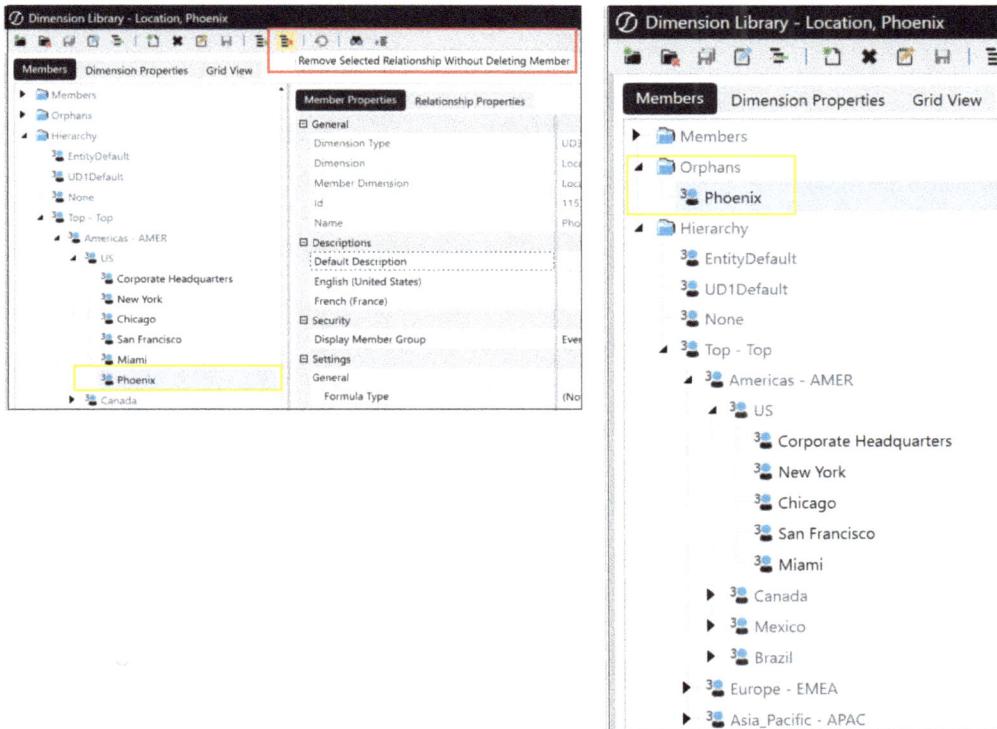

Figure 3.27

Changing the member's spot within the hierarchy can also be done in the Relationship Properties tab where, relative to its siblings, various dropdown options to move the member exist.

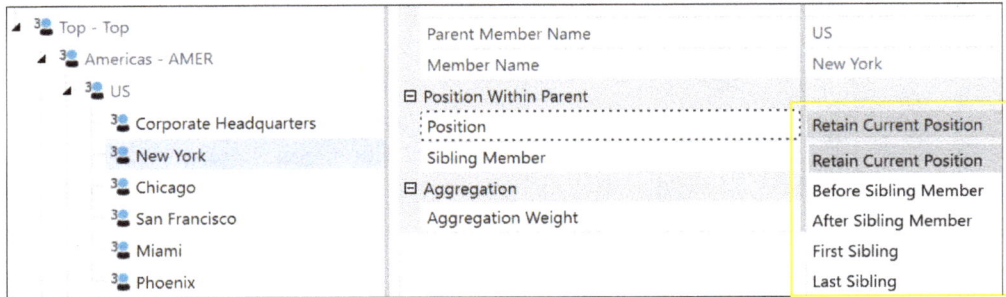

Figure 3.28

Using The Grid View for Multiple Configurations

After the project build, the dimension members' configurations may require changes. This may be the administrator's responsibility or be delegated to the team who are managing their respective hierarchies. Configuration can be done one member at a time, or the grid view may be the preferred option when configuring multiple members. Located in every dimension, Grid View is the third tab, and after applying the grid settings (and possibly Member Filter options, too), we can change the property settings of multiple members in one update.

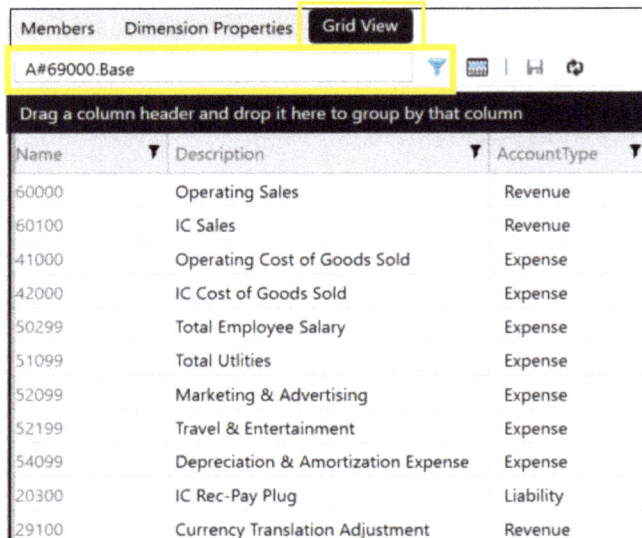

Member Filter used to select base members to display in the Grid View

Figure 3.29

Importing Dimension And Members

Dimensions and member hierarchies are part of a wider terminology known as **application artifacts**. These can be imported into the application by loading XML files in the **Load/Extract menu**.

XML files can be formed by using the Excel Metadata Builder Tool, which is ideal for creating many dimensions and members in an application.

Dimension Type:	Entity
Dimension Name:	200_Americas
Description	Americas
Access Group	Everyone
Maintenance Group	Everyone
Inherited Dimension	100 Corporate

Member	Description	Formula Type	Allow Input	Is Consolidated	Alternate Currency For Display	Workflow Channel	In Use
210	US	(Not Used)	TRUE	Conditional		Standard	TRUE
220	Canada	(Not Used)	TRUE	Conditional		Standard	TRUE
230	Mexico	(Not Used)	TRUE	Conditional		Standard	TRUE
240	Brazil	(Not Used)	TRUE	Conditional		Standard	TRUE
		(Not Used)	TRUE	Conditional		Standard	TRUE

Parent	Child	Aggregation Weight	
200 AMER	210	1	
200 AMER	220	1	
200 AMER	230	1	
200 AMER	240	1	

Figure 3.30

Once the cells are populated with the member names in the main body of the Spreadsheet, the right-hand side will convert the characters into the XML format required, which can then be copied from top to bottom and pasted into, for example, a NotePad++ document, saved as an XML file, and then imported into the application using the Load/Extract menu.

```
1   <?xml version="1.0" encoding="utf-8"?>
2   <OneStreamXF version="4.1.0.7407">
3   <metadataRoot>
4   <dimensions>
5   <dimension type="Entity" name="200_Americas" description="Americas" accessGroup="Everyone" maintenanceGroup="Everyone">
6   <members>
7   <member name="210" description="US" displayMemberGroup="Everyone"><properties><property name="FormulaType" value="(Not U
8   <member name="220" description="Canada" displayMemberGroup=""><properties><property name="FormulaType" value="(Not Used)
9   <member name="230" description="Mexico" displayMemberGroup=""><properties><property name="FormulaType" value="(Not Used)
10  <member name="240" description="Brazil" displayMemberGroup=""><properties><property name="FormulaType" value="(Not Used)
11  <member name="" description="" displayMemberGroup=""><properties><property name="FormulaType" value="(Not Used)"/><prope
12
13  </members>
14  <relationships>
15  <relationship parent="200 AMER" child="210" aggregationWeight="1"></relationship>
16  <relationship parent="200 AMER" child="220" aggregationWeight="1"></relationship>
17  <relationship parent="200 AMER" child="230" aggregationWeight="1"></relationship>
18  <relationship parent="200 AMER" child="240" aggregationWeight="1"></relationship>
19  <relationship parent="" child="" aggregationWeight="1"></relationship>
20
21
22  </relationships>
23  </dimension>
24  </dimensions>
25  </metadataRoot>
26  </OneStreamXF>
27
```

Figure 3.31

Member Properties

As newcomers to OneStream, we have managed to understand a broad range of metadata concepts. As our learning progresses, the likes of member property configurations further add to our understanding of the platform's capabilities. Member properties are discussed in a lot more detail in *the Foundation* and *Administrator Handbook* publications. But at this stage, as we have discussed all the dimensions, it is also worth going over a select few member properties that are unique to certain dimension types.

As a start, all dimension types have a common theme of properties such as name, description, and text 1, 2…8 (a way of identifying a member in, say, a rule, by applying what has been assigned to the text fields in the rules expression).

Security settings in the dimension library for entity and scenario will quite rightly be either Read and Write Data Group, Read Data Group or Display Member Group, with remaining Account, Flow, and UDs having just the Display Member Group option, that limits member access.

Constraints Member Property

The constraint property is found in the Entity, Account, and UD1 dimensions. It is used to restrict entering data to only certain intersections set on the Flow, Intercompany or User Defined members. For example, in Figure 3.32, the Top Training US entity is restricted to only entering data for the US locations in the UD3 dimension member intersections.

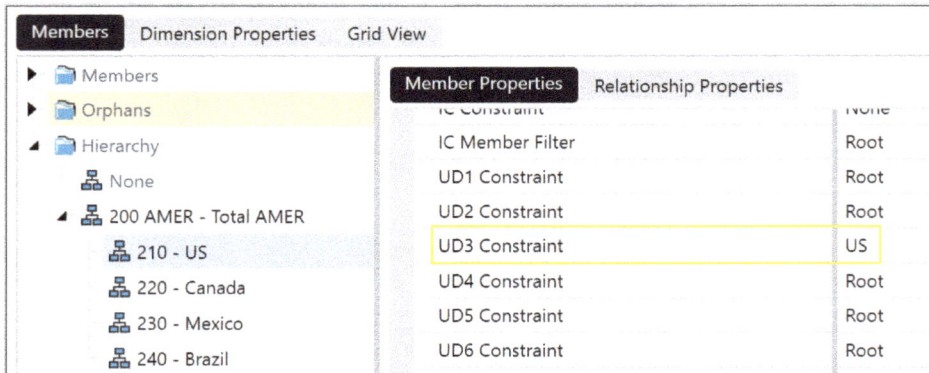

Figure 3.32

Conclusion

Dimensions and metadata overall are the foundation of other artifacts and the backbone of OneStream. The process of creating them – along with their associated members – is very logical in the OneStream platform. Through the design phase of an implementation project, it is important to establish the business areas that will represent the entities and then structure them for a legal statutory hierarchy, as well as an internal alternate hierarchy for management reporting.

The chart of account members will be a unified set of accounts in the OneStream platform, with each of the group subsidiaries mapping their legacy system accounts to OneStream Account dimension members for group consolidation, planning, and reporting.

The scenarios establish the type of data being analyzed and reported on: Actuals, Budget, and Forecast. The remaining configurable dimensions will be organization-specific if required.

Finally, we have established that the final two dimensions – Origin and View – are system-defined dimensions with a mandatory requirement of a member selection from both for a data point to be established.

4

Cubes
(Hexahedrons
Sounds Smarter!)

Let's Make Cubes

After building our dimensions, we shall be working on our cube types and how best they can serve each business area.

Here is this chapter's learning journey:

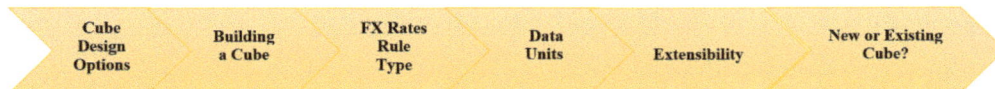

Figure 4.1

Using the jigsaw analogy, we now know that dimensions are the tiles created for us, which are then pieced together to form a cube. A cube, therefore, is a multi-dimensional (two or more dimensions) structure that controls how data is stored and then used for calculations, translations, and consolidations.

Back in the design phase of the implementation project, there would have been a discussion about cubes, from their initial requirements for Top Training to using them for reporting purposes.

To distinguish types of cubes within OneStream, the scoping session in the project uses an implementation methodology to describe cube design options. This is not related to selecting anything in the platform; it is a way of labelling the functional workings of the cube. Explored in detail – in both the *Foundation* and *Administrator Handbooks* – a summary of our options is:

Super Cube Linked to Detail Cubes

A super cube is a common setup for workflow and consolidation where a top-level cube is linked to the detail business area cubes. With Top Training, Figure 4.2 shows that the super 100 Corporate cube links the three business area detail cubes of Americas, Europe and Asia Pacific. An alternative approach can also be a single detailed cube, which contains all three business areas, linked to the super cube.

Exclusive Cube

As the name suggests, an exclusive cube will be a standalone cube that could be populated by another cube through business rules and possibly used for the purpose of complex reporting. This type of setup could be considered if data is of a sensitive nature and security can easily be applied to the isolated build.

Monolithic and Specialty Cubes

Monolithic cubes are considered simple in design and not linked to other cubes. They can be part of a phased approach, from capturing Top Training's requirements to eventually being updated with further design features. Ultimately, a monolithic and exclusive cube could serve the same purpose with no differences.

Off the back of the monolithic option, an administrator can create a **specialty cube** which, in effect, is a simpler version of the monolithic cube but used for a specific purpose (for example, a driver-based function or for inventory). It can be separated from other cubes and secured to grant access and maintenance.

These are the cubes that have been designed in Top Training Inc.

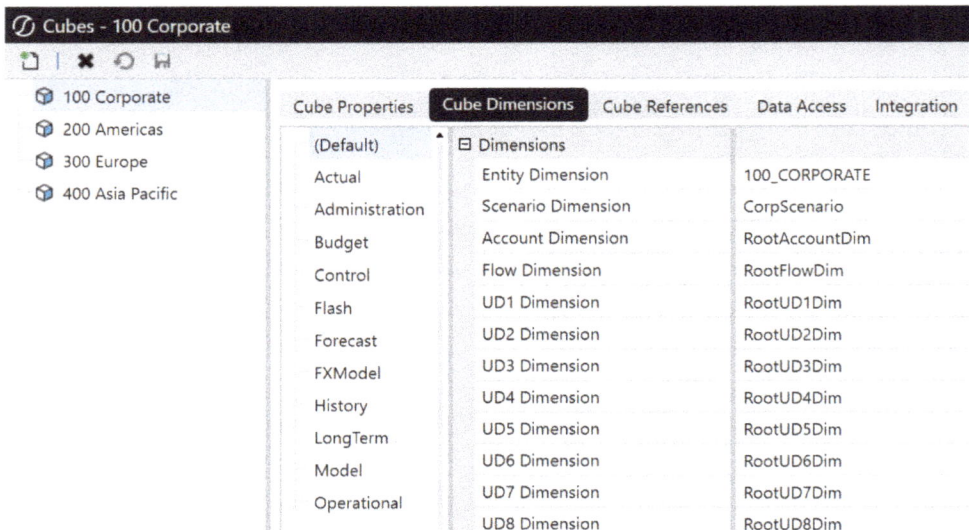

100 Corporate is the Super Cube with 200 Americas, 300 Europe, and 400 Asia Pacific the Detailed Cubes

Figure 4.2

Building a Cube

The cube's design and build will be the responsibility of the implementor or the administrator for Top Training. At the start of the project, all the required cubes will be built, but once the platform is up and running and maintained by the administrator, then a decision needs to be made for any further business requirements. Business requirements may mean adding new cubes, or (after speaking with the stakeholders) the administrator may conclude that the new requirement can be captured in an existing cube. Let's start off by building a new cube before we tackle the second option.

Cubes are built in the Application tab, and once the cube menu is selected, there are five tabs that will be worked through to complete the construction of said cube. These are Cube Properties, Cube Dimensions, Cube References, Data Access, and Integration.

Don't Forget Your Cube Properties Tab

The Cube Properties tab has six sections: General, Security, Workflow, Calculation, Business Rules, and FX Rates. It is important to get the core settings correct first time, as some cannot be changed once the cube is live. For example, unlike other artifacts, the name of the cube cannot be amended.

In the General section, we assign a Time dimension profile (the standard Time Profile will be assigned by default), as well as the name and description of the cube and the selection of the cube type. The cube type selection ranges from Standard, to Tax, Treasury and What If, as well as cube types 1 to 8. Consider using a **tag** to group cubes with similar characteristics. Tags are also a great way when applying constraints on dimension members (as mentioned in the previous chapter) to vary constraints by cube type.

The Security section controls read and write access, as well as maintaining the cube object, but – regardless of the access setting – the user will be able to select the cube in the Cube POV.

The additional setting – Parent Security for Relationship Consolidation – can restrict access to parent-level consolidation members, such as share, elimination, OwnerPostAdj, and Top, by selecting True.

As per Figure 4.3, the next section is about workflow, which we will get into – in depth – later in the book. The Workflow section in the cube is a starting point for selecting which cube will be the top-level cube used by the Workflow Profiles to assign tasks and entities to.

The Suffix for varying Workflow by Scenario Type option will only be available if the top-level cube is set to True and provides a mechanism to create further instances of top-level cubes in the Workflow Profile type (see chapter on 'Let Your Workflow').

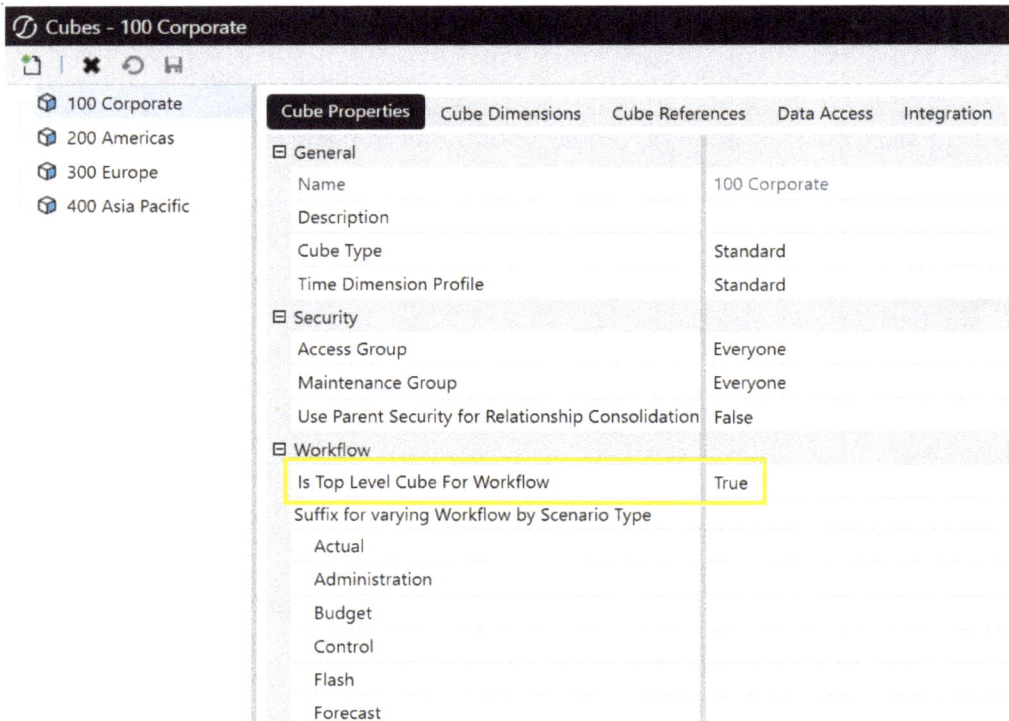

Figure 4.3

The Calculation section determines the options used for the consolidation and translation algorithm engine (the Standard option is the default, working with Consolidation dimension members as per the previous chapter, and the FX rates setting shown in Figure 4.4, below; this can be switched to Custom consolidation to use a business rule instead). Other options include performing a calculation when there's no data in the cell. This ensures data being copied into empty time periods or scenarios through a calculation will run.

The Business Rules section determines the order in which rules are run. This is referred to as the Data Unit Calculation Sequence (DUCS), explored further in a later chapter on 'Figuring Out Calculations'. For reference, the *Finance Rules and Calculation Handbook* book covers calculations and business rules in depth.

The FX Rates section allows for the selection of the **default reporting currency** that entities will translate to, with the rate and rule types for income and balance sheet accounts. The default currency is also the driver for the system to triangulate rates.

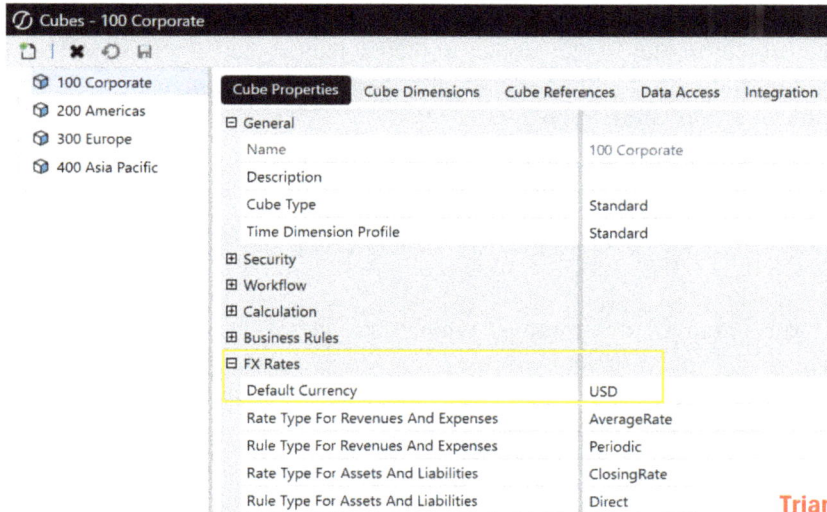

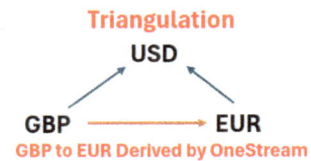

Figure 4.4

As part of my learning journey, I now understand the **Periodic** and **Direct Rule Types**, and I love sharing, so here is what I have learned.

The direct method is straightforward. Whatever the YTD local value is for the entity for a particular month, just multiply it by the exchange rate. So, the direct rule is like a spot rate.

The periodic method, on the other hand, first takes the month's movement and multiplies that local value with the exchange rate, and then adds last month's translated YTD value.

	Direct Method		Periodic Method	
	Jan	Feb	Jan	Feb
Exchange Rate	1.20	1.15	1.20	1.15
Local Currency YTD Value	1,000	1,200	1,000	1,200
Translated YTD Value	1,200	1,380	1,200	1,430

Movement is 1,200 - 1,000 = 200   200 x 1.15 = 230   230 + 1,200 = 1,430

Figure 4.5

Figure 4.5 shows the direct method translates the local value by the exchange rate, whereas – for the periodic method – the movement from January to February is 200, which is multiplied by the 1.15 rate with the result added to 1,200 (January's translated value) for the final value to be 1,430.

This is all extensively covered further in the *OneStream Administrator Handbook*.

Pick Your Dimensions Carefully in the Cube Dimensions Tab

After we have established in the design phase which dimensions should be assigned to the cube per Scenario Type, it is here – in the Cube Dimensions tab – where the dimensions are now selected. This will provide structure to the cube and how the cube will organize the data within the application.

For each Scenario Type required, we assign as many of the Account to UD8 dimensions as per the design phase. Further, if any dimension is not needed, it is recommended that the root option be selected. For the Default Scenario Type, we select which Entity and Scenario dimensions are required for this cube, as shown in Figure 4.6; then all the other Scenario Types for this cube will also use them (note that we could continue in the Default Scenario Type with the selection of other dimensions or leave it to just Entity and Scenario with the others set to Root).

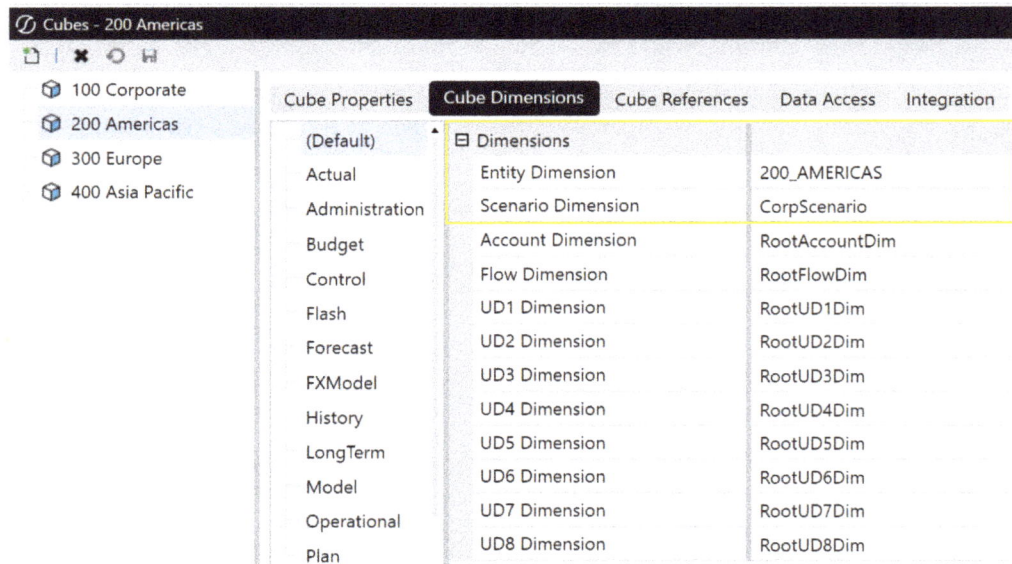

Figure 4.6

Selecting the root option on the dimensions which are not needed is important. Why? Because once dimensions have been assigned and data is loaded into the cube, it is not possible to change any dimensions assigned to that cube (unless a complete data clear-out is done on the cube).

But if root has been the original selection, then as the value is sitting in the root's None member and should a new dimension be required, this can be easily changed to the new dimension name.

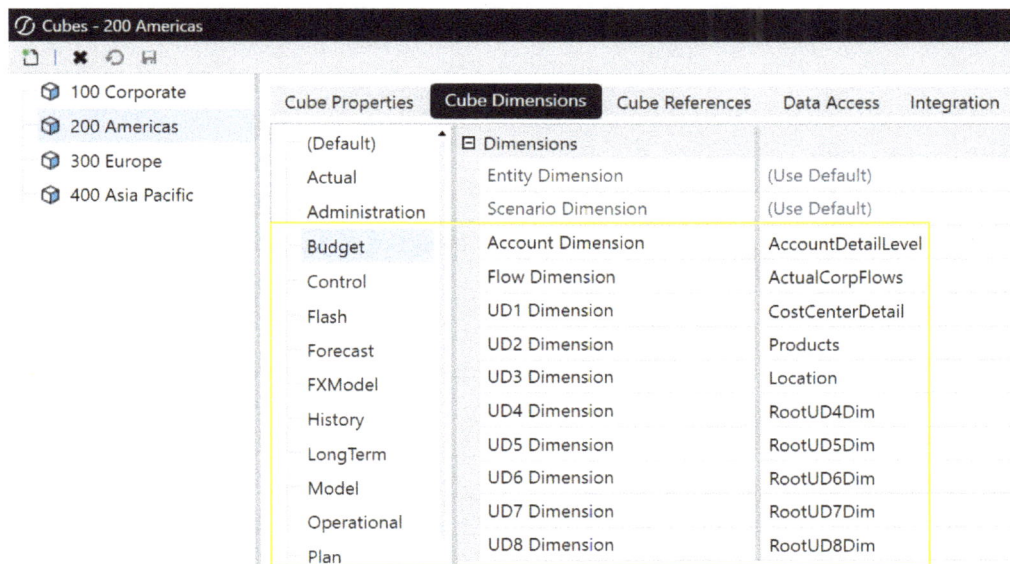

Figure 4.7

Cubes References Tab

When confirming what our cube design options were, specifically the super cube linked to detailed cubes, this tab completes that design. The options available in this tab have come about from a chain of events starting firstly with the creation of the entity hierarchy where in Top Training, the Corporate entity has a relationship with Americas, Europe and Asia Pacific entities. Then, the 100 Corporate cube has True for Is Top Level Cube For Workflow, in the Workflow section of the Cube Properties tab (the first tab).

In our example, it will only be the 100 Corporate cube that has options in the Cube References tab and not 200 Americas, 300 Europe, or 400 Asia Pacific, as these are the detail cubes.

To complete the selection for the 100 Corporate cube in Cube References, it is just a case of selecting which cube from the right-hand dropdown is assigned to the left-hand Entity dimension. For convenience, we labeled the cube name the same as the entity name, but this may not always be the case.

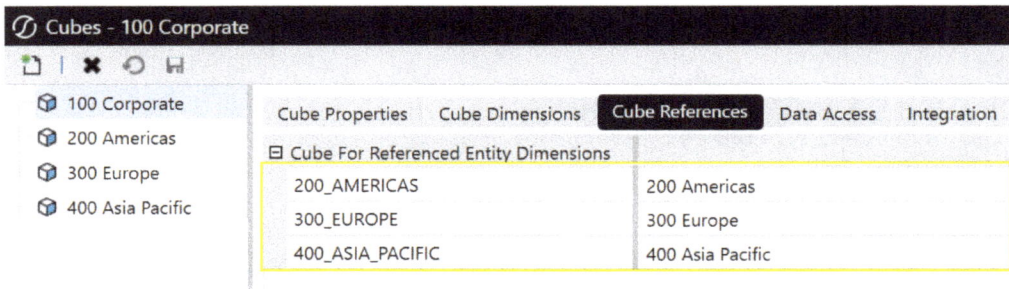

Figure 4.8

Data Access Tab

The first layer of cube security was in the Cube Properties tab, with the next layer in the Data Access tab, providing access to the data stored in a cube. The Data Cell Access Security, also known as **slice security** (access to specific slices of data), provides the mechanism for the user not to have access to every data cell for, say, a particular entity or account-related dimension. The combination of security settings involved here is beyond the scope of this book but can be found in the very helpful *OneStream Documentation Release* and the *OneStream Security Essentials* book.

Integration Tab

Configuration settings in the Integration tab will impact the data source and transformation rules menu options (discussed in detail later in the book), which are both in the Application tab, and ultimately control what is seen for the data load in the OnePlace workflow.

It is in the Cube Dimensions tab where the selection of the dimensions for each dimension type will, in turn, provide the driver in this Integration tab to disable dimension types not being used. For example, in the Cube Dimension tab, the 200 Americas cube for the Budget Scenario Type, has UD4 to UD8 set to Root as they are not being used. This means they do not need to be part of a selection in the data source and transformation rule profile menus. For this to happen, all five User Defined dimension types can be set to False in the Enabled setting in the Integration tab as per Figure 4.9.

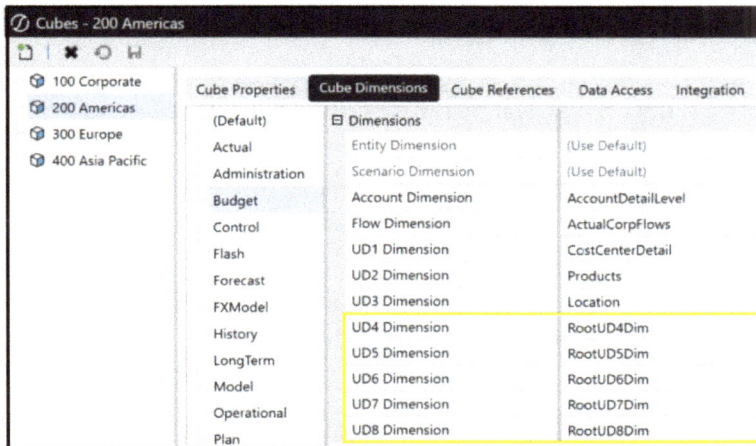

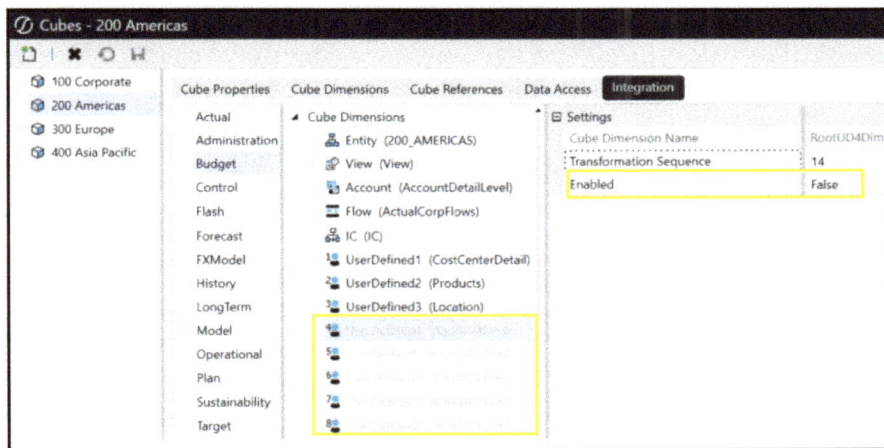

UD4 to UD8 set to False in the Integration tab as these are not needed for the Cube

Figure 4.9

Once set, these dimensions are still part of any data load, with the None member automatically being used. This would also mean the None member should now be selected for these dimensions when running reports.

With the super cube plus a range of detail cubes now built, the data from various sources to load into OneStream will follow and be discussed in the next few chapters. For the remainder of this chapter, a few technical aspects of cubes – together with content on design efficiency – will enhance our learning experience of cubes and make for a good segue to the *Administrator Handbook* publication.

Did Someone Mention Data Units?

Important knowledge, when it comes to the design of a OneStream application and measuring the efficiency of cubes processing various tasks, can be encapsulated with the term **Data Unit**.

Within OneStream's multi-dimensional engine, the work tasks carried out range from clearing data, loading data, calculating data, translating data, copying data and consolidating… you guessed it… data!

All of these tasks are performed within a Data Unit. This Data Unit is created in the server's memory and the size of that unit will determine the processing time.

If we were to look at the cube as a whole, with so many data intersections and records, it would be difficult to gauge the processing time for various tasks the cube performs. Therefore, taking smaller chunks (or subsets) of the cube would be easier, hence the Data Unit metric. The analogy I have in mind for this is that of a large house. It may be difficult to gauge how many days would be needed to refurbish the whole house, but if we split it down room by room, this would be easier to assess.

So, what is the make-up of a Data Unit? It is the Entity, Parent, Consolidation, Scenario and Time dimensions, as well as the cube, that make up a Data Unit (this is commonly known as a Level 1 Data Unit… bear with me!).

Why is this important for the user? Knowing how the size of the data impacts performance for, say, good report building would be one example. When a report is built and run, the server is assessing how many members from Entity, Parent, Consolidation, Scenario and Time need to render (basically the number of intersections or slices of data to render) to produce the report (i.e., one entity or two entities, one year or two years). The multiplying of members from these specific dimensions adds to the number of Data Units that are being processed at one time, and in this case one Data Unit or two Data Units.

This is why a consolidation report containing multiple entities on the rows may perform more slowly than an income statement with a single entity in the Cube View POV, because entity belongs to a Level 1 Data Unit.

The Data Unit we are describing is known as Level 1, and its size is of a higher granular level than Level 2 or Level 3 Data Units, both of which slice the monitoring of the performance at a more detailed level. Level 2 considers all of the Level 1 dimensions mentioned, *plus* the Account dimension. Level 3 is all of Level 1 and 2 and then a selected User Defined dimension. These two levels are discussed further in the *Administrator Handbook*.

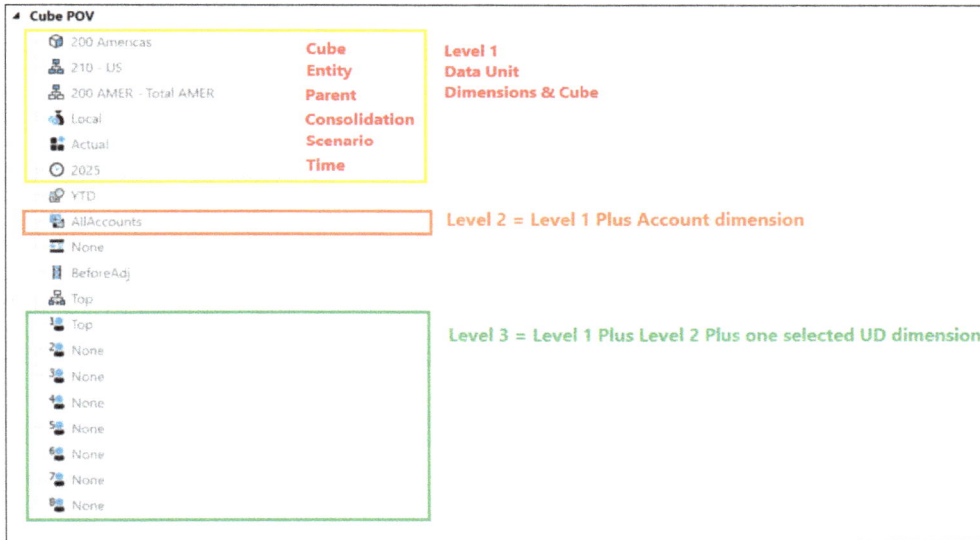

Figure 4.10

Let's Fall in Love with Extensibility

Top Training's platform administrator is responsible for correctly maintaining the application to provide flexibility and high-level performance. One of the key design features for this is **Extensibility**.

Extensibility is the sharing, inheriting, and extending of dimensions by entity across business areas or across Scenario Types. This type of design helps to contain different requirements for Top Training's business areas all in one application.

Extensibility provides the flexibility of a single member serving multiple purposes, as well as the ability to use multiple cubes, with each one tailored to a different business and each one possibly using different levels of the same dimension. Ultimately, performance gains can be seen when breaking up the Data Units; in Figure 4.11, the 100 Corporate uses the summary level for the Account and UD1 dimensions, whereas the 200 Americas cube is at the detail level of the same dimensions.

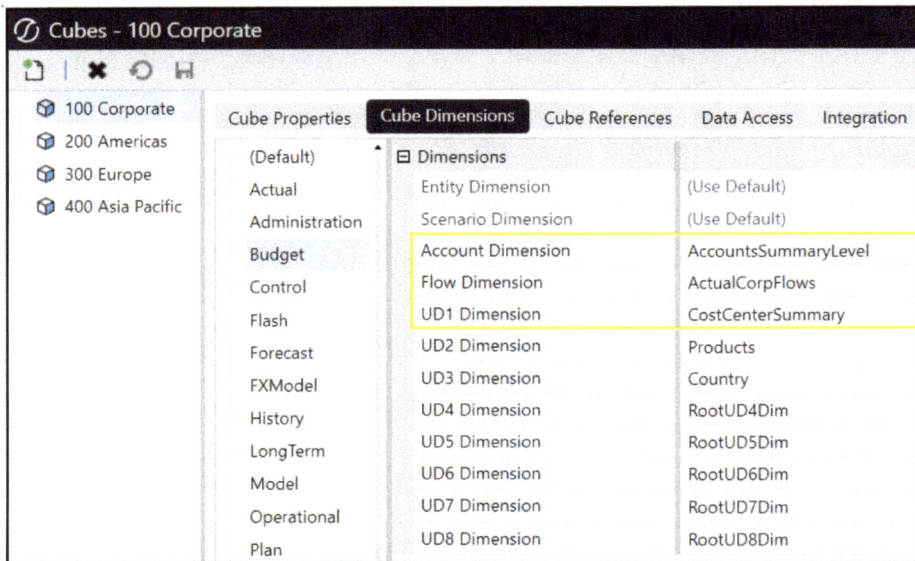

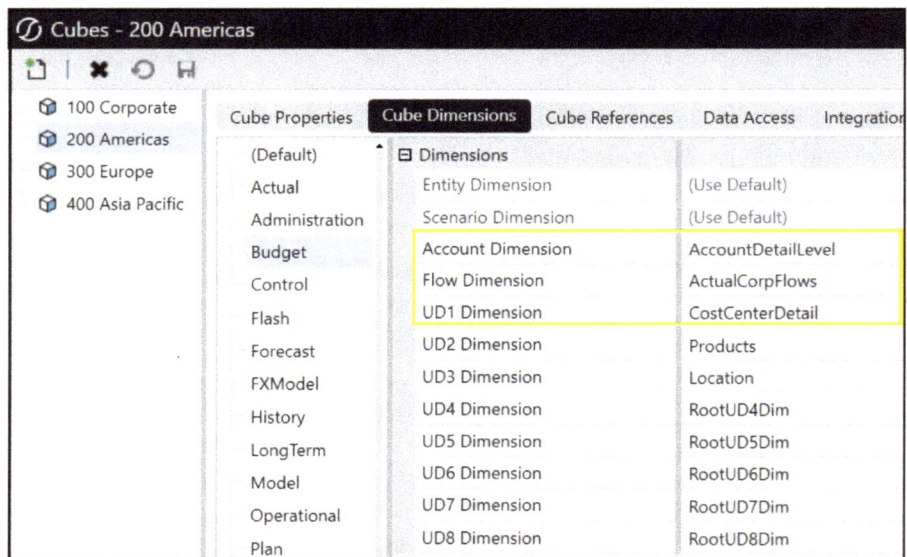

Figure 4.11

Two types of extensibility designs are discussed in the implementation project – **vertical extensibility** (which can reduce the Data Unit size) and **horizontal extensibility** (which does not reduce the Data Unit size).

Vertical Extensibility

The purpose of vertical extensibility is to consolidate an entity structure. This is set up with a single Scenario Type across entities and multiple cubes. As the entity is the only dimension that cannot extend (you cannot have Entity dimensions inheriting other Entity dimensions), we are instead able to create relationships between members from different Entity dimensions and then connect them using multiple cubes. Figure 4.12 sketches out Top Training's `100 Corporate Cube` consolidating the detail business area of cubes `200 Americas`, `300 Europe`, and `400 Asia Pacific`.

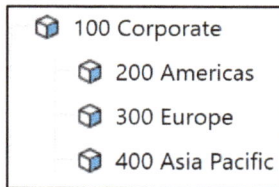

Figure 4.12

As other dimensions are able to extend, there is then the ability to have different Account, Flow or User defined dimension members for different areas of the business, so those areas can report on what is relevant to their results. Looking at Figure 4.13, for operating sales, BU1 has related detail members that are different from the BU2 detail member requirements.

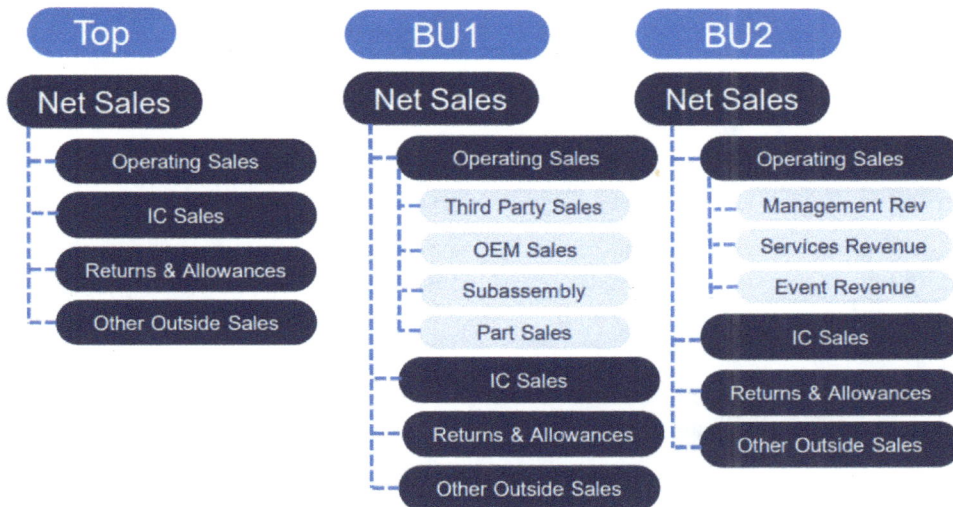

Figure 4.13

This type of design suits an organization that is a conglomerate (a group containing some businesses that are not related in terms of industry or markets).

Horizontal Extensibility

Possibly, with just one cube, horizontal extensibility will take that cube and use the concept of dimension levels over a range of selected Scenario Types. For example, in Figure 4.14, a cube's Budget Scenario Type has been built with the Account dimension showing net sales at a summary level, and for the same cube, its Actual and Forecast Scenario Types use the Account dimension at a detail level, and in this case, different base-level members for operating sales. There is still the ability to use variance analysis between scenarios, as there will still be some common members.

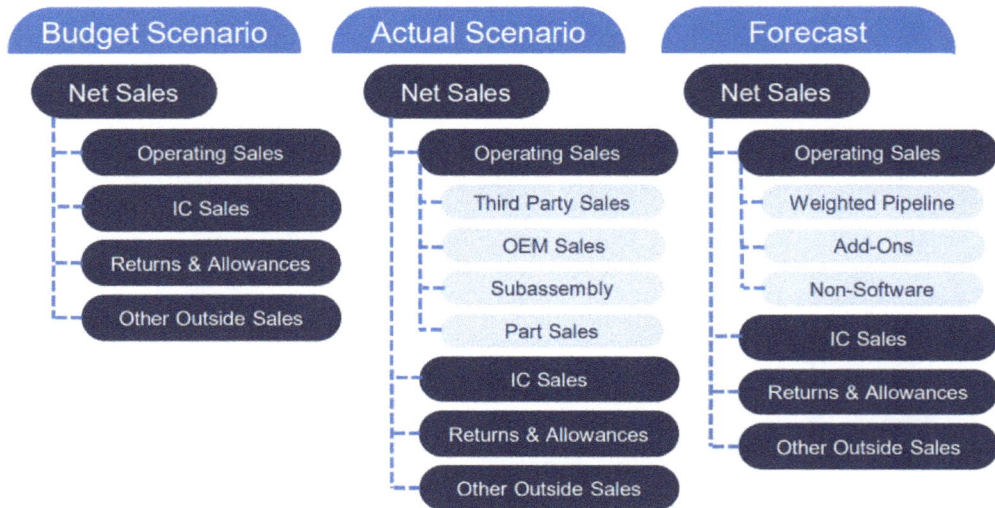

Figure 4.14

Existing OR New Cube? That is the Question!

In Top Training, the administrator will face changing business requirements that require new members in existing or new dimensions altogether. The obvious question is whether the business change can be worked into an existing cube or whether a new cube will need to be created.

It will be the role of the administrator to determine the answer to this question, considering things such as:

Is the new business requirement involving an acquisition that is in the same industry, or a completely different industry?

The same industry only requires additional members to a dimension and, therefore, lies within an existing cube. But with a new industry, new dimensionality will be required and (as mentioned above) existing cube dimensions cannot be changed once data is in the cube. Therefore, a new cube is required.

Is the new business requirement referring to new products that are similar to existing ones, or referring to a complete diversification of the product range?

Similar products can be added to an existing Product User Defined dimension, but diversification will be a new User Defined dimension that will ultimately require reporting from a new cube setup.

Other factors will come into the decision, with each OneStream client having specifics that may warrant a new cube; for example, a reorganization of entities or reducing the Data Unit size.

Conclusion

A cube will hold most of the data required for reporting. There are various types of cubes, from detail business area cubes rolling up to a super cube or exclusive cube for complex reporting, and monolithic cubes, which could also act as placeholders during the project's implementation. Specialty cubes can be used for specific purposes, such as storing driver-based data for other cubes, or an inventory cube can be used where calculations can be isolated to this particular cube, not affecting the rest of the application.

Building the cube will initially require good dimension design, as will selecting which dimensions are required and if the members for the cube need to be at a summary or detail level. Each cube built can have a default currency as part of the entity translation. The default currency is also used as part of the currency triangulation calculation.

Data Units are made up of selected Level 1 dimensions that are considered subsets of the cube and used as a metric to measure performance.

Cubes are built using extensibility, either vertical where each business area cube rolls up to a super cube for consolidation or planning purposes; or horizontal extensibility, which can be one cube over many Scenario Types.

This chapter on understanding cubes in OneStream is the foundation for upcoming chapters on importing, workflow, and reporting, which will then lead us to the bigger picture about cubes... so keep going; you're doing great!

5

Importing That
All-Important Data

Data Import Preparation

Now that the cubes are built, we turn to prepping the data that will be imported into them. The setup and the final import can be broken down into stages. These are:

1. Set up the data source artifact.

2. Create the transformation rules artifact that maps source items and target members.

3. Add the data source and transformation rule artifacts to the Workflow Profile.

4. The end-user can now import data from OnePlace into the cube.

This chapter will focus on creating the data source and creating the transformation rules, which can then be used in the later chapter on workflow setup.

The learning journey for this chapter is:

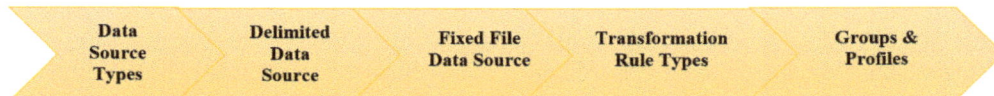

Figure 5.1

As a reminder, in chapter 4, when discussing the cube integration tab, we have already decided – during our cube design – which dimensions will be part of the data load by leaving the Enabled configuration as True. These dimensions will then be seen in our data source creation. The remaining dimensions that are not used will be set to False and will not be seen when it comes to the data source.

Before embarking on the mapping of dimensions to a source file, it is worth looking at what types of data sources OneStream handles.

Knowing Your Data Source Types

The creation of the data source tells OneStream how to interpret incoming metadata and data for the import required during the end-user's workflow tasks. The blueprint defines how the data should be parsed and imported and is based upon the cube and Scenario Type data source assignment. There are four different types:

Fixed Files

A consistent format with the fields mapped by column ranges, based on the number of characters within source files. Usually a text (.txt) file. Example to follow.

Delimited Files

Data is separated by a special character such as a comma or a semi-colon, though – typically – a comma separator variable (CSV) file. Example to follow.

Connectors

Connectors use a business rule to import data directly from either an external system using an Application Programming Interface (API), or from custom tables within the OneStream application. The data source requires a connector business rule that contains custom .NET code.

Connectors are used to attach directly to either Structured Query Language (SQL) sources, or a file-based setting that connects to a FTP/SFTP (secure file transfer protocol), Azure, or Amazon type service. Other options for connectors are a webservice connection (databases that use XML or JSON, for example), or smart integration connections (SIC) which connect to items that are non-public facing IPs but which need a direct connection to OneStream.

Connector data source types are created to have, for example, a direct connection to an ERP system (enterprise resource planning), where data can then be pulled into OneStream seamlessly. Or from web sources, to pull, for example, FX rates from a website.

This data source type is beyond the scope of this book, but discussed further in the *Foundation Handbook.*

Data Management Export Sequences

Used to copy data from one cube or scenario into another through a workflow's import task. For more advanced jobs, this data source type can be used to extract data from OneStream for backup reasons or to import to other systems.

Creating a Data Source

For Top Training, we will be loading a delimited file. The first step is to create the data source and use an example template file to assist with our mapping. (Using the connector option would not require a template file, as this directly queries a source database) .

The template file and its format will mirror the end-user's file, that will eventually be uploaded as part of their import workflow task. The idea is to create the correct mapping of each column in the source to the dimensions in the cube to which we are loading data.

For the load to take place, we must make sure the items in the source file columns match the members in the dimension. This is discussed in the transformation rules section later.

Creating a Delimited File Data Source

The Application tab has a subsection called Data Collection where the Data Sources menu sits. Once the source type has been established, we create the data source.

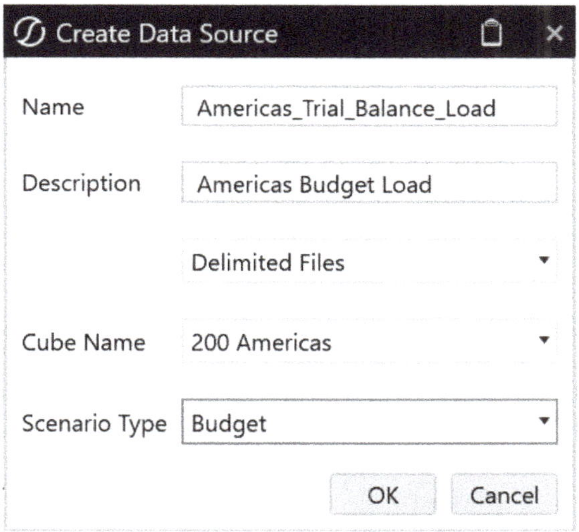

Figure 5.2

With the data source now created, the template file is then uploaded using the Upload File icon as seen in Figure 5.3. The file name prompt then lets you select the file, and see it previewed as shown. Next, select each dimension type and map it to its corresponding source column.

Note in Figure 5.3 that only the three User Defined dimensions are showing, and we don't see the dimensions UD4 to UD8 that were set to False in the Enabled settings of the cube Integration tab.

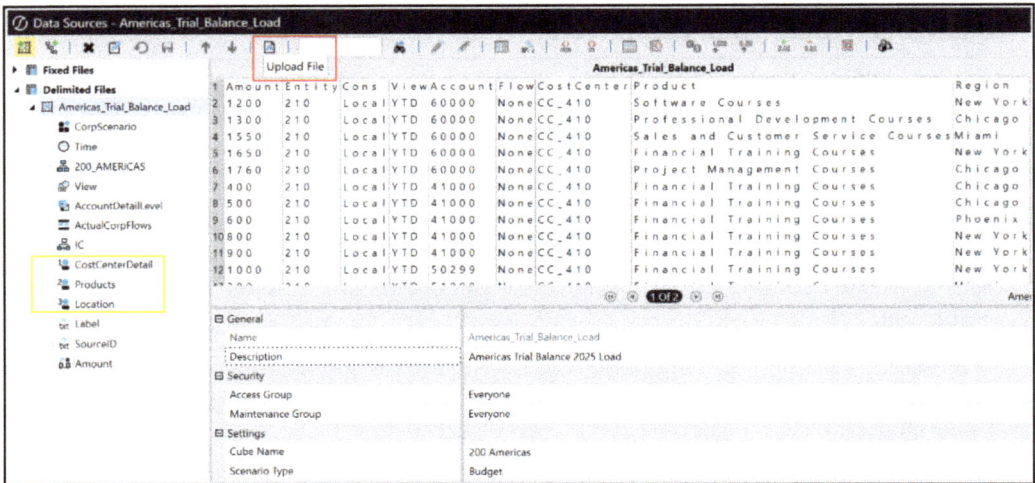

Figure 5.3

Assigning Dimensions To Source File

The first two dimensions – Scenario (dimension named CorpScenario) and Time – require a corresponding match in the source file. But, as there is no column to match in the source file, we can select Current DataKey Scenario and Current DataKey Time for the Data Type setting; this will mirror the current workflow Scenario and Time selection when the end user imports the data.

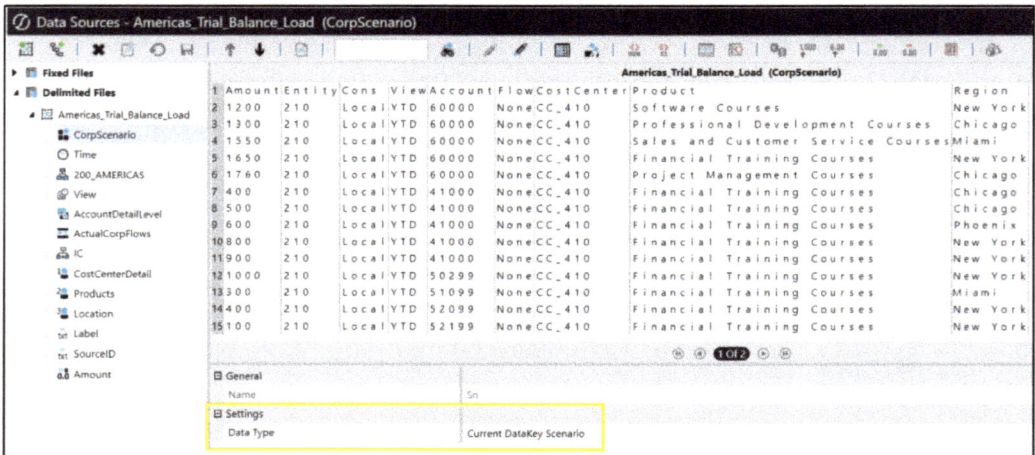

Figure 5.4

Next, we tell OneStream that the Entity members in dimension 200_AMERICAS will find their corresponding Entity in the second source column as shown in Figure 5.5. OneStream's feature of selecting a character in the corresponding source column and selecting Apply Selection assists with the configuration. Alternatively, the column number can be typed in.

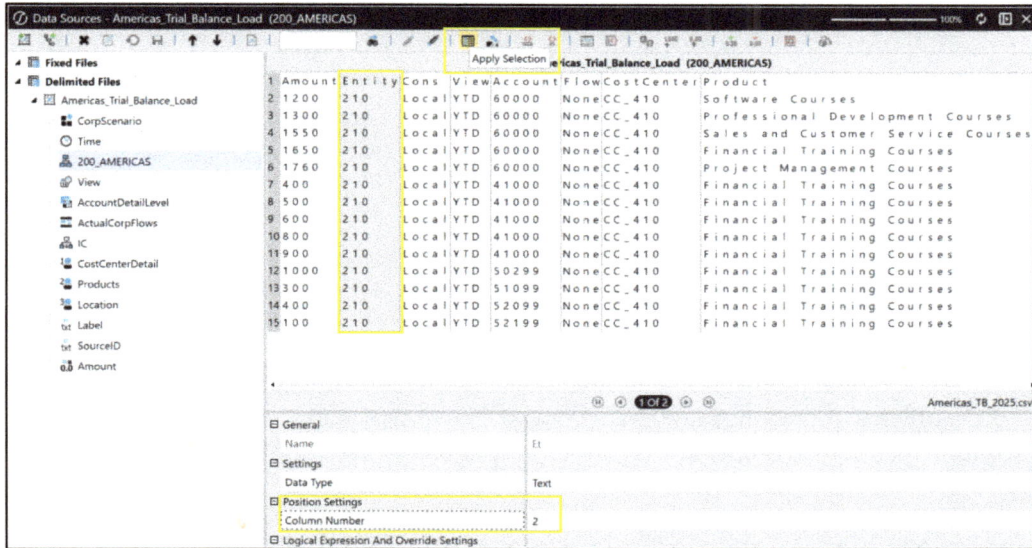

Figure 5.5

The View dimension will be configured to the View source column which, in this case, has YTD (Year to Date) items.

The AccountDetailLevel configured to the Account column.

The ActualCorpFlows configured to the Flow column. In Figure 5.6, the source Flow column items are all None. This can map to the None member in the cube's Flow dimension, but as this is a template – when the end-user performs the import task and uploads their file – the Flow source column can be other items, such as Activity or EndBalance to map to the Flow dimension Activity or EndBalance members in the cube.

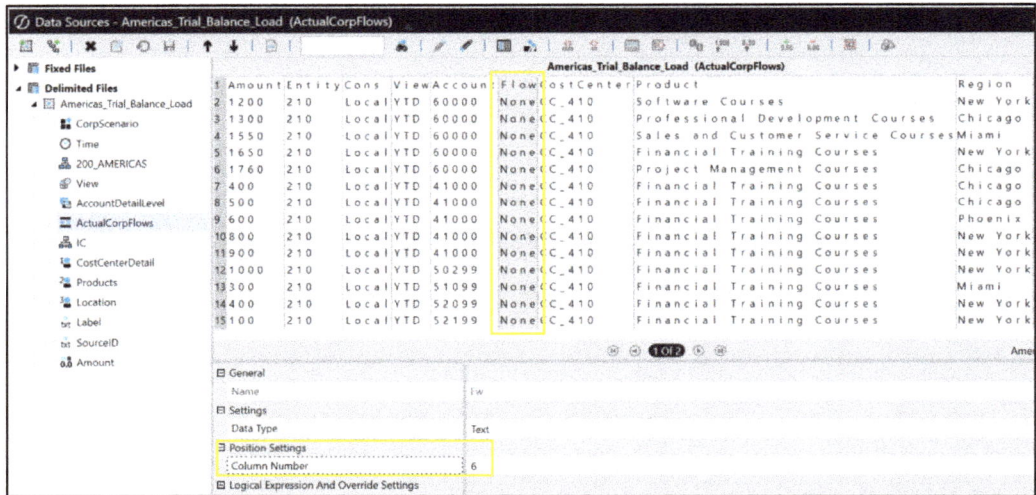

Figure 5.6

For the IC (Intercompany) dimension, this data source template will have a Static Value of None, embedded under the Logical Expression And Override Settings. Unlike the Flow option, where the None was in the source file and acted as a placeholder, in this case there is no flexibility, and None will always be the target member option, as we believe there will be no intercompany transactions for this import task.

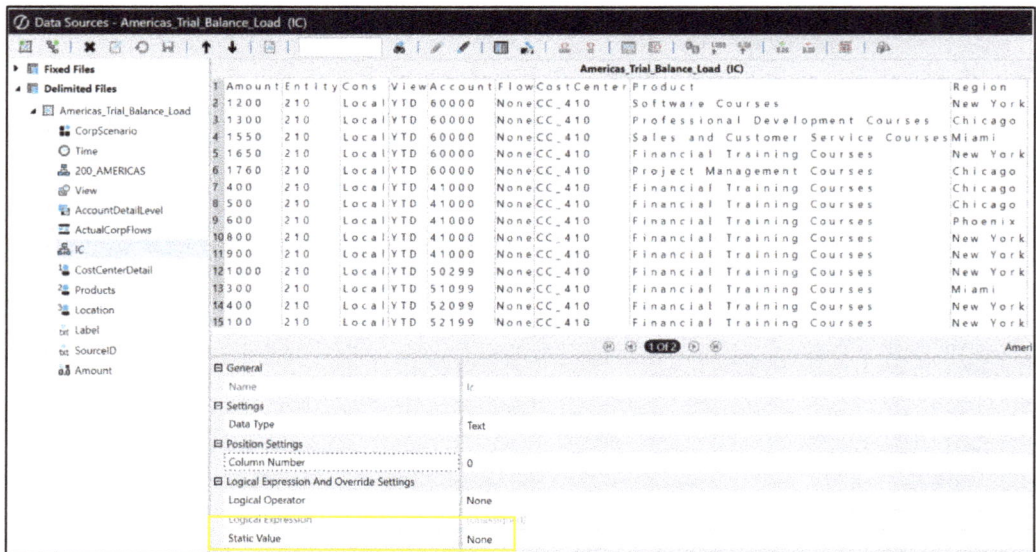

Figure 5.7

All three User Defined dimensions for Cost Center, Products, and Location can map to their corresponding column in the source file.

The Label dimension provides an opportunity to load a description against it. Details such as a bank statement description or trial balance statement might be applicable. In this case, there are no descriptions in the source file.

The SourceID can have the file name populated in the Static Value field. This provides a unique identification of each file. In the event that more than one file is used to load data in our workflow import task, any reload can target the specific file for clearing and loading, rather than having to look through all the files to clear.

Figure 5.8 shows the Text Fill and Substitution Settings that can also be found on other dimension configurations. Text fill settings allow you to define how text values are processed during data import. Options include leading fill values, which prepend specified characters to text values; for example, leading fill value '000' to a data value of '34' will result in '034'. The substitution settings will replace characters with others. These settings help ensure that the imported data matches the target format within OneStream.

Finally, the Amount column must be configured for the import to be able to execute. The Amount field is unique because OneStream's default settings will only import a line if the value in this field is numeric. This ensures that non-numeric rows – such as header lines, which are typically alpha numeric – are automatically skipped. Figure 5.8 illustrates how the numeric settings for the amount source dimension enable precise control over the formatting and characteristics of the imported values.

The thousand, decimal, and currency indicators provide the option to enter which characters separate thousands and decimals in the amount value, as well as the currency symbol for the value.

The positive and negative sign indicator pinpoints which characters in the file – if any – indicate the value is a positive or negative.

The Debit / Credit Mid-Point position allows the user to separate an amount column in the file that has both debits and credits in the same field. The mid-point character entered will then set amounts as debits to the left of it, and credits to the right.

The Zero Suppression feature allows the import values to not include any zero values. The recommendation in most cases is to leave it at the default setting of True.

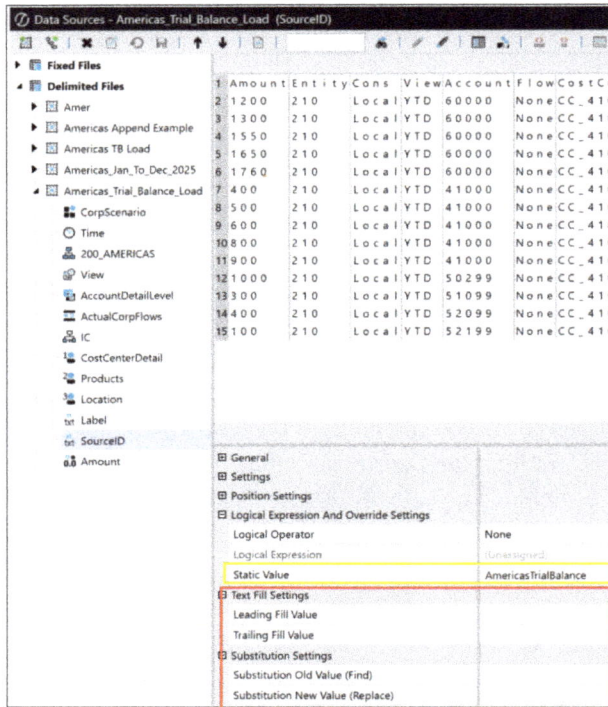

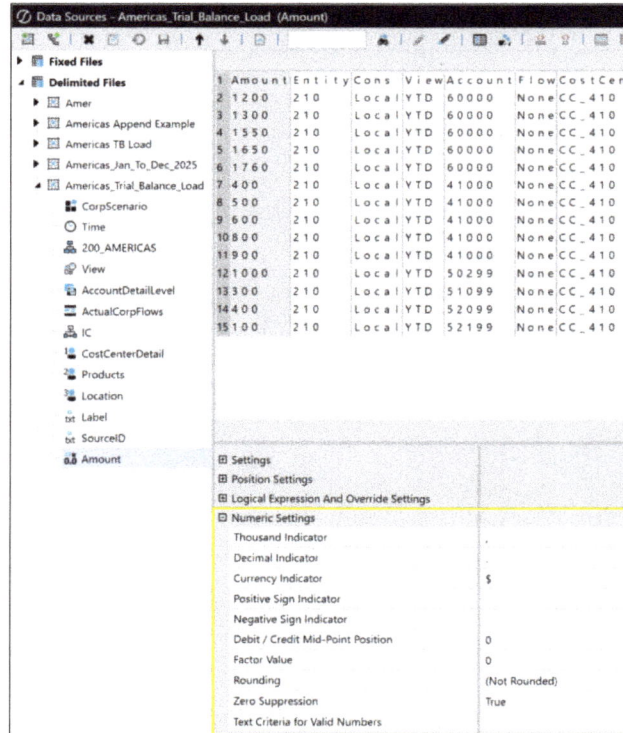

Figure 5.8

Creating a Fixed File Data Source

With fixed file mapping, the columns are set by position settings, identifying the start position of the source item and the number of characters for its length.

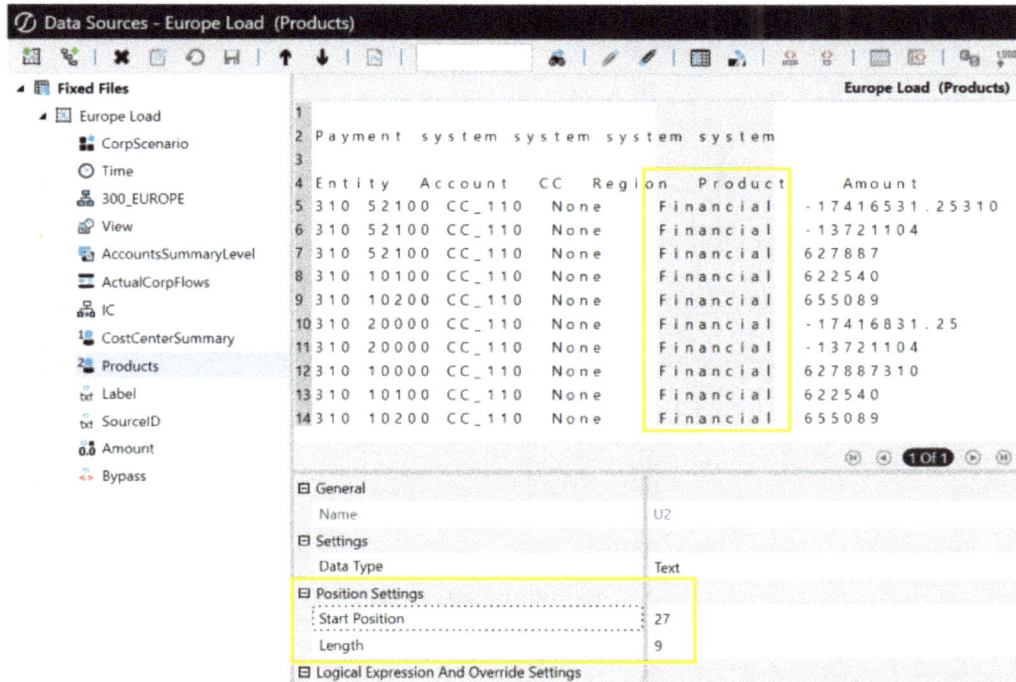

Figure 5.9

There may be a need to ignore items in the files, such as text or numerical data. This can be done by creating a Bypass and selecting which text values to ignore.

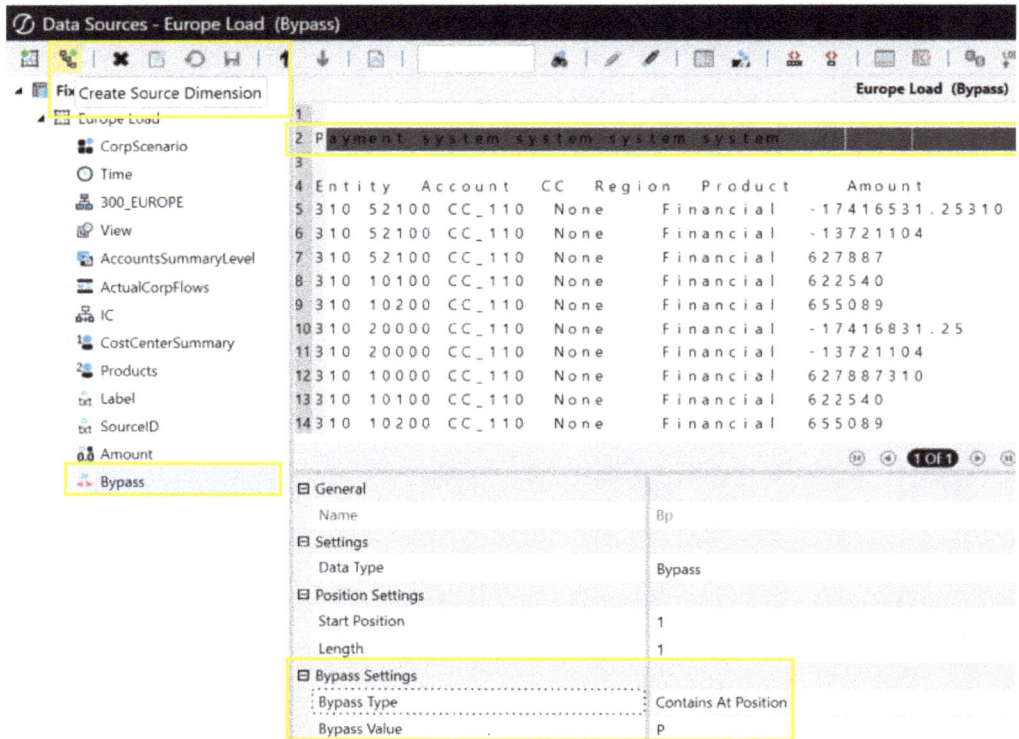

Figure 5.10

Matrix Data Source

A matrix data type is used when a fixed or delimited data source has multiple amount columns, as opposed to just one. For example, if each month is a separate column, then all 12 months can be loaded at once. This is useful for budgeting or planning scenarios where work is done on multiple months in the same cycle. The data structure type when the data source is created is required to be set to Matrix Data (as opposed to the Tabular Data setting for amounts in just one column).

A **matrix data key** is used to map each column to a dimension. Additional source dimensions can be created; in this case, additional Time dimensions can be created for each column in the data source.

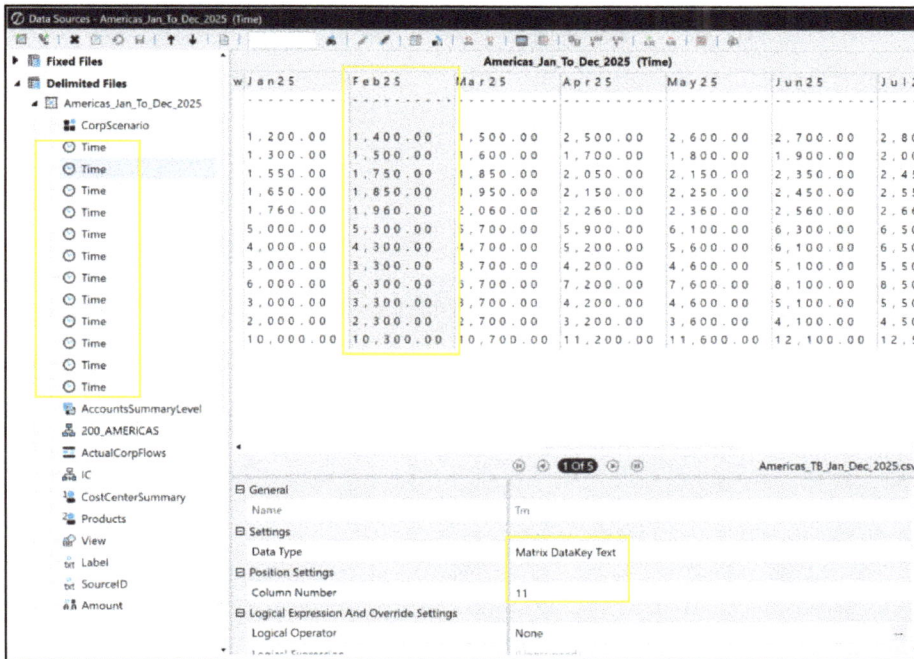

Figure 5.11

Transformation Rules

The data sources we have just created direct OneStream on where to find the metadata and data within a file or via a connector. Now, in the next step of the process, we will create transformation rules that direct OneStream on where the data should go.

The need for transformation rules arises because the items in our source file columns may not be the same as the members we use in OneStream.

Why does this situation arise? The reasons why source file contents are different to the target members – and don't align – are to do with the fact that various entities around the group are using source systems unique to them. Accordingly, as OneStream has been set up to provide a unified set of descriptions – representing the whole group – there will be a mismatch that administrators will have to map.

Also, as we don't require transactional detail in the cube, mapping rules are set to collate the source detail values to load to summary members in the cube.

Figure 5.12

Types of Transformation Rules

The five main types of transformation rules are:

- One-To-One
- Range
- List
- Mask
- Composite

One-To-One

The rule maps one source item explicitly to one target dimension member. This makes it the best rule for audit purposes and the only rule used for Scenario, Time, and View dimensions. Figure 5.13 shows that even though the source may be a different code to the target, the import can still take place in the mapped target member.

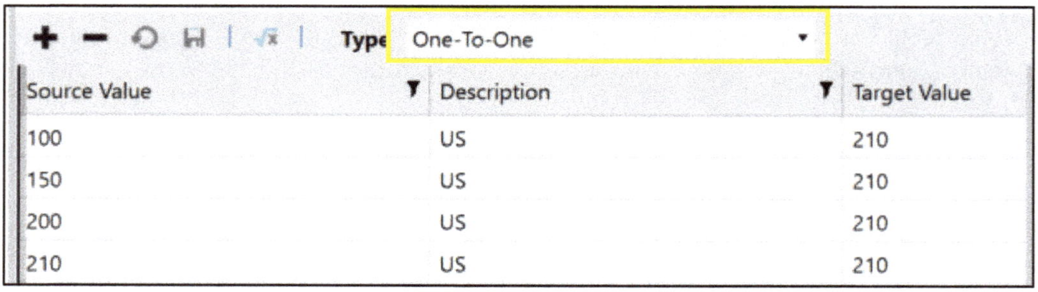

Source Value	Description	Target Value
100	US	210
150	US	210
200	US	210
210	US	210

Figure 5.13

Composite Mapping

These are intended to be conditional mappings, with the set-up showing a combination of members mapped to a target value. In Figure 5.14, the rule expression states that all source item accounts that begin with `52` when aligned with entity `210` should be mapped to `New York`.

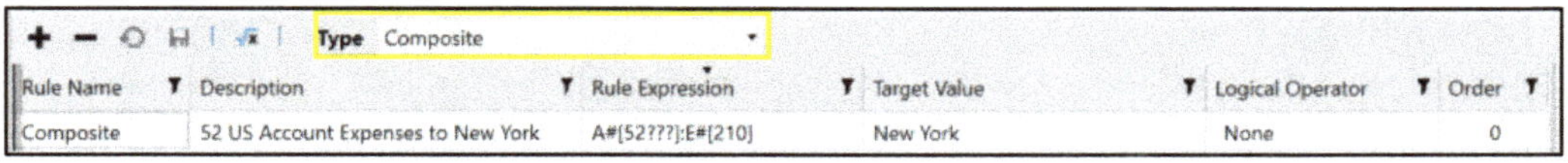

Type: Composite

Rule Name	Description	Rule Expression	Target Value	Logical Operator	Order
Composite	52 US Account Expenses to New York	A#[52???]:E#[210]	New York	None	0

Figure 5.14

Range

As the name suggests, this is a defined lower to upper limit source, whereby any target member within this range will be mapped to. The range is indicated with the use of a tilde `~` sign.

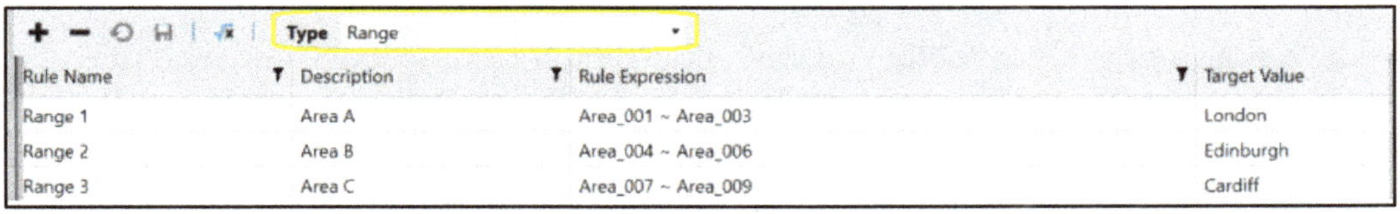

Type: Range

Rule Name	Description	Rule Expression	Target Value
Range 1	Area A	Area_001 ~ Area_003	London
Range 2	Area B	Area_004 ~ Area_006	Edinburgh
Range 3	Area C	Area_007 ~ Area_009	Cardiff

Figure 5.15

List

Uses a delimited list of source members, each separated by a semi-colon, that all map to the same target member.

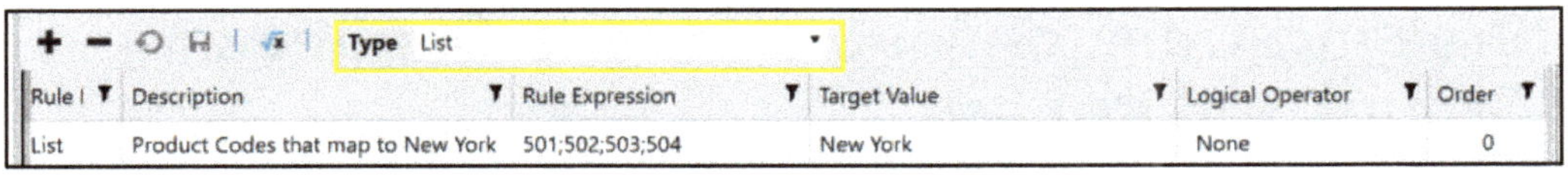

Type: List

Rule I	Description	Rule Expression	Target Value	Logical Operator	Order
List	Product Codes that map to New York	501;502;503;504	New York	None	0

Figure 5.16

Mask

Uses the question mark (?) to represent a single character and star/asterisks (*) to represent multiple characters as wildcards (can also be stacked, for example, to capture numbers before and after defined characters). These will then map into the target member specified.

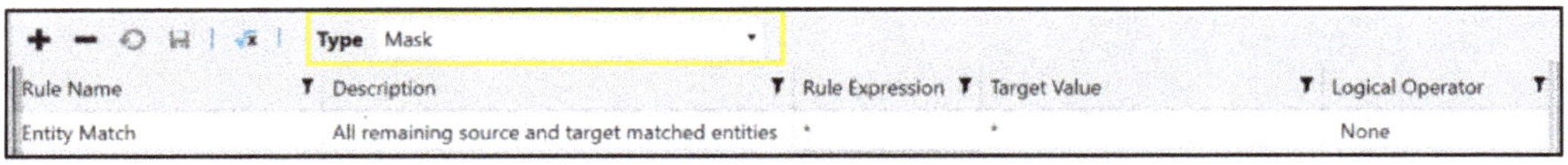

Figure 5.17

> **Note:** There is a processing order with transformation rules, which means no account will clash. For example, the mappings for one-to-one are worked on first by OneStream, followed by composite, range, list, and mask. Known as the **first trap method**, an account dealt with (or trapped) by a rule will be ignored by subsequent rules.
>
> It is also possible to set the order of processing for every line inside each rule. This is done in the order column and provides the opportunity to, for example, deal with more specific mappings first. For example, 821* to run before 82*.
>
> When deciding which rule to use, consider the execution order, how easy it will be to maintain future additional members, and overall performance. In terms of performance, a one-to-one will process faster than, say, a mask rule, which could run less efficiently due to the use of question mark and asterisk characters.

Creating Transformation Rules in OneStream – Groups and Profiles

Groups and **Profiles** are commonly used across the OneStream platform, enabling artifacts built by the administrator to be easily distributed and accessed by the end-user.

A group is a method to organize artifacts. For example, transformation rules are created within a transformation rule group.

A profile is a method of organizing groups and can contain one or many groups. The same group can also be shared across profiles. This prevents an identical group needing to be created for each new profile. Security can be applied to isolate maintenance to just one team, if required. Then, the profiles are assigned to various functions in OneStream (as shown in the example at the end of the chapter).

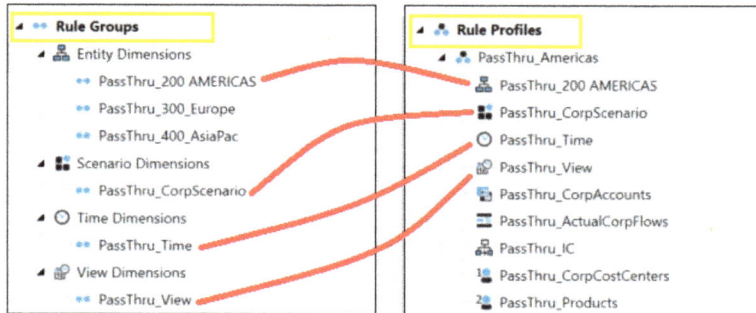

Figure 5.18

Preview Of When The Import Setup Is Used

For completeness, let us preview some of what we will discuss in the Workflow chapter on how the use of data sources and transformation rules end up in the hands of the end user for that all-important final import.

The administrator will add the Data Source and Transformation Profile Name to the Import Workflow Profile, as shown in Figure 5.19.

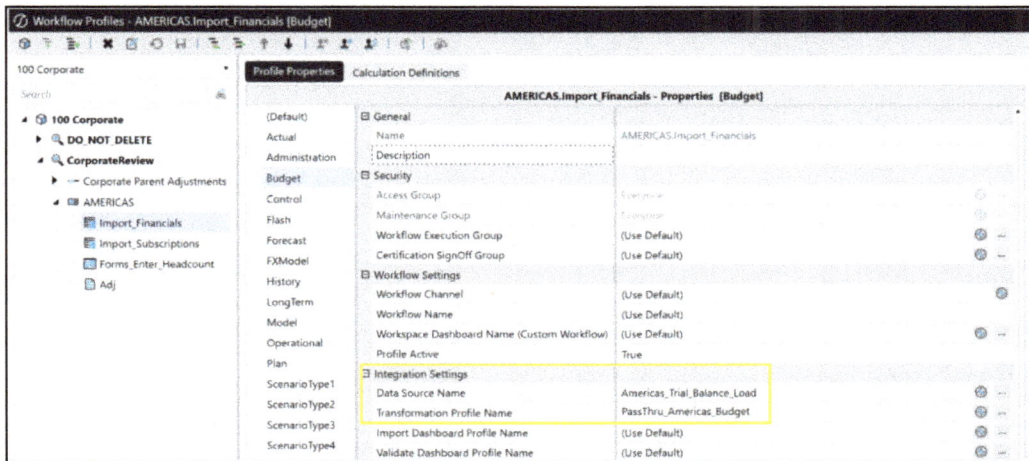

Figure 5.19

This becomes ready for the end-user to import – in OnePlace – when the import task is selected.

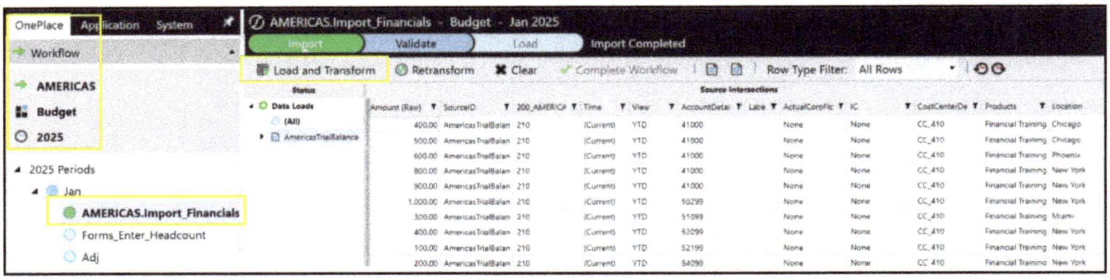

Figure 5.20

Summary of Data Source and Transformation Rule Process

In this chapter, we covered a lot on the setup of the data source and transformation rule. This will eventually lead to the grand finale of importing data when we get to the chapter on Workflow.

Therefore, let us pause for a moment and summarize what we have learnt so far:

1. Go to the Data Source menu under the Application tab and create one of four types of data source (which can be from a fixed file, delimited file, connector, or data management export sequence). This will also identify the cube where the data will eventually load to, from the OnePlace workflow import task by the end-user.

2. Assign the dimensions to the source columns.

3. Create any Bypass additional dimensions (if needed) to ignore text or numerical values in the file.

4. Create a transformation rule group, building a group for each dimension enabled in the Cube Integration tab.

5. Define the mapping rule for each transformation rule group that covers each dimension required for the final import.

6. Create the transformation rule profile and add the rule groups.

7. Now add both the data source and the transformation rule profile to the import Workflow Profile (discussed later in the book). This will be the final step when importing data.

Conclusion

As we have seen, the preparation is twofold for an import to take place. Firstly, the creation of the data source using a file as a template; and then the transformation rules that are built as groups for each dimension before gathering the relevant ones together in a profile.

The data source types range from fixed or delimited files to more advanced connectors, which pull data directly from a source system. When setting up a data source, the source dimensions available (that get configured to the source file columns) all depend on the dimensions that were left enabled when the cube was built, specifically from the Integration tab.

Transformation rules vary from one-to-one (where ongoing maintenance is required, but which provide a good audit trail), to the more integrated forms of mapping, such as composite mapping.

With our initial data import preparation complete, we will now be able to progress – over the following chapters – on taking these artifacts and making them work for us in Workflow Profiles and finally the OnePlace tab, where the data import will take place to eventually get to reporting… our end result.

6

Figuring Out Calculations

What is a Calculation in OneStream

Cubes are referred to as the financial model in OneStream. Within this model, we calculate (which means, in simple terms, using our imported or manually entered data to compute further for financial reporting), store, and dynamically view the data. Calculations within an application are a core function and can be written within members (known as Member Formulas), or as a rule (known as business rules), or in Cube Views (known as Cube View Math or expressions).

The more advanced way calculations can also be performed are through Assemblies. These are found under the Workspaces menu and are useful for handling complex calculations and processes. They work by organizing and managing business rules and other source code files, and used by the developer community when, for example, building solutions or creating dashboards.

The administrator chooses the method that is the most appropriate for the calculation task at hand.

This chapter will discuss calculations at a beginner's level, and administrators will be able to use the knowledge acquired as a springboard to further learning and as a segue to the *OneStream Finance Rules and Calculations Handbook*.

Here is this chapter's learning journey:

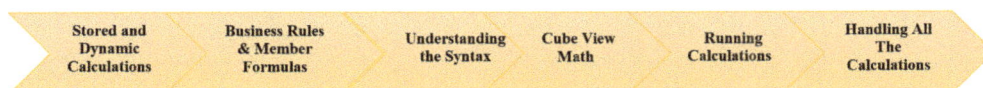

Stored and Dynamic Calculations	Business Rules & Member Formulas	Understanding the Syntax	Cube View Math	Running Calculations	Handling All The Calculations

Figure 6.1

We have just mentioned the four ways in which calculations can be written. Before we delve further into some of these methods, it is worth mentioning how calculations can be performed. These can be either stored calculations or dynamic calculations.

Stored Calculations

As the term suggests, these types of calculations have been derived from data in the cube, with the calculated value stored in the database. Our understanding of Data Units will help us further here. If we recall, a Data Unit is a subset of the cube. This Data Unit is made up of cells, and a subset of these cells is known as a data buffer.

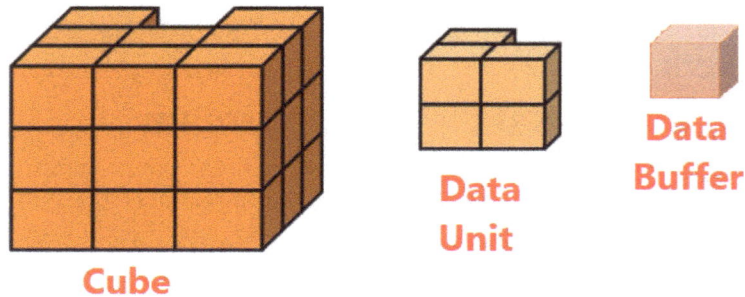

Figure 6.2

The data buffer can consist of all the cells of the Data Unit, or as a subset of cells of the Data Unit.

When a calculation is executed, a first set of data buffers is calculated together with a second set of data buffers. The results are then stored in the database as a third set of data buffers.

For example, in Top Training, for the revenue calculation, we will multiply price by volume. This will comprise of the course prices (data buffer one) multiplied by their volumes sold (data buffer two). The result is the revenue by course (data buffer three).

	Price	Volume	Revenue
Software Courses	1,500.00	200.00	300,000.00
Professional Development Courses	900.00	300.00	270,000.00
Management Training Courses	500.00	500.00	250,000.00
Sales and Customer Service Courses	600.00	200.00	120,000.00
Financial Training Courses	700.00	250.00	175,000.00
Project Management Courses	800.00	100.00	80,000.00

Figure 6.3

Dynamic Calculations

Unlike stored calculations, dynamic calculations process results **in-memory** (on the fly) when requested by the user. The result is not stored in the database.

The calculation syntax can be created in the dimension library, specifically in the Account, Flow, or User Defined dimensions. It is performed on a cell-by-cell basis (unlike stored calculations working on data buffers), and therefore can run slower for very large reports or complex dynamic calculations.

With our example of price multiplied by volume, the data cell calculation uses a singular value to return another singular value.

We could think about creating a repository of common dynamic calculations that are specific to the organization's requirements. This is usually done on the UD8 dimension, where each member is a reporting metric that can be used in Cube View rows or columns.

For example, Figure 6.4 shows the VariancePY member, with its Formula Type set to DynamicCalc.

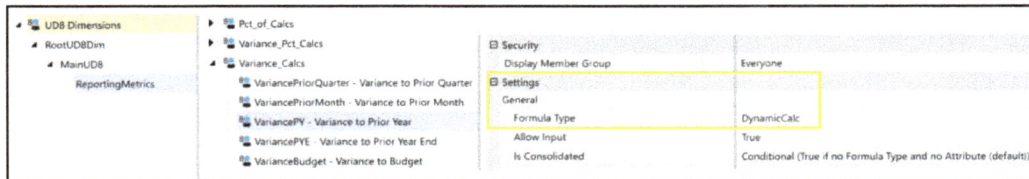

Figure 6.4

Figure 6.5 shows the VariancePY member's embedded formula. Later, we will look at understanding syntax calculations. As a starting point, though, this formula condition checks the View dimension, and proceeds to run the calculation if the cell is not a text value, and deduces the prior year value from 12 months ago. This then brings back the variance result.

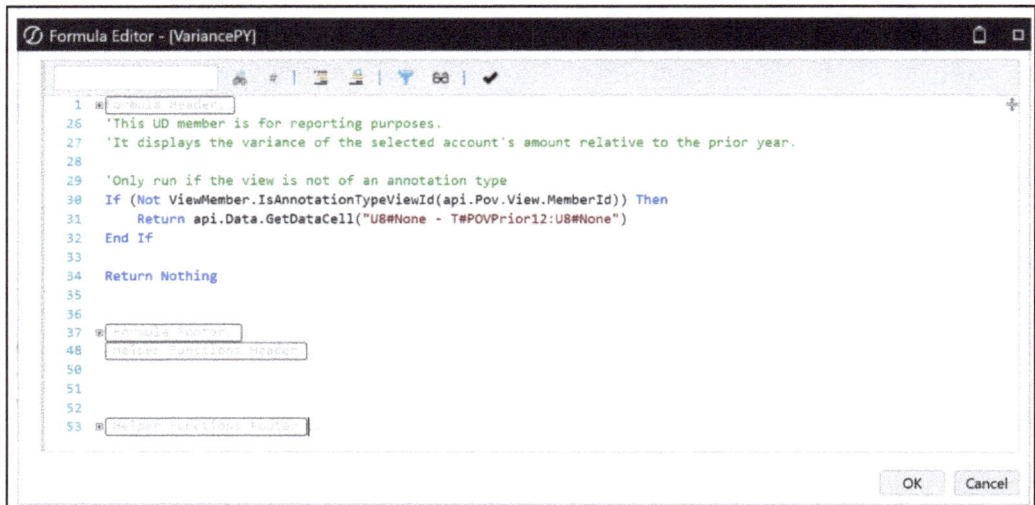

Figure 6.5

Dynamic calculations can also be utilized to pull relational information, such as transactional details, into cube-based and Analytic Blend (data from various sources) reports.

What Are Rule Types And Expressions

When it comes to learning OneStream's rule types and expressions (used within the rule types), knowledge is acquired over time. Administrators will come across scenarios that help understand how syntax gets structured, or how expressions and function names are used.

Let us walk through some rule types, expressions, and functions we will encounter in OneStream documentation.

Business Rules

Business rules are written in the Business Rules menu option, found in the Application tab, and contain multiple calculations for different members within the same business rule. Business rules run in sequence, which may mean a longer process time, but have the ability to span across many members.

Figure 6.6 shows an example of a finance business rule type multiplying accounts. These are shown by the red characters. Any green characters are a result of being commented out and are either for supporting narrative or the line is not currently used. These can be uncommented and worked on, if required, for further calculations in the future.

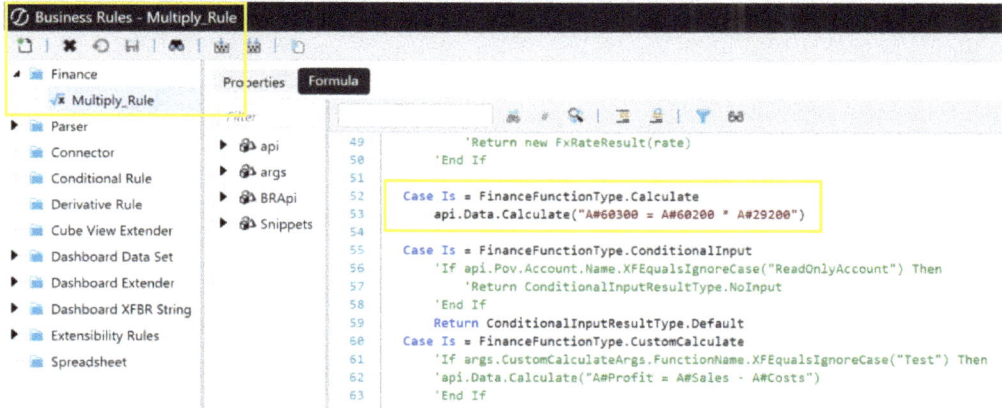

Figure 6.6

A **Finance rule type** is used for multi-dimensional financial calculations, but there are other rule types within the business rules menu that cater for specific scenarios; for example, the **Parser rule type** cleans and transforms data before it is loaded.

The **Connector rule type** assists with mapping and transferring data from external systems, and the **Conditional rule type** filters out unwanted or irrelevant data during imports, ensuring only clean, usable data is imported into the system.

Business rules can use variables instead of hardcoding string values. This reduces redundancy and makes calculations easier to maintain, and can be used, for example, in complex scenarios such as allocations, cash flow, and custom eliminations.

Member Formulas

Member Formula syntax is written on individual dimension members, specifically on Scenario, Account, Flow, or User Defined dimension members in the formula property. If required, the formula within this individual member can reference multiple members. This would then function the same way as business rules.

Using Member Formulas means it is easy to pick individual members and apply a formula; for example, a Sales account calculation or Cost account calculation.

A key feature is the ability to vary the Member Formula by Scenario Type. For example, the calculation formula can be embedded for the Forecast scenario but not for, say, the Actual scenario, where Actuals just need to be loaded from the general ledger system rather than calculated.

We also have the ability to vary the Member Formula by time period. For example, a formula can be applied for Months 1 to 6, before changing in Month 7. The change does not alter the first six months' calculation, worked on by the initial formula.

Member formulas are processed in parallel, and for general calculations, can be the better performing option.

A unique feature for Member Formulas, compared to business rules, is the ability to add a formula for calculation drill down. This gives the user the capability to drill down on a calculated member in a Cube or Quick View, and can also be varied by Scenario Type and time. The formula works by stipulating a new variable, for example `DrillDownFormulaResult()` that then stores the result of the drill down operation. Upon drill down, OneStream will check to see if the requested data cell is a calculation and – if so – will provide the source data cells.

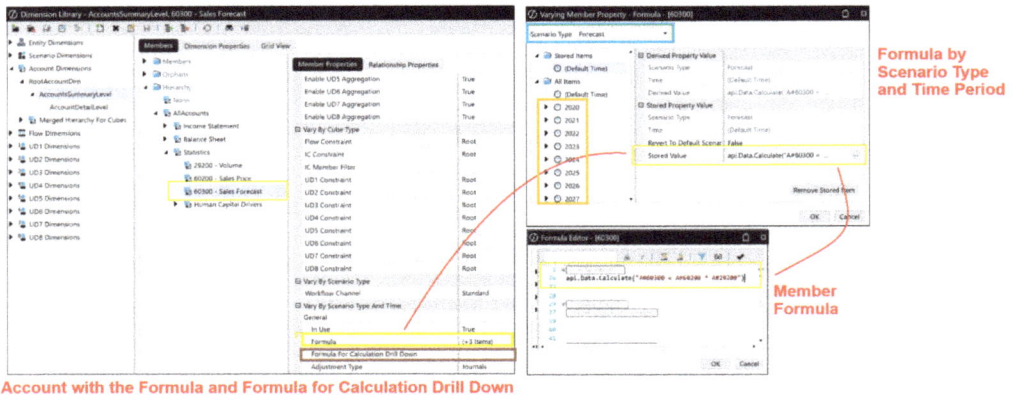

Account with the Formula and Formula for Calculation Drill Down

Figure 6.7

Cube View Calculations

Cube View calculations are dynamic calculations that are executed when the Cube View is run. The type of calculations that work well with this method (instead of using Member Formulas or business rules) are Key Performance Indicators (KPIs) and variances.

The Member Filter Builder guides the user with predefined syntax options that are useful for calculations on rows and columns.

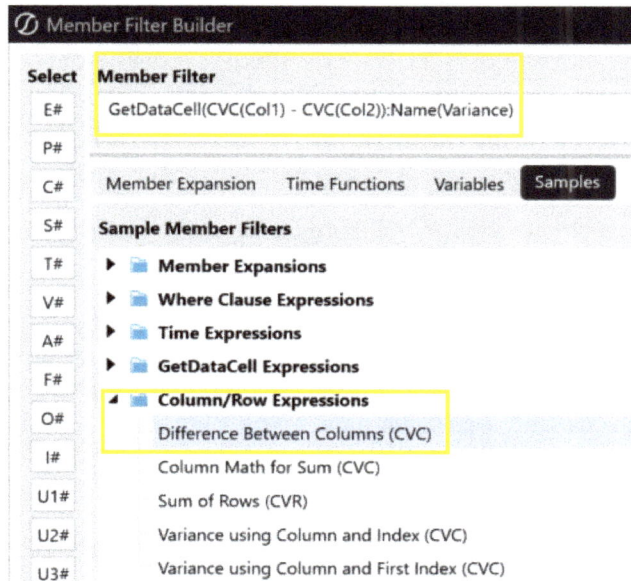

Figure 6.8

When writing calculations, deciding whether it's a business rule, Member Formula or Cube View calculation will be looked at on a case-by-case basis.

Expressions are used to form the business rule, Member Formula or Cube View calculations. Let's look at some examples, starting with frequently used GetDataCell.

GetDataCell Expression

The `GetDataCell` expression is commonly used in Cube Views. The calculation is dynamic (but can also be found in business rules). `GetDataCell` can use specific dimension members to return a data point, and this is a good way to make use of members in the syntax that are not actually in the Cube View. Examples include:

Calculation of the difference between two scenarios:

```
GetDataCell(S#Scenario1-S#Scenario2):Name(Difference)
```

Calculation of multiplying two accounts:

```
GetDataCell(A#Account1*A#Account2):Name(Total)
```

> **Note:** `Name` is a function that will label the column with the word Difference or Total.

In Top Training, after calculating two accounts using the `GetDataCell` expression, we have labelled the column Sales Forecast, as shown in Figure 6.9:

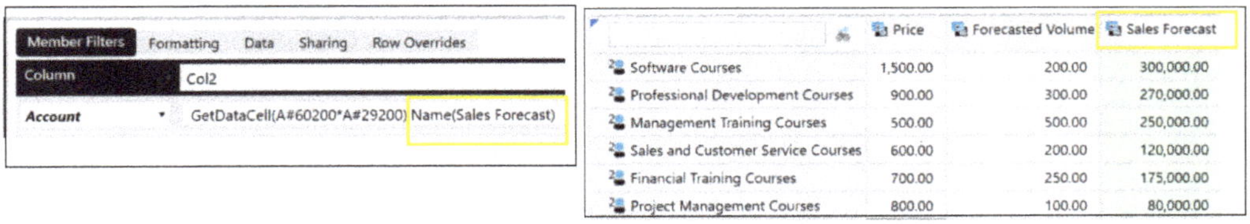

Figure 6.9

With the expression, we can also utilize functions. These are designed to improve performance and shorten the formula as well as avoid errors, such as handling zeros, where for example, dividing by zero will return a null value rather than an error. Sample expressions can also be found in the **Cube View Member Filter Builder**. Let us take the GetDataCell expression further and marry it with functions:

Divide Function

Divides two accounts to provide the ratio value.

```
GetDataCell(Divide(A#Account1,A#Account2)):Name(Ratio)
(Note: standard math operators can be used as an
alternative,i.e. GetDataCell(A#Account1/A#Account2).
```

Variance Function

This calculates the difference between the two scenarios as a ratio.

```
GetDataCell(Variance(S#Scenario1,S#Scenario2)):Name(Variance
)
```

VariancePercent Function

Calculates the difference between two scenarios and then multiplies the result by 100.

```
GetDataCell(VariancePercent(S#Scenario1,S#Scenario2)):Name(V
ar %)
```

api.data.calculate Expression

This expression makes extensive use of data buffers to calculate many values at once, and stores the final value in the database.

For example, if there are 100 numbers in Account1, the below expression takes all 100 numbers that are stored in this data buffer, copies them to a new data buffer, changes the account to Account2, and stores the new set of 100 numbers in the database.

```
api.data.calculate("A#Account2=A#Account1")
```

Hopefully, you are getting some idea of how the syntax is structured. Shall we take it up one notch? Let's see if you grasp this next one.

Firstly, you may be familiar with conditional functions, such as IF, THEN, AND, AndAlso, ELSE, END… well, these are no different in OneStream and can be used with expressions.

In the next example, we want to copy our entities' actual values to a What_If scenario member for us to manipulate further. But we should only copy the base level entities (at their local currency) because we want OneStream to translate and consolidate the What_If scenario parent members from their newly-copied base values. This is as opposed to having the parent member values just copied from one scenario to another. We can structure the formula as follows:

```
If (Not api.Entity.HasChildren())
AndAlso(api.Cons.IsLocalCurrencyForEntity()))

Then api.Data.Calculate("S#What_If = S#Actual)

End If
```

> **Note:** To keep this example simple, the chosen dimension levels (which, in effect, refer to the extensibility), are the same for both Actual and What_If, otherwise the formula would require further work.

The interpretation for this, once again, is for Actual values. If the Entity member does not have children (i.e., it is base level and at that entity's local currency), copy the value to the What_If scenario.

If you're feeling good about this last one, then your OneStream formula writing is well underway.

Column / Row Expressions

Another type of expression that will be taken further (when we embark on the Reporting Chapter) is to use column names, rather than specific dimension members. This type of formula can be found in Cube Views, referencing what has been used for the column or row name to return a data point. Commonly known as **column/row math**, this can be helpful for more complex queries.

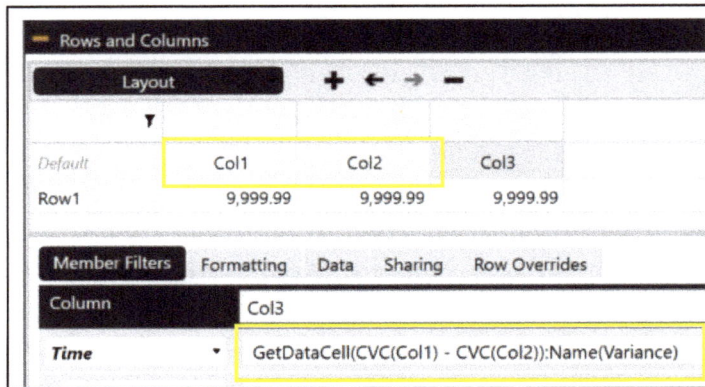

Figure 6.10

Understanding The Syntax and Functions

As part of your OneStream learning, writing and understanding calculation syntax (the way the code is structured) helps with the platform's efficiency, as well as making you a better troubleshooter.

The OneStream platform uses VB.Net (Visual Basic) or C# (C Sharp) for writing rules. For all the non-coders (including the author), it is reassuring to know that a lot can be managed in OneStream without coding, but if the need arises, there are many resources and templates to guide you. Coding is typically done for specialized requirements that don't fit out-of-the-box configurations or where performance is better with code.

One of the key templates is **Snippets,** which can be downloaded from the Solution Exchange. It holds a broad range of syntax structures for a particular requirement, where the member placeholders will need replacing with the actual ones required for the calculation to take place. In Figure 6.11, in the left-hand box, we see the full range of the Snippets templates, and the right-hand box shows a sample structure that adds two account members.

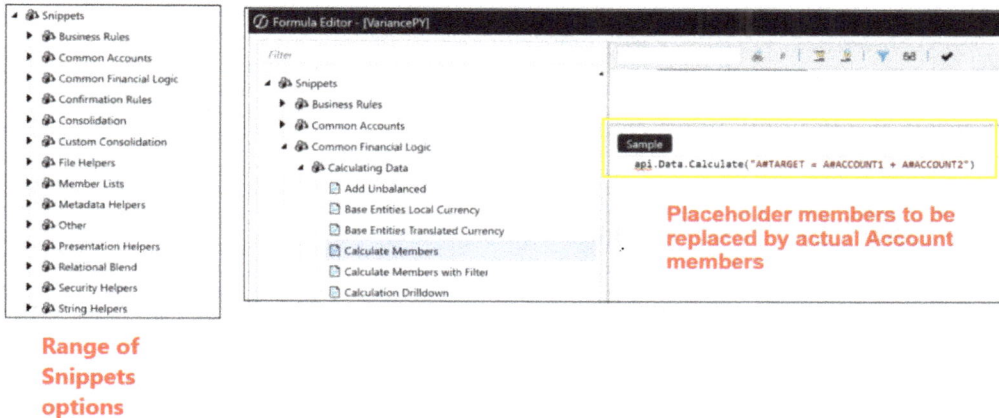

Range of Snippets options

Figure 6.11

Other Areas Using Calculations

In previous chapters, we discussed certain artifacts having features that allow the user to execute calculations by simply selecting a menu option rather than being required to write syntax. This is worth revisiting in this chapter.

The View Dimension

The View dimension has predefined members that cannot be deleted, renamed, or have additional members added. The data is stored at the YTD member, and then calculations such as Trailing Month Totals, Averages, or Summations are performed just by the user selecting the required member.

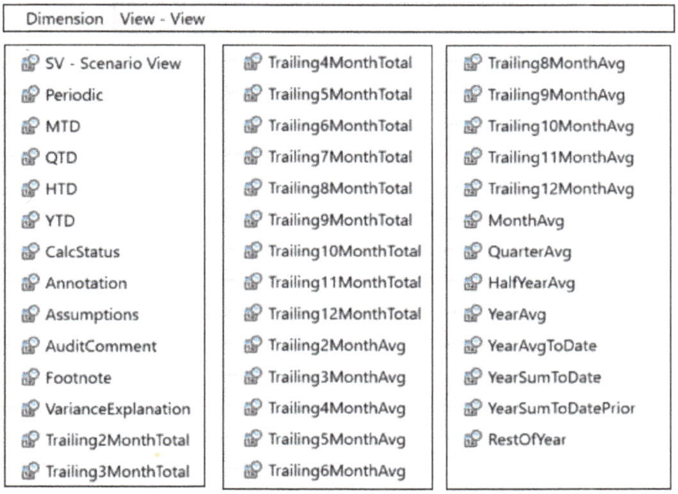

Figure 6.12

119

Account Type and Aggregation Weight

The Account dimension's parent member's value is calculated by their child members' Account Type selection. This is the built-in financial intelligence that determines how child members' values will roll up to the parent cell. This depends on the type of parent member (i.e., if it is a revenue or expense member). For our example in Figure 6.13, a Revenue account type is a positive roll-up, and an Expense account type a negative roll-up, in the Net Sales parent member.

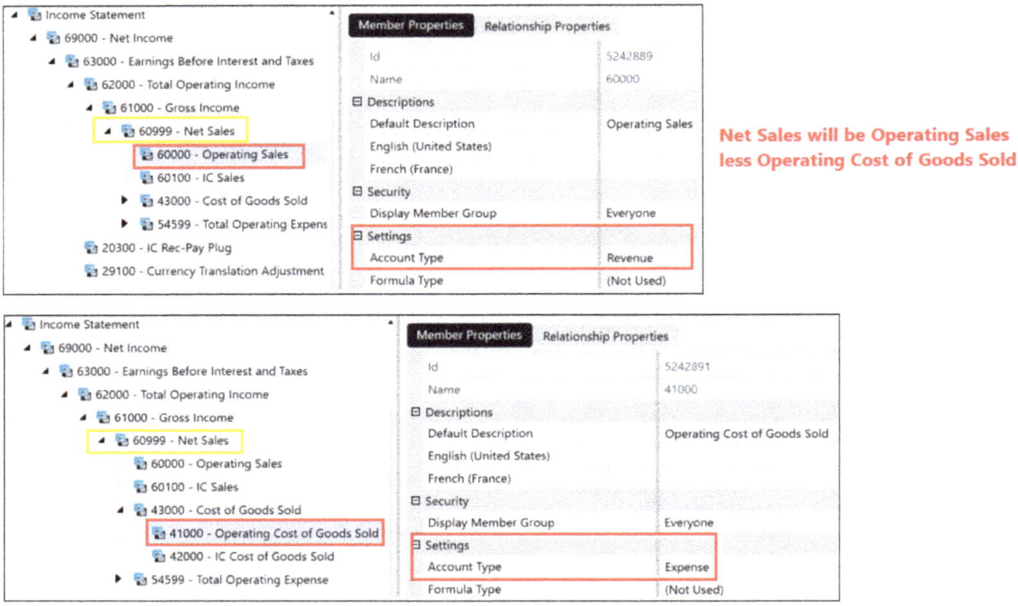

Figure 6.13

Alternatively, the parent value is derived from the child members' Aggregation Weight in the Relationship Properties tab. This option is found in Account, Flow, and User Defined dimensions.

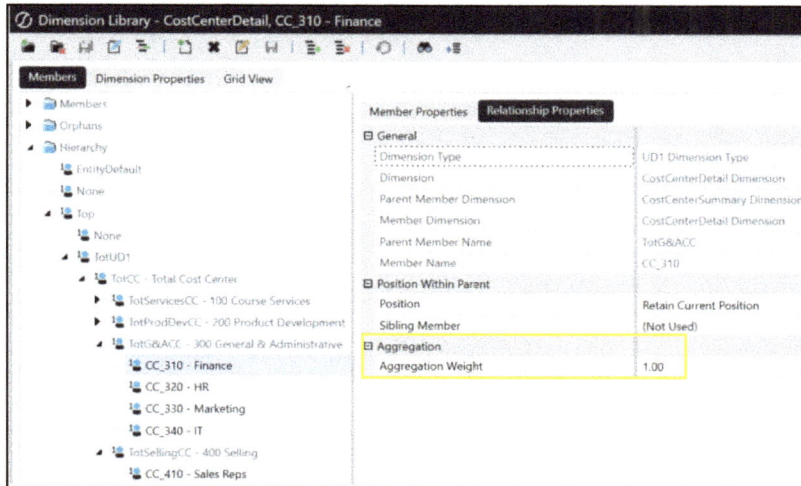

Figure 6.14

Figure 6.14 shows the weight determining how the finance cost center `CC_310-Finance` will roll-up to `TotG&Acc - 300 General & Administrative`. The `1.00` signifies a positive roll-up.

Calculation, Translation, Elimination, Consolidation

The calculation types that can be executed in the OneStream platform (for example, by clicking the Process button in a workflow) are:

Calculate

This will run all the calculations that are assigned to members in their Member Formula, or on the cube for each required Data Unit (running through a Data Unit calculation sequence, see below).

Translate

This will run the calculation, as above, plus – following the calculation run – the data will be translated into the currency of the parent entity (or a selected currency chosen by the user to translate to).

Consolidate

Consolidate runs calculations and translations for the Data Unit as per the above two steps, and then consolidates data up to the parent entity.

In the OneStream platform, the user can select a few ways to access the menu option to execute standard calculate, translate, or consolidate processes, or use force calculate, force translate, or force consolidate.

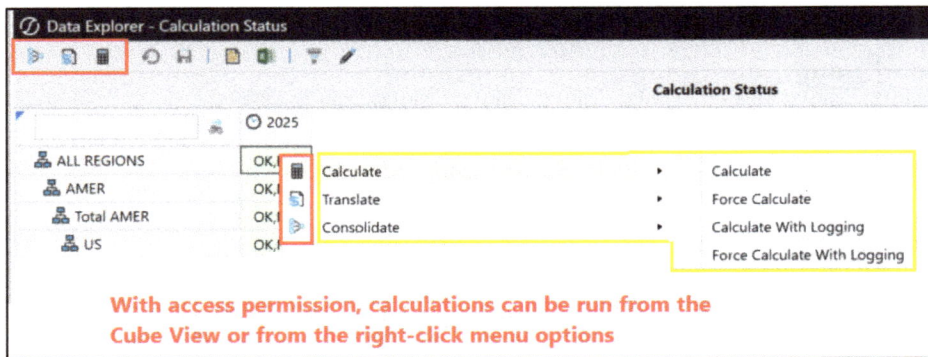

Figure 6.15

The difference between standard calculations and force calculations is that the standard will first check any prior periods (starting with the first period in the current year) to ascertain if the engine needs to execute on each period up to and including the current period. This is determined by what is known as the **Calculation Status** (see below). If the status is OK, then the calculation will not execute. But with a status of CA, for example, a calculation needs to be applied.

The standard is useful for statutory scenarios where Actuals are being reported for the current month, and prior period Actual values will not have changed.

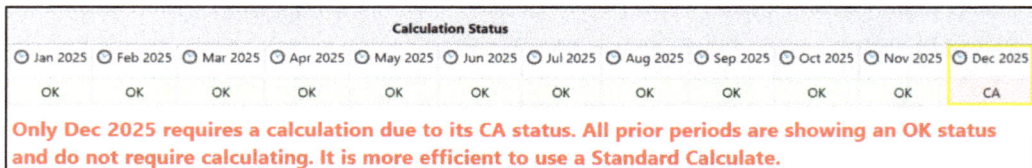

Figure 6.16

With the force option, prior periods – from the first period in the year onwards – will automatically be worked on by the engine, *irrespective of status*. This is useful for planning cycles where multiple periods are being worked on by many departments, and new data is then loaded, spanning the year. Using force is the most efficient option, because each period does not require to be checked first.

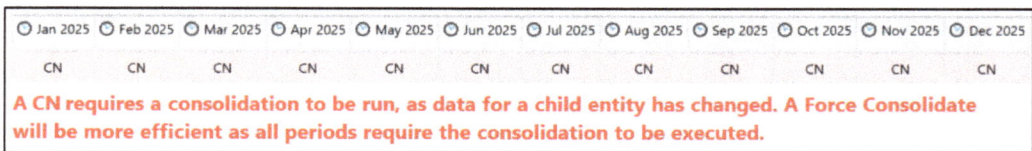

Figure 6.17

Calculation Status

To ascertain calculation status before running standard or force, a Cube View can be built where the View dimension has the built-in CalcStatus member. The row and column options will use a defined dimension hierarchy (for example, entities in rows and time in columns). The calculation status is shown by a code that is determined on the data and metadata, and the code status will change when there are changes to either of these.

On the left of Figure 6.18 is an illustration of how a Cube View presents the status. The right-hand box displays what the codes stand for. With codes relatively straightforward to understand, it is worth pointing out OK,MC, which indicates that the calculation has been performed, but due to artifacts related to the Cube, formulas, FX rates, or business rules (all considered metadata changes), then it is advisable to run the calculation again as the results may be different.

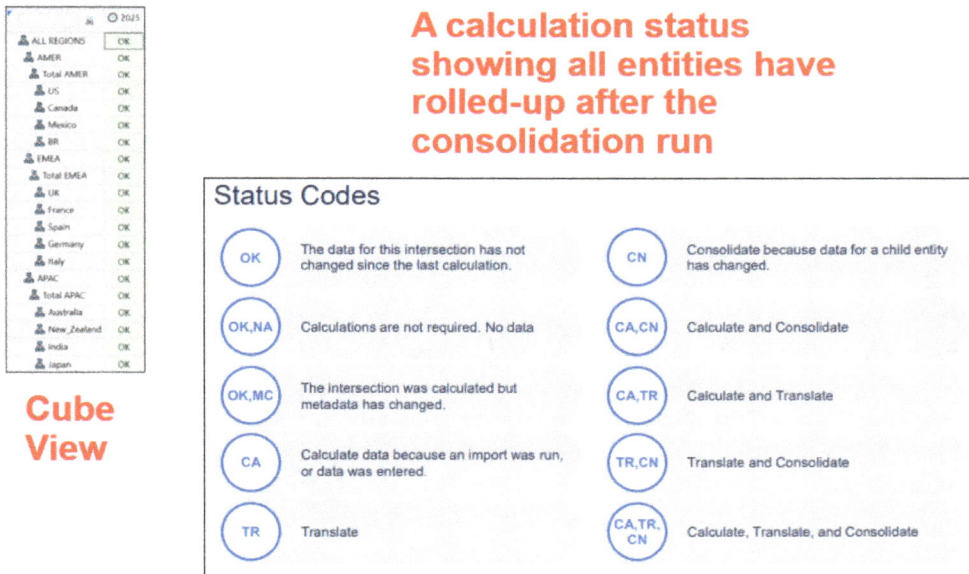

A calculation status showing all entities have rolled-up after the consolidation run

Cube View

Status Codes

Code	Description	Code	Description
OK	The data for this intersection has not changed since the last calculation.	CN	Consolidate because data for a child entity has changed.
OK,NA	Calculations are not required. No data	CA,CN	Calculate and Consolidate
OK,MC	The intersection was calculated but metadata has changed.	CA,TR	Calculate and Translate
CA	Calculate data because an import was run, or data was entered.	TR,CN	Translate and Consolidate
TR	Translate	CA,TR,CN	Calculate, Translate, and Consolidate

Figure 6.18

How Calculations Are Run

Once business rules have been created, they can be embedded in various places around the platform, waiting to be executed, the Cube Properties tab being one of them. At Top Training, we have the business rule named Multiply_Rule in the 200 Americas cube, as shown in Figure 6.19.

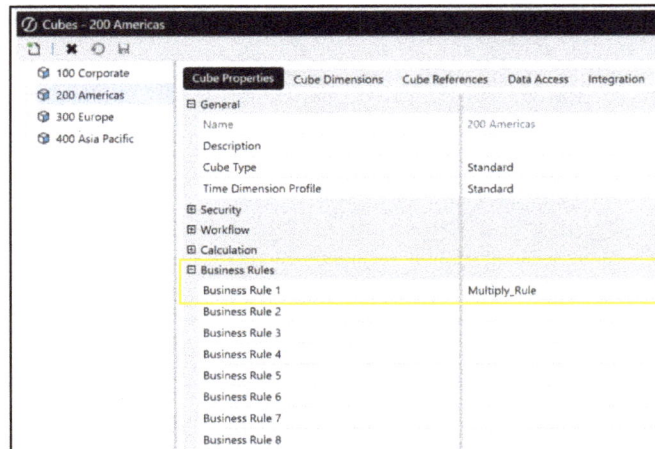

Figure 6.19

We also now know that Member Formulas are embedded in a specific Member Formula field (as previously mentioned and shown earlier in Figure 6.9).

Now, it is a case of knowing where the business rule or Member Formula can be run from. This would have been part of the design, as it may be the administrator who runs it, or the end-user who has been given permission to.

Let's look at areas where calculations can be run.

Cube View Icons

The three icons highlighted in Figure 6.20 (usually grayed out by default) can be set to True in the General Settings of the Cube View (with security settings determining the final access), and the end-user can click to consolidate, translate, or calculate values. The right-click option also then becomes available and is typically used by administrators.

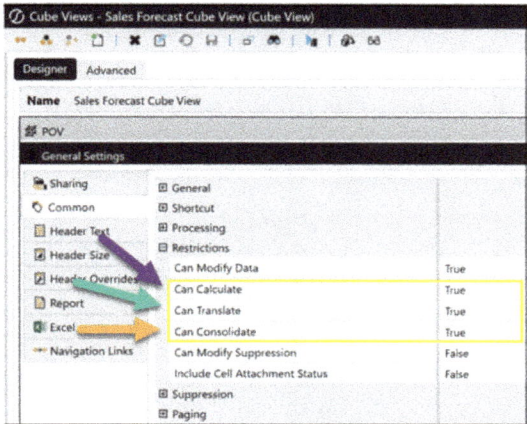

Figure 6.20

Data Management Job

A data management job is a convenient way of executing tasks such as calculate, translate, and consolidate, as well as other tasks such as clear, copy, or export data. The data management artifact is made up of a data management step (or steps) that have been embedded into a data management sequence.

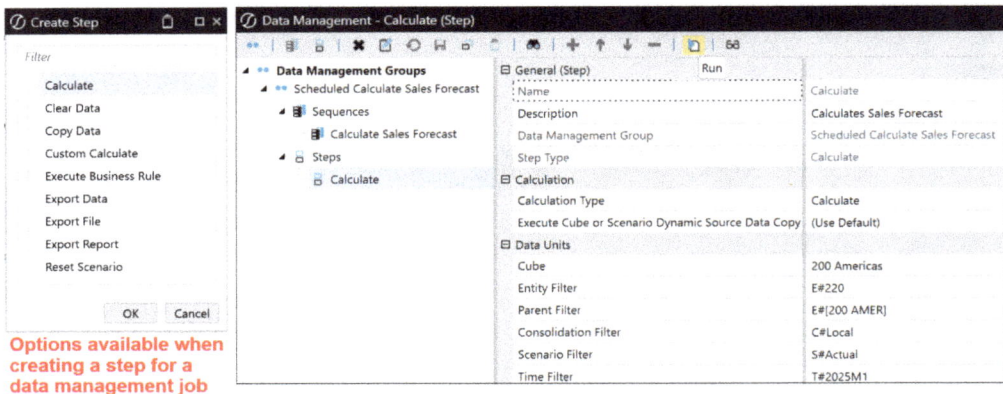

Figure 6.21

A data management job can be executed from:

- The Data Management menu

- The data source; Data Management Export Sequence option

- The calculation definitions within a Workflow Profile. The data management job name can be embedded in the Filter Value field in the Calculation Definitions tab. The data management job will run when the end-user executes the Process task in the OnePlace tab.

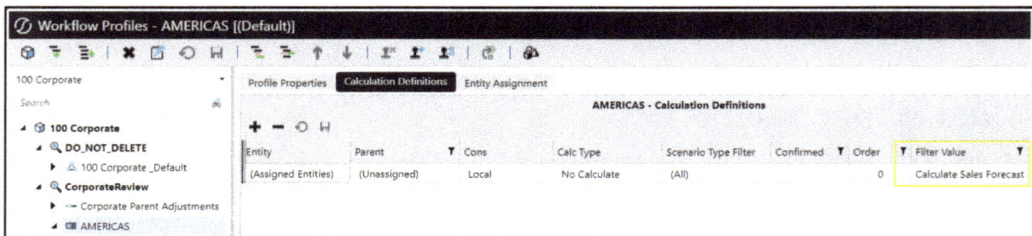

Figure 6.22

- Embedded in a business rule. This is discussed in the *Finance Rules and Calculations Handbook*.

- In the Task Scheduler. This is found in the Application tab and can be used to schedule the running of a data management job on a particular day and time.

- Dashboard components (see below). The data management job has the option to be run as part of an action for a dashboard button.

Workflow Profiles – Calculation Definitions

The calculation is set up as part of the workflow task, specifically when the user executes the process step. This is set up in the Calculation Definitions tab of the Workflow Profile, where a selection of Calc Types is available from a drop-down menu.

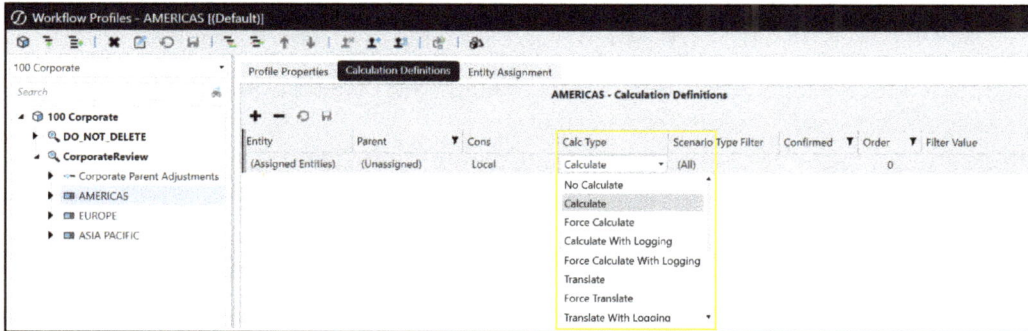

Figure 6.23

Other Options Where A Calculation Can Be Run From

Dashboard Button

A dashboard button is a component for a dashboard that allows the user to execute a step. When constructing a button, the action section allows for the selection of a calculate option, or (as mentioned in the data management job above) a data management sequence can also be selected.

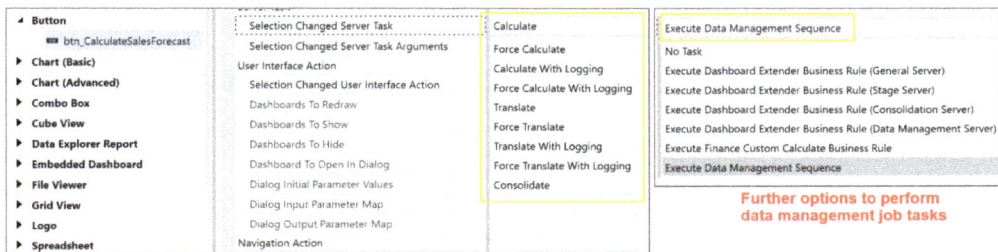

Dashboard button with actions to perform either calculate, translate, or consolidate tasks

Figure 6.24

Data Unit Calculation Sequence (DUCS)

Data Unit Calculation Sequence (DUCS) is a term used to outline the steps involved when a business rule or Member Formula script gets executed.

A DUCS occurs each time a calculation or consolidation is run on a cube. In short, the steps range from clearing the existing calculated, non-durable data in the Scenario (depending on its settings) , checking for any scenario Member Formula, and then alternating between executing groups of business rules and groups of formula passes (e.g., executing business rules 1 and 2 assigned to the cubes then formula passes 1 through 4 for Account, Flow, UD1, then UD2 to UD8. Then business rules 3 and 4, and formula passes 5 through 8, and so on).

As many calculations have dependencies on other calculations, the DUCS will run all the steps each time. This ensures the whole Data Unit is processed before the data is then consolidated. Calculations such as initial allocations, for example, need to be processed first and will therefore be in business rules 1 or 2, before period activity in formula passes 1 to 4.

There may be occasions when running all the steps to only calculate a few values will be over-processing; therefore, methods focusing only on items that need to be part of the calculation are used. For example, a **Custom Calculation** option has been developed. This function narrows the scope to specific members populated in the Data Unit section of a data management step. This can be more efficient when only specific entities, business areas, or departments need to be processed, rather than the whole Data Unit.

Also, using the `If` statement preceding the calculation (Member Formula or business rule) will mean the DUCS not being run many more times than it needs to be. In an earlier example, we made sure the calculation only ran for the Local Consolidation Member and Base Entities:

```
If api.Cons.IsLocalCurrencyForEntity() AndAlso Not
api.Entity.HasChildren()
```

Detailed steps on the DUCS and more on methods to scope calculations are in the *Finance Rules and Calculations Handbook*.

Handling All The Calculations

Calculation Documentation Matrix

Capturing all the initial calculations required is a discussion that starts in the design phase. Further calculations are then added when the application is live, with all of this captured in good documentation. A calculation matrix can be created, with headings related to the calculation, such as:

- Name of calculation; e.g., Margin

- Category of calculation; e.g., Key Performance Indicators

- Type of calculation (stored or dynamic)

- Location in OneStream (business rule or Member Formula)

- Syntax, expression (outlining source and target dimension and members), or function (e.g., Profit / Revenue)

- Comments; e.g., calculation in Income Statement.

Application Reports And Administrator Solution Tool

Another way to keep track of calculations is by using a suite of standard **Application Reports**. The key reports are the **Formula Statistics Report** which provides a breakdown of each dimension with members that have Member Formulas, and a **Formula List Report** that shows each Member Formula and its syntax.

The **Administrator Solution Tool** provides a business rule viewer which allows for the viewing of current and historical business rules and Member Formulas. It provides a historical audit trail of all the rules that have been added, edited, or deleted. Further to this, in the Administrator Solution Tool, there is a **Member Formula Builder** that helps you to create calculations through a guided approach in a user-friendly interface.

Conclusion

A lot of OneStream's functionalities are performed through menu options for both administrators and users. But when calculations are required, the initial design is key since it looks at the most efficient way of doing so. The chosen option may be a Member Formula that targets specific members, or business rules that provide the ability to cover a large area of dimensions and members.

Calculated values can be stored within OneStream, in which case data buffers drive the process, or dynamically calculate on the fly when a report is run.

The way code is structured is referred to as syntax. This can contain expressions, functions, or both. The status code will indicate whether the calculation needs to be run, and this can be initiated from menu options, Cube View icons, a workflow process step, or data management jobs.

This chapter has covered the basics you need when starting to think about rule writing. It is not hard to write syntax, as there are many resources that help, including business rule Snippets, Member Filter builder expressions, or the Member Formula Builder.

7

Let Your Workflow

How a Workflow Helps Bring It Together

In organizations, 'workflow' refers to a structured sequence of tasks designed to achieve a specific goal. In OneStream's case, this is mainly the movement of data or information. On an operational level, this is the set-up of the right tasks for the right users at the right time, while helping to ensure data integrity in the financial model (cubes).

Here is this chapter's learning journey:

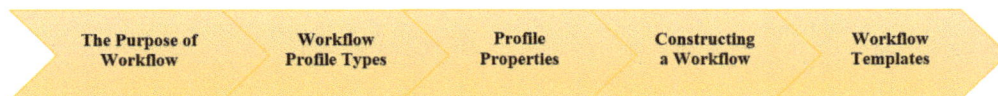

| The Purpose of Workflow | Workflow Profile Types | Profile Properties | Constructing a Workflow | Workflow Templates |

Figure 7.1

The Purpose of Workflow

Workflow in OneStream is the platform's backbone that drives most user interaction. It can be seen as the business process that is used to model and analyze data in a cube, and sometimes referred to as the responsibility hierarchy.

Simply put, end-users cannot do anything without tasks, which shows how important the workflow component (that provides the tasks) is. It controls all user activity, guiding them through tasks to complete data loads, adjustments, analysis, and data certification.

At Top Training's group level, the workflow assists with the data consolidation process.

Workflow Profile Types

Workflow Profiles are found in the Application tab and are the building blocks of a workflow hierarchy. These are the task items that need to be performed by the users. The profiles, like other artifacts in OneStream, differ by Scenario Type.

The tasks within a Workflow Profile can be configured to each organization's requirements, additional ones can be added, or existing ones removed. Each Workflow Profile name created must be unique.

Base Input Profiles

Base Input Profiles have three tasks, which are Import, Forms, and Adjustments (Journals), and are worked on by the operational team within a business area. These tasks can be renamed, additional ones added, or individual ones deactivated. The profile establishes the relationship between the workflow hierarchy and Entity members.

The tasks of Import, Forms, and Adj will be automatically linked to members in the Origin dimension, as shown in Figure 7.2.

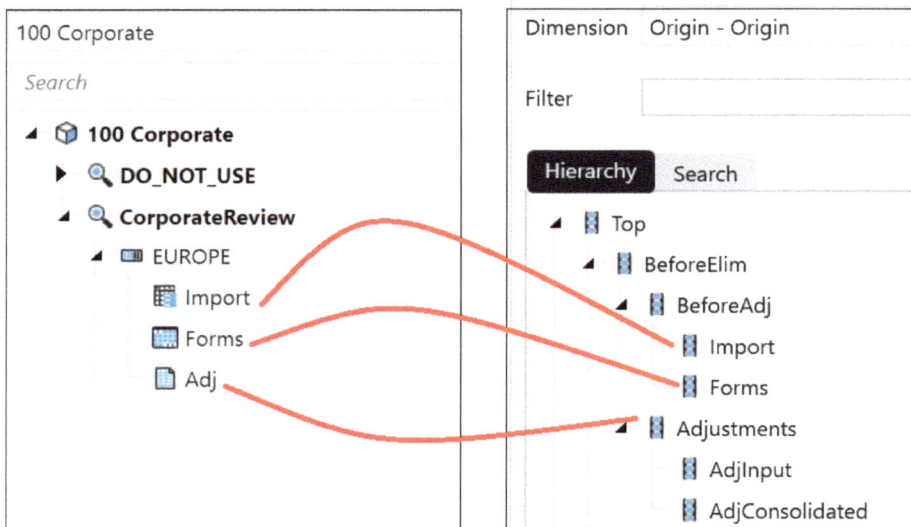

Figure 7.2

Parent Input Profiles

Parent Input Profiles have two tasks, which are Forms and Adjustments (Journals), used for top-side adjustments to parent entities.

As per the Base Input Profiles, the parent input also has a relationship with the Entity members, and the two tasks are linked to the Forms and Adj members' Origin dimension.

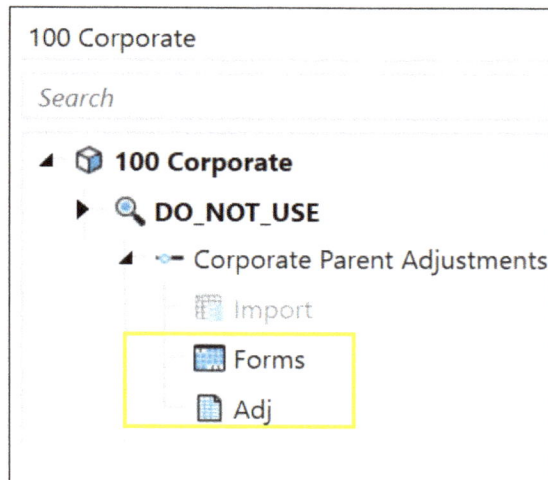

Parent Workflow Profile only has Forms and Adjustments.

Figure 7.3

Review Profiles

Review profiles do not have any tasks, but the profile facilitates reviewing of the data and sign-off certification. It will be read-only and is usually worked on by an area or group manager.

The review profile acts as a good checkpoint for the base and parent Workflow Profiles and does not have any direct relationship with entity or origin members. It is also possible to have cube calculations in review profiles that help control the sign-off process.

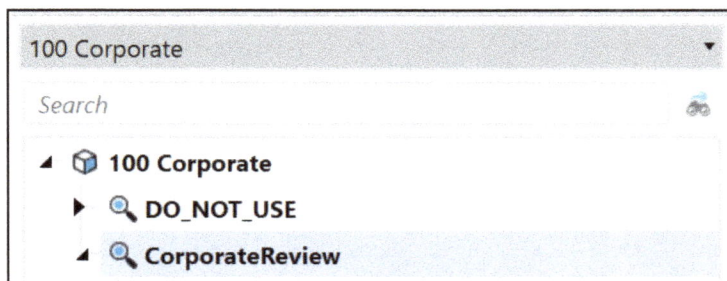

Figure 7.4

Chapter 7

Constructing The Workflow

Building a workflow structure starts with creating a **Cube Root Workflow Profile**. To create a cube root, we must remember the particular setting that needs to be applied. This was discussed in a previous chapter, specifically the one on cubes. Need a reminder? It is the Is Top Level Cube For Workflow setting, under the Workflow section of the Cube Properties tab, as per Figure 7.5.

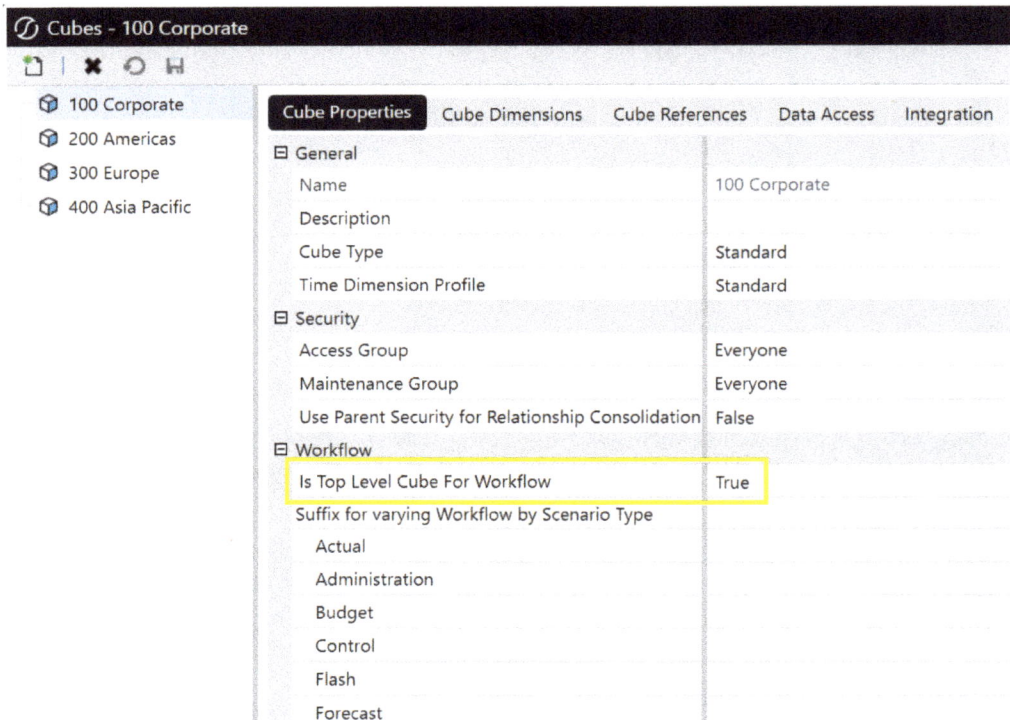

Figure 7.5

When designing the workflow, we can sketch out a draft of workflow hierarchies beforehand, which in turn will show the entities that are responsible for each segment of the workflow, as shown in Figure 7.6. By doing this, it becomes apparent which of the cubes in our model will drive all the hierarchies. That cube will have a relationship with the entities required and, therefore, will have the Is Top Level Cube For Workflow set to True. In Top Training, the setting has been applied to the 100 Corporate Cube.

Workflow Hierarchy Sketch

Cube Root Workflow Profile: 100 Corporate

Hierarchy	Entity
Corporate (Review)	N/A
Corporate Parent Adjustments (Parent)	200 AMER, 300 EMEA, 400 APAC
AMERICAS (Base Input)	210 - US, 220 - Canada, 230 - Mexico
Import Financials	
Import Subscriptions	
Forms Headcount	
Adj	
EUROPE (Base Input)	310 - UK, 320 - France, 330 - Spain
Import	
Forms	
Adj	
ASIA PACIFIC (Base Input)	410 - Australia, 420 - New Zealand, 430 - India, 440 - Japan
Import	
Forms	
Adj	

Figure 7.6

We can now create our Cube Root Workflow Profile. Once this has been done, note how the platform creates what is known as a **Default_Workflow**.

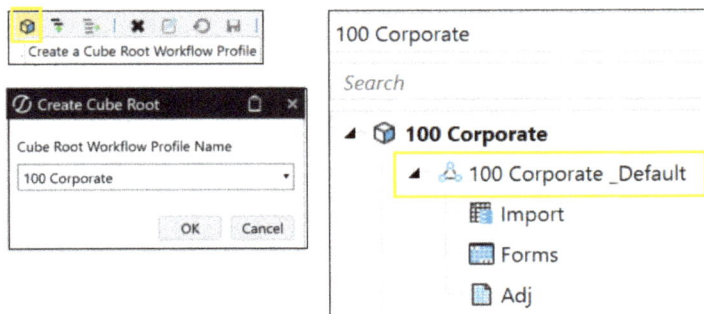

Figure 7.7

This is the platform's go-to for calculating workflow status, by establishing a relationship between the workflow hierarchy and the Entity members, and is therefore required for each workflow hierarchy.

All entities are initially assigned to the default profile automatically (and then reassigned as and when new workflows are created).

Any modifications made to properties in the default profile will affect entities that remain within it, causing issues when later reassigned to their respective workflows. For example, if the Adj is deactivated in the default profile, this will now not be available to any of the entities within it, that have not yet been assigned elsewhere.

For its purpose to remain intact, it should not be used or deleted. Instead, it will be better to house it under a DO_NOT_USE structure that can be created from a review Workflow Profile type. Further to this, security can be applied to limit access to the default profile.

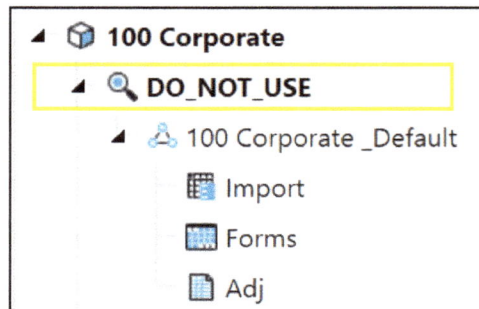

Figure 7.8

Workflow Profiles can be created by selecting the Create Child Under Current Workflow Profile and opting for either a Base, Parent, or Review profile.

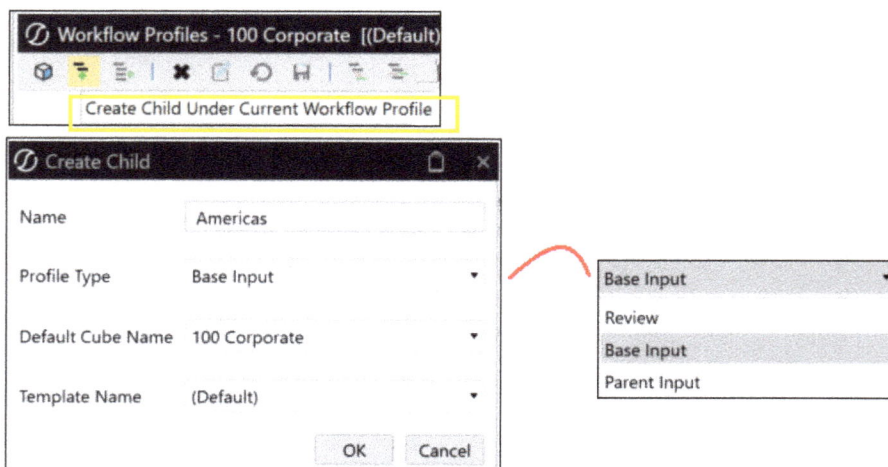

Figure 7.9

For the base and parent profiles, the tabs that are available are Profile Properties, Calculation Definitions and Entity Assignment. For the review profile, it's Profile Properties and Calculation Definitions.

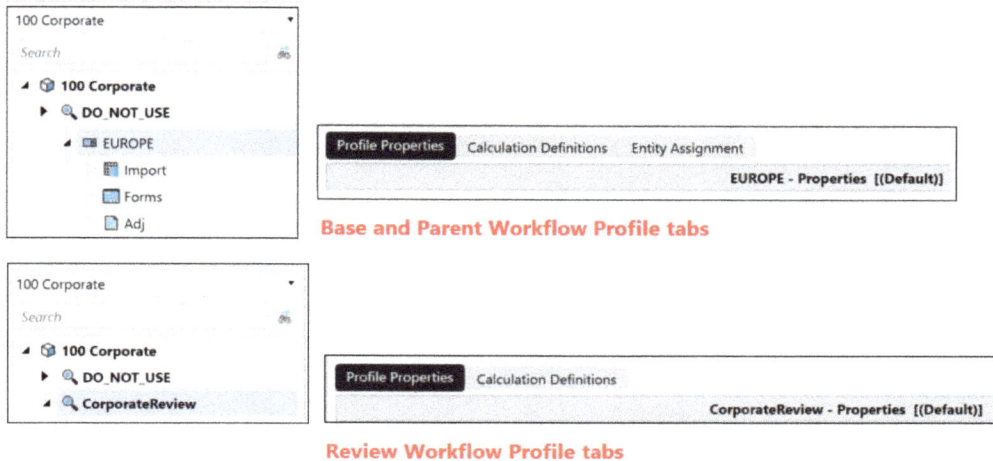

Base and Parent Workflow Profile tabs

Review Workflow Profile tabs

Figure 7.10

Profile Properties

This is the primary tab for workflow configuration. Profile Properties will vary by Scenario Type. The key configuration fields are:

Security

At the default Scenario Type, an **Access Group** can be created. The users in this group will have access to the Workflow Profile at run time to view results, as well as a **Maintenance Group** (who are also part of the Access Group) that controls which users can administer the profile.

By individual Scenario Type, the **Workflow Execution Group** and **Certification Signoff Group** allow for the loading of data and sign-off on the workflow, respectively.

For further understanding on workflow security, refer to the *OneStream Administrator Handbook* where this is extensively covered.

Workflow Name

These are the tasks that users need to complete in the workflow. As there are a lot of combinations here, the selection will be based on the workflow design. The list drop-down selection will vary depending on which input type is being worked on; for example, an Import type will have import-related tasks, and an Adj type will have journal-related tasks.

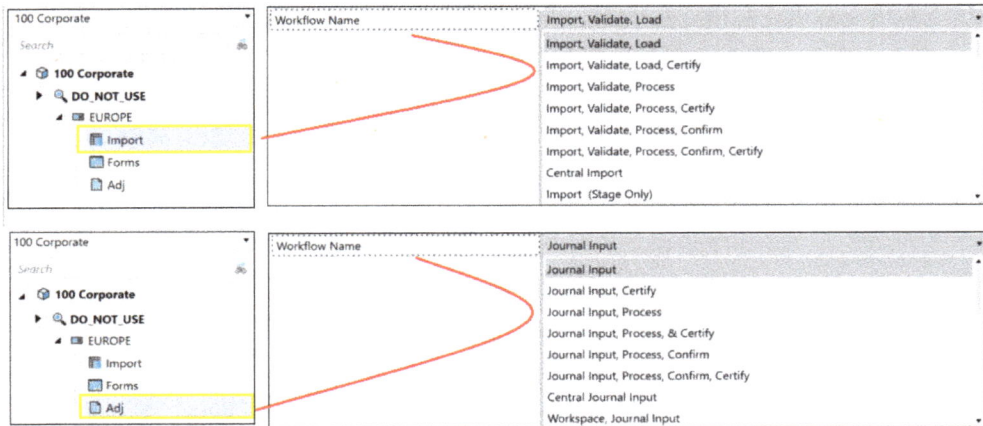

Figure 7.11

The tasks chosen will then reflect what the user will see in the navigation pane in the OnePlace tab. For example, in Figure 7.12, the tasks are Import, Validate, and Load.

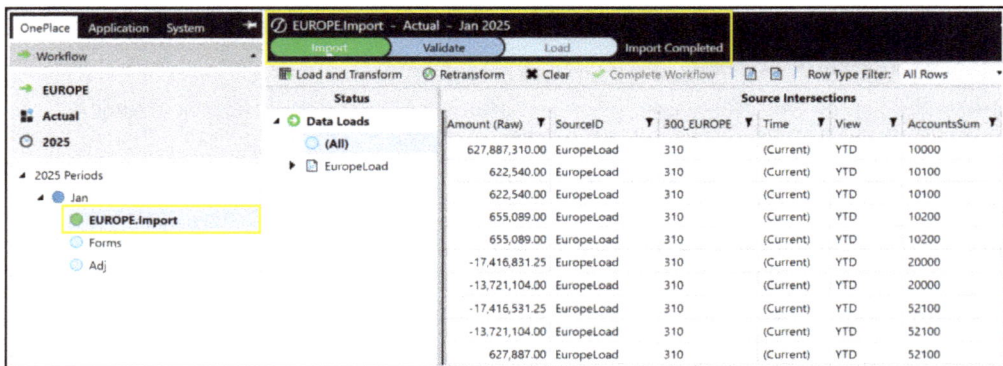

Figure 7.12

Note: When importing data, the four data load methods available to the user are: Replace (clears existing values then loads new values from the file), Replace (All Time) (clears existing values and then replaces values in all time periods for a selected year), Replace Background (All Time, All Source ID's) (clears existing values, replaces all periods for a selected year and also replaces all the source IDs), and finally Append (the existing values are unchanged and rows of data are added, not included, in the previous data load file).

Profile Active

This is where a True / False setting determines if the active profile will be seen on the workflow page or not. Deactivating the profile should always be the preferred option to deleting it altogether.

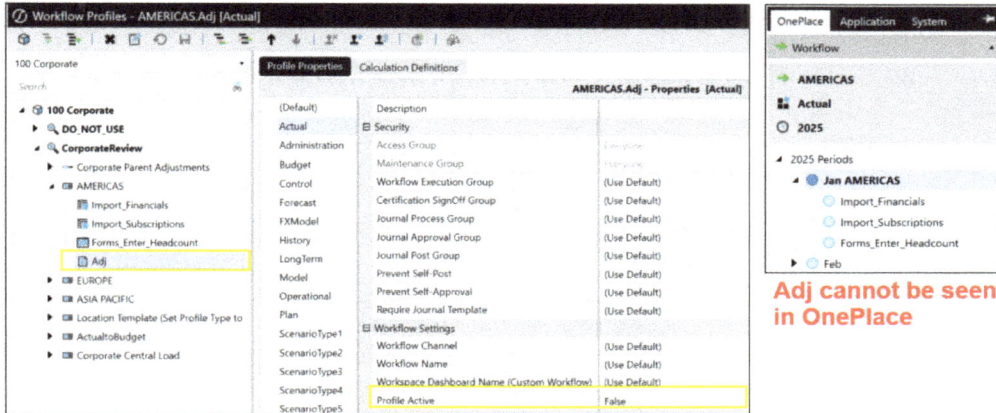

Adj cannot be seen in OnePlace

The Adj Profile Active has been set to False

Figure 7.13

Data Source and Transformation Profile Name

Previously, in the chapter on 'Importing that all Important Data', the data source type was created. Remember, this was telling OneStream how to read the source file. Then, the transformation rules were assigned, which was the mapping of the source items to the target members.

Both artifacts can now be added to the import task of the Workflow Profile, as in Figure 7.14.

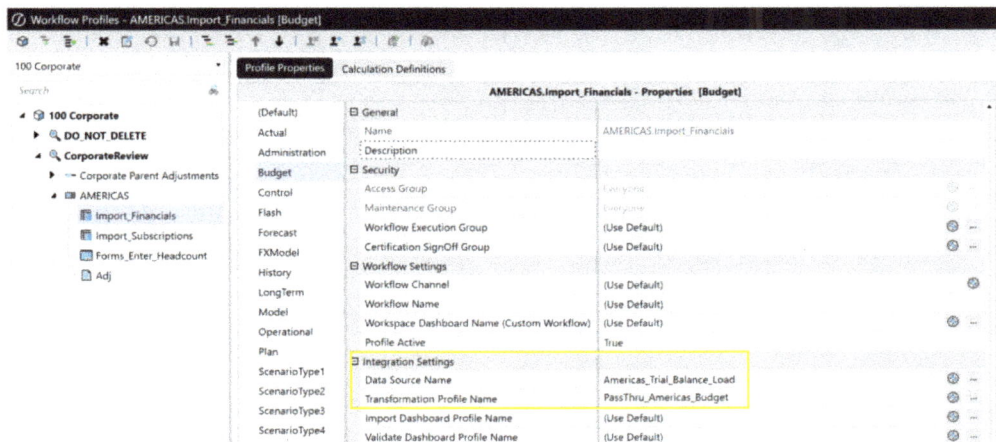

Figure 7.14

Chapter 7

Input Forms Profile Name

The **Form** input type is a data entry form. This is created from the Form Templates menu. In this menu, the data entry form can use a Cube View or Spreadsheet to be the method of entry, and created within a Form Template Group and then put in a Form Template Profile.

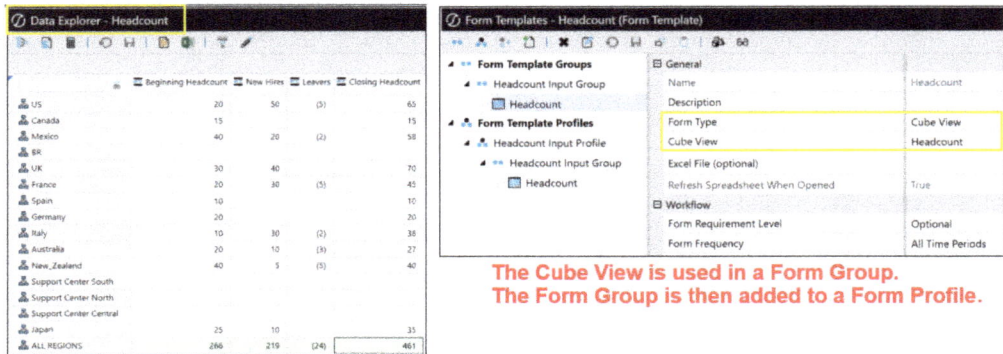

A Cube View created to be used as a Form

The Cube View is used in a Form Group.
The Form Group is then added to a Form Profile.

Figure 7.15

The Form Profile is then selected in the Workflow Profile, allowing users to access the form from the OnePlace tab.

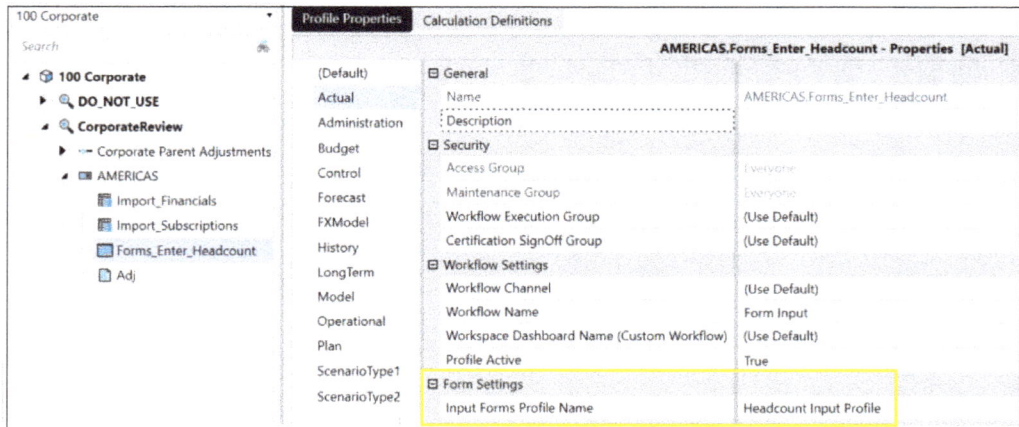

Form Profile is selected in the Form Settings Workflow Profile

Figure 7.16

140

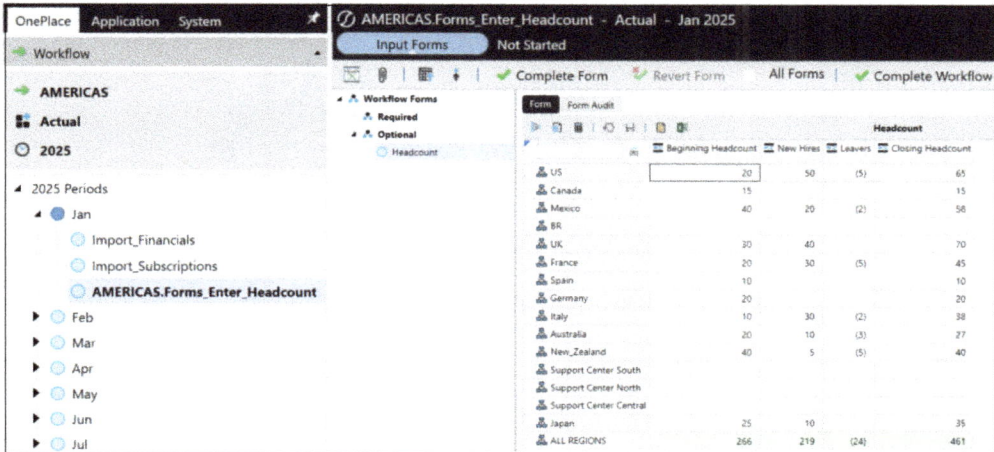

The Form is accessed by the user from OnePlace to input values

Figure 7.17

Journal Template Profile Name

Like the Form Template, a Journal Template is created in a Journal Template Group and then slotted into a Journal Template Profile.

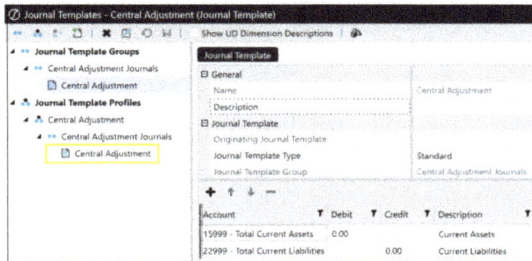

A Journal Template is created in a Journal Template Group and then added to a Journal Template Profile

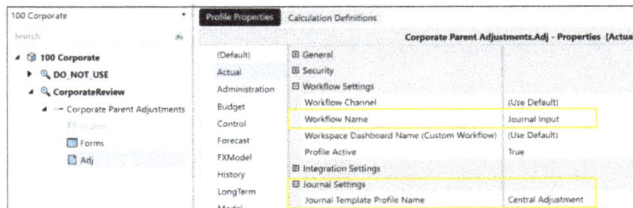

The Journal Template Profile is selected in the Journal Settings Workflow Profile

Figure 7.18

The Journal can then be accessed by the user from the OnePlace tab.

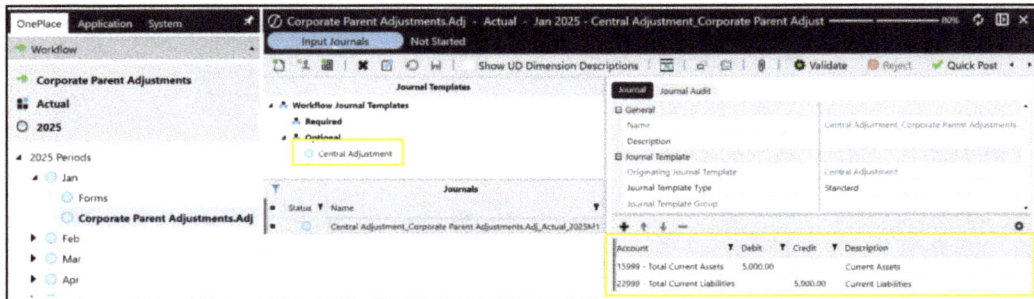

Figure 7.19

Confirmation Profile Name

Confirmation rules are visual checklists embedded within the workflow and used to verify whether data is breaching a threshold, by either providing a warning, or an error that prevents the user from moving forward. A confirmation rule can be configured to get the user to attach a file or comment.

All confirmation rules are optional to have as part of the workflow but – if used – will place more ownership to ensure the integrity of the data, together with the choice for documentary or commentary evidence.

To run the rule, the workflow must have a workflow name containing Confirm with a Process task required before it (together with the calculation definition having Confirm selected as well).

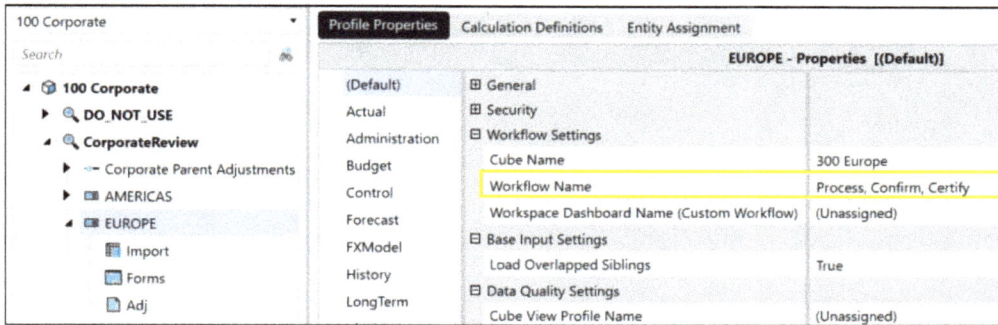

The Workflow Name with Confirm must have Process before it

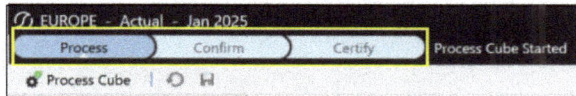

The result in OnePlace

Figure 7.20

Once run, the status for each rule is shown with green representing passed, orange representing warning, and red representing fail.

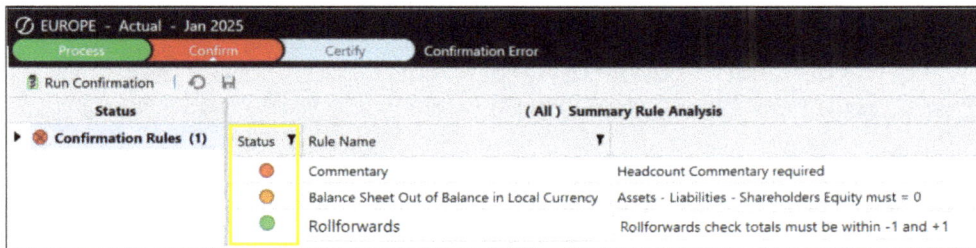

Figure 7.21

The rule is created in a group. Each rule is a line consisting of the rule name, rule text and an embedded business rule that performs the integrity check.

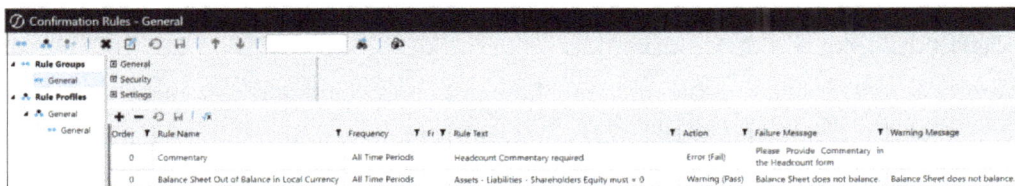

Figure 7.22

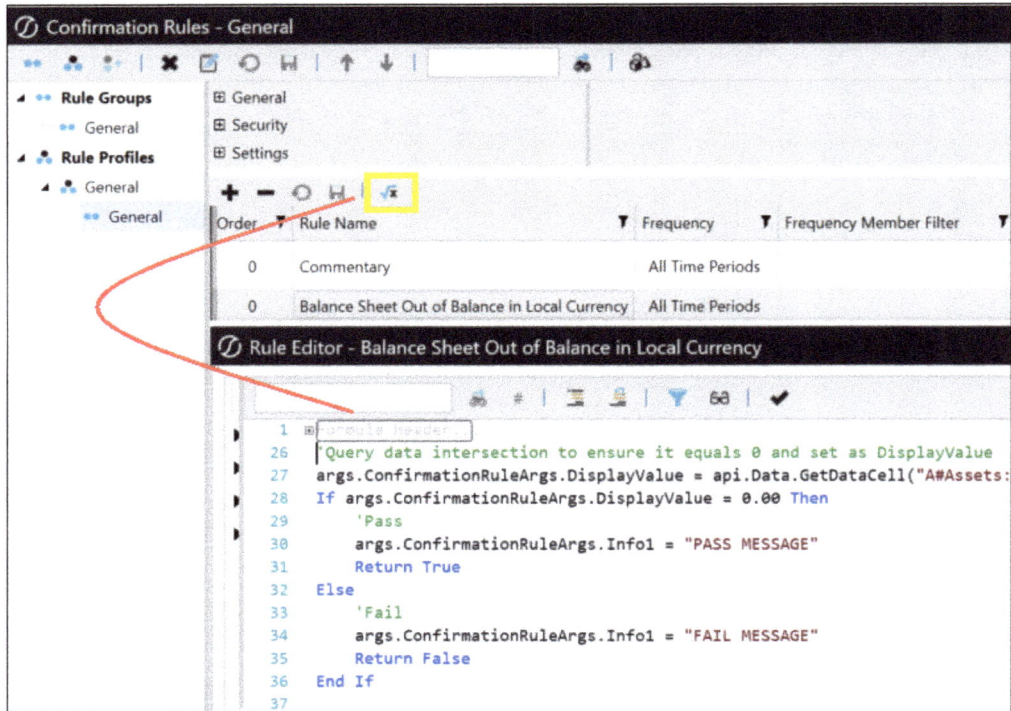

Figure 7.23

The group is then attached to a profile in the Confirmation Profile Name setting.

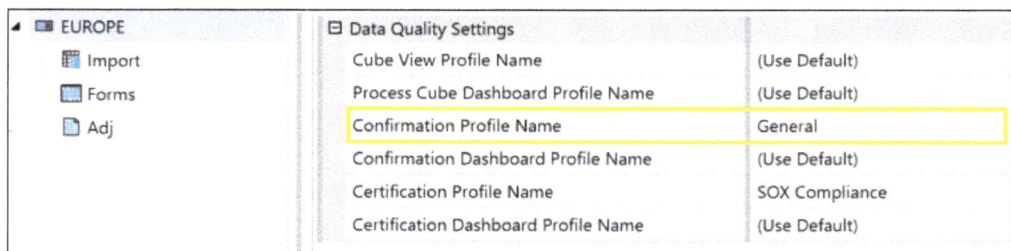

Figure 7.24

Certification Profile Name

Certification is usually considered one of the last tasks in a workflow, consisting of specific questions to sign off the data.

Once again, like confirmation rules, a certification questionnaire is optional but may provide added data integrity for organizations that have to comply with external requirements. Created in a Question Group that consists of Name, Category, Risk Level, and Question Text, it can then be added to a Question Profile, where the profile is embedded in the workflow that uses a Certify task in its workflow name.

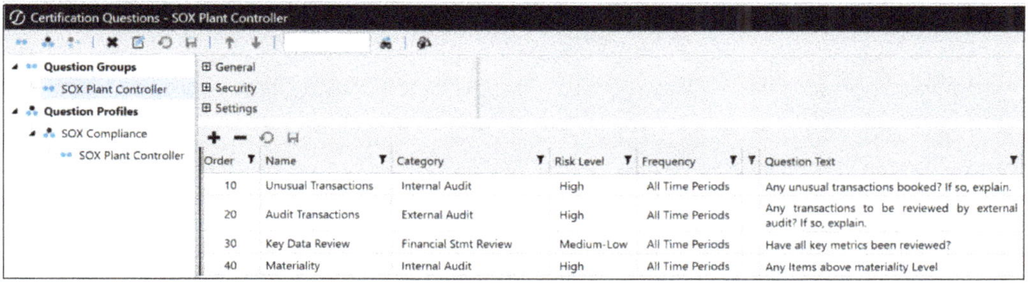

Figure 7.25

If no questions are required, a Quick Certify can be used if there is a certification task in the workflow (the Quick Certify option is selected in the workflow). This will only need a response to Is the workflow complete?

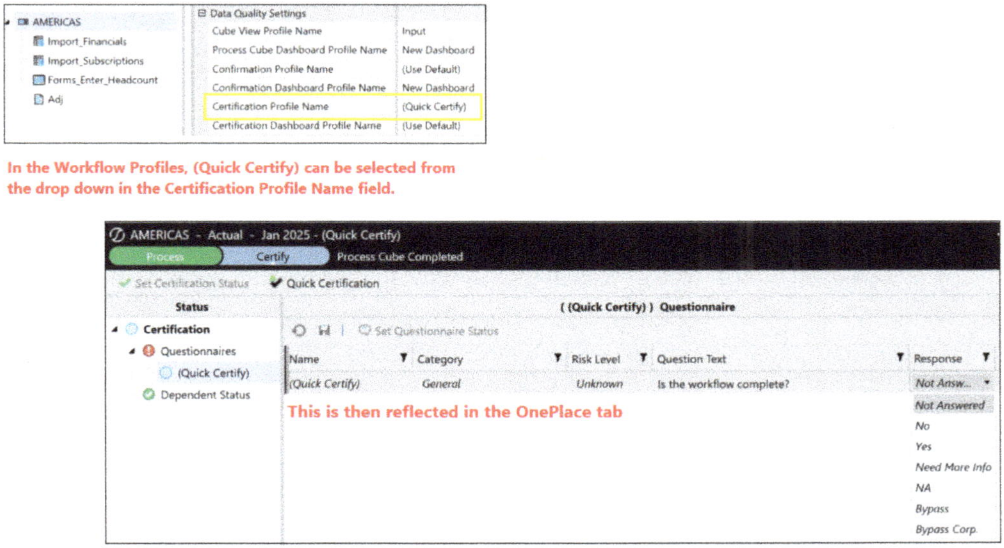

In the Workflow Profiles, (Quick Certify) can be selected from the drop down in the Certification Profile Name field.

This is then reflected in the OnePlace tab

Figure 7.26

Intercompany Matching Settings

This is where intercompany matching is initiated. When Matching Enabled is set to True, the Matching Parameters section needs to be configured. For Top Training, we would like to set up the US, Canada, and Mexico entities to be able to trade with each other. Figure 7.27 shows the matching parameters.

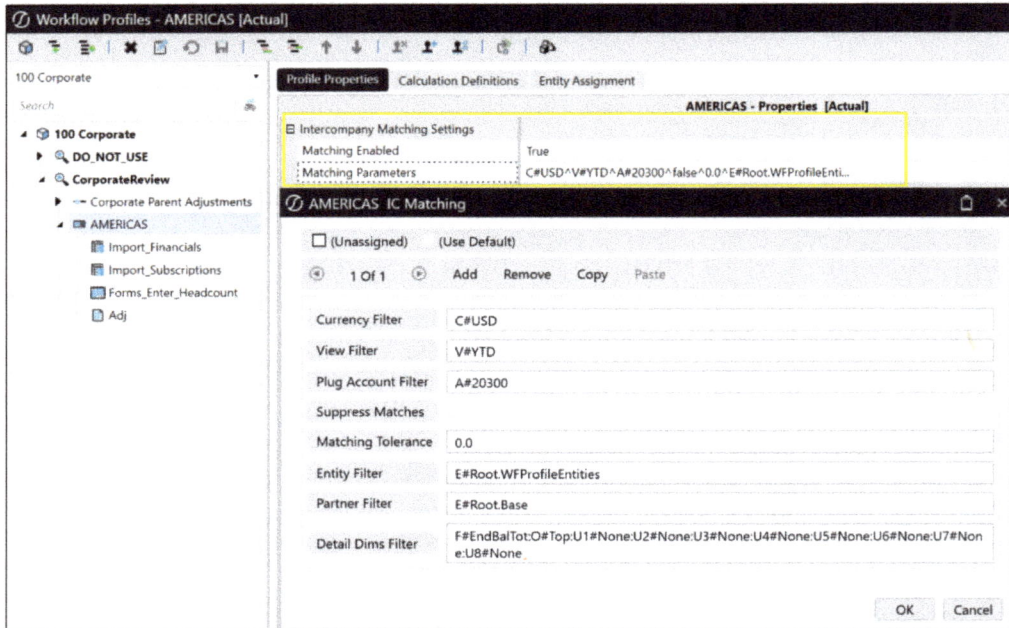

Figure 7.27

For intercompany to take place, entities would have been assigned the is IC Entity as True, in the Entity dimension. Then, intercompany accounts will need to have been set up for IC Sales and IC Purchases, as an example, and a Plug that will hold any differences (the Plug Account will have been embedded in the IC Sales and IC Purchases settings).

Account Type	Revenue
Formula Type	(Not Used)
Allow Input	True
Is Consolidated	Conditional (True if no Formula Type (default))
Is IC Account	True
Use Alternate Input Currency In Flow	False
Plug Account	20300
Input View For Adjustments	Use Scenario Setting (Default)
No Data Zero View For Adjustments	Use Scenario Setting (Default)
No Data Zero View For NonAdjustment	Use Scenario Setting (Default)

60100 - IC Sales
42000 - IC Purchases

20300 - IC Rec-Pay Plug

Account Type	Liability
Formula Type	(Not Used)
Allow Input	False
Is Consolidated	Conditional (True if no Formula Type (default))
Is IC Account	True
Use Alternate Input Currency In Flow	False
Plug Account	
Input View For Adjustments	Use Scenario Setting (Default)
No Data Zero View For Adjustments	Use Scenario Setting (Default)
No Data Zero View For NonAdjustments	Use Scenario Setting (Default)

Figure 7.28

The intercompany values are entered in an intercompany data entry form, created from a Cube View or Spreadsheet.

Data Explorer - Intercompany Americas

		Form Input		
		IC Sales	IC Purchases	IC Rec-Pay Plug
US	⊞ Canada	20,000.00		
Canada	⊞ US		18,000.00	
Mexico	⊞ US			
Total AMER	⊟ Top	20,000.00	13,320.00	6,680.00

Figure 7.29

In OnePlace, we can see the IC Matching when we select the workflow where the matching has been enabled.

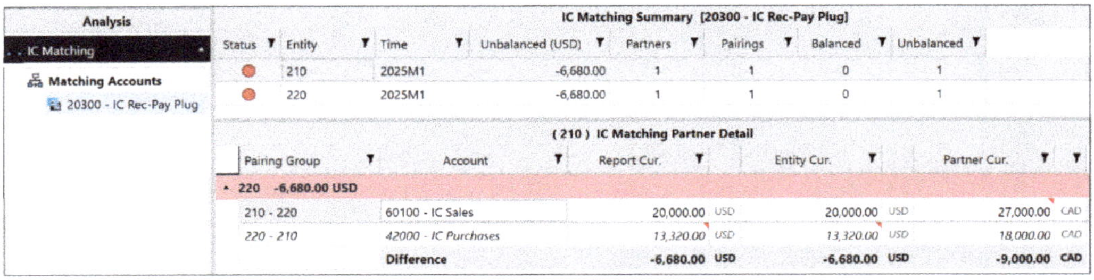

Figure 7.30

We can also run **Application Reports** that provide intercompany details and status.

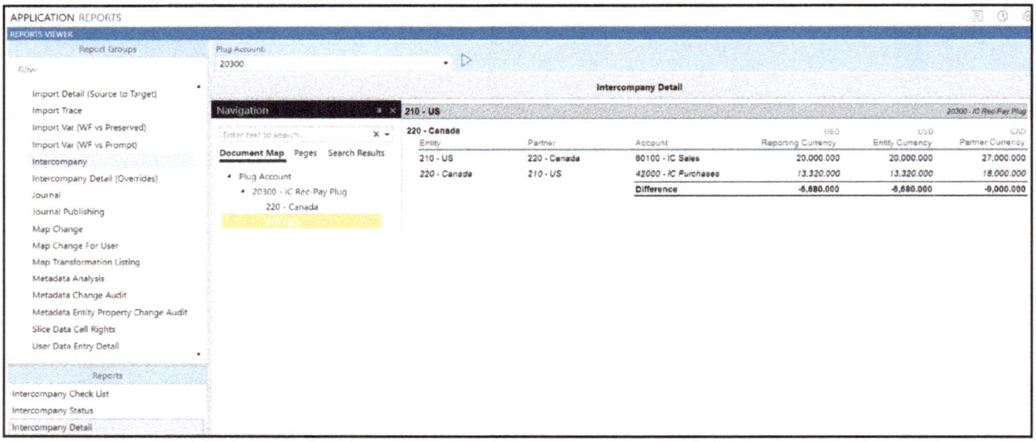

Figure 7.31

Calculation Definitions

This is the second tab (which we briefly discussed in the previous chapter on Figuring Out Calculations). This is where the administrator assigns the calculations required when the user selects Process in the OnePlace tab.

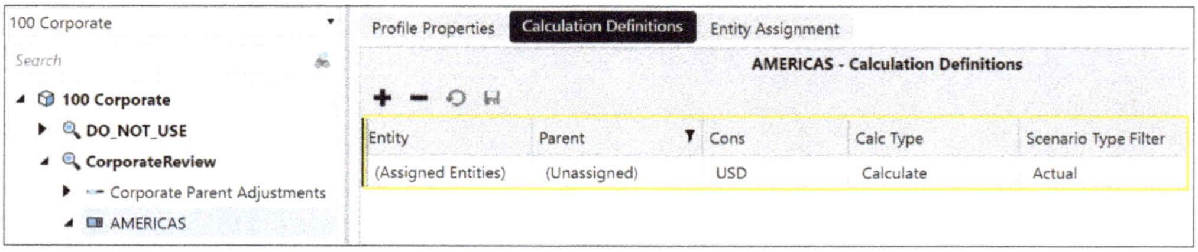

Figure 7.32

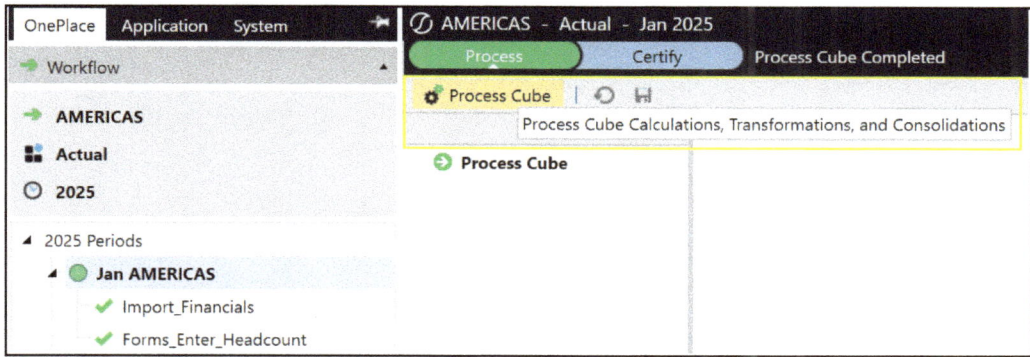

Figure 7.33

The calculation definition can be used to run a combination of calculations, translations, and consolidations, as well as just being set up to run a data management job in the Filter Value field. If using a data management job, then set the Calc Type to No Calculate, as shown in Figure 7.34.

> **Note:** An **Eventhandler** rule will have been created in the business rules menu. This is the trigger to run a job after, say, a task has been performed. In this case, a **DataQualityEventHandler** business rule will run the data management job after the process cube task has been executed.

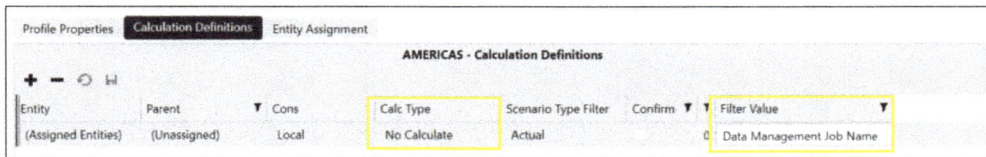

Figure 7.34

Entity Assignment

This tab is where the entities are assigned to the workflow. As entities can only be assigned once to a particular cube's workflow (a cube can have many base, parent, or review workflows), the Unassigned Base Entities section on the right will not show any entities that have already been assigned to another workflow within the same cube.

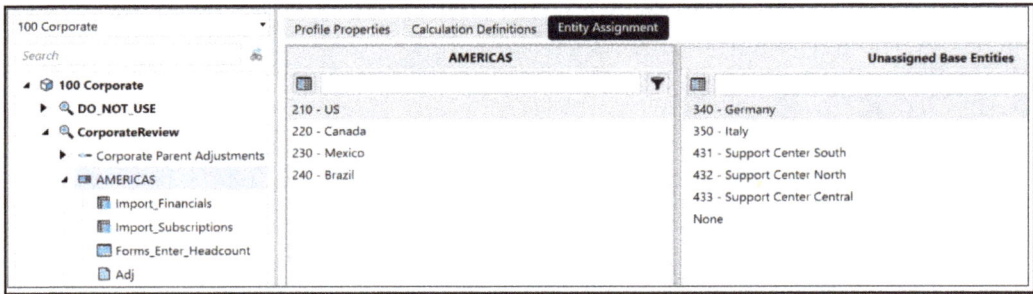

Figure 7.35

Assigning entities to the workflow will then mean items such as calculation definitions and confirmation rules will be processed, as well as the locking mechanism for the workflow.

Workflow Suffix

As we are initially limited to entities only being assigned to one workflow from the same cube, creating workflow suffixes allows for separate workflow structures in the same cube, and this will allow entities to be reused. The separate workflow structure allows for different data collection points, security, and approval processes.

There are points to note when working with suffixes. They can be seen as the workflow's version of extensibility, and as such, suffixes should be the backbone of a proper design of extensibility; it's precisely because of suffixes that OneStream can be tailored to each business process that helps reduce the maintenance.

They should only be used for Scenario Types being implemented. A workflow suffix for any Scenario Type cannot be added or updated once data is loaded, so suffixes should be added early on when creating workflows.

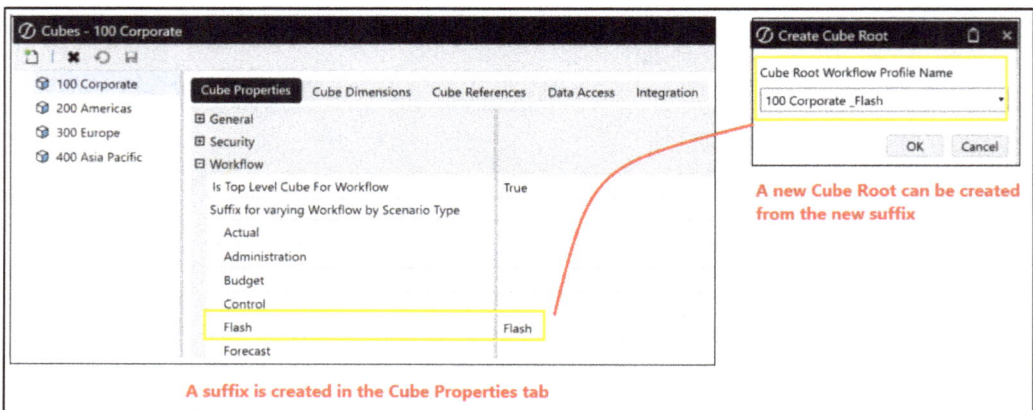

Figure 7.36

150

Not every Scenario Type needs to have a separate suffix. If Budget and Forecast follow the same process, they can be grouped together under the same suffix.

Keep A Workflow Template Handy

A nice feature when creating Workflow Profiles is a **Workflow Template**. As the name suggests, an administrator can create a template to a bespoke standard version, and then select it every time a new Workflow Profile is constructed.

A bespoke version might require additional base input types that will need renaming. Or some input types that need to be disabled. A workflow template is useful when required to build a series of, for example, base input Workflow Profiles with similar settings.

Workflow templates are found in the Work With Templates menu. A new template can be created by using the option Create a Sibling of the Current Workflow. If additional inputs are required, then the Create Child Under Current Workflow Profile option is used.

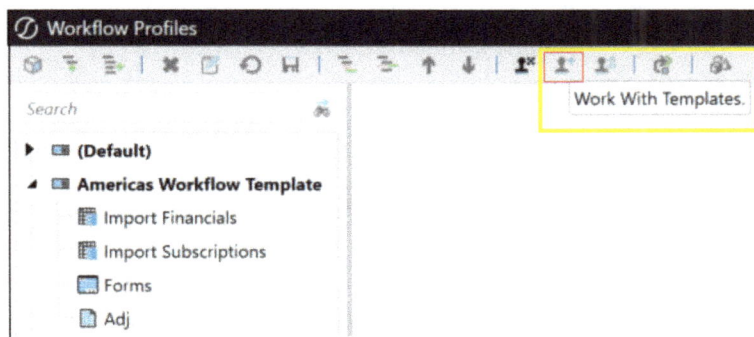

Figure 7.37

Once a template has been completed, back in Work With Profiles the option of using a Template Name is available when building the base or parent profile type, as in Figure 7.38.

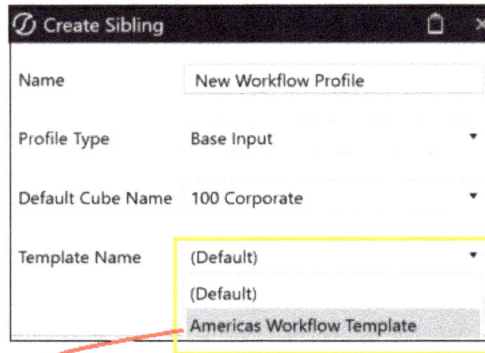

Figure 7.38

If the workflow template is updated, this can be reflected back in the Workflow Profile by using Update Input Children Using Template. By selecting the Input Profiles on the left of the window, and the Input Templates on the right, the existing Workflow Profile will be updated with the template's changes.

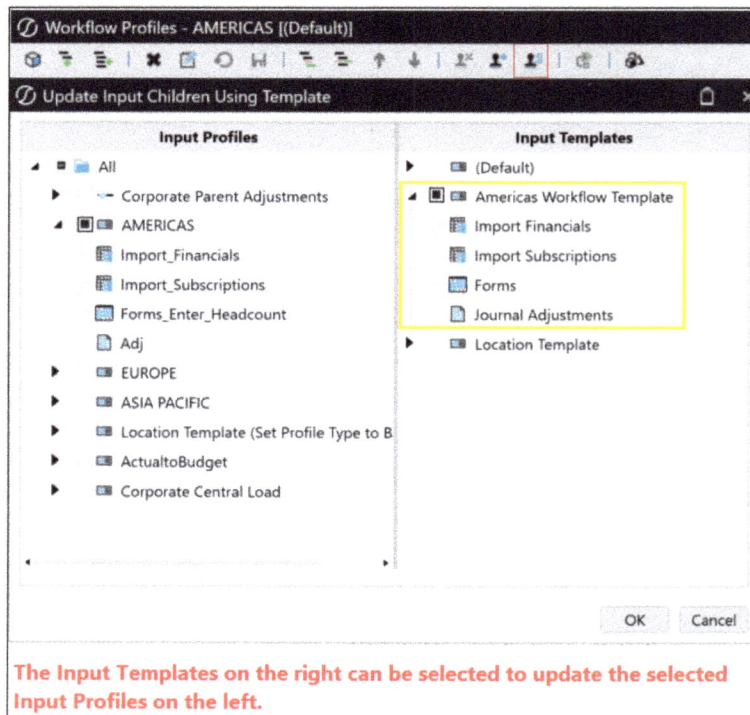

Figure 7.39

Conclusion

A lot of what we have learned in the previous chapters has led to this point where the likes of cubes (and not forgetting the dimensions required to build them), data sources, transformation rules, and calculation artifacts have all come together to form part of the construction of the workflow.

From this really important chapter, we have seen that workflow is how an end-user interacts with the platform, providing the user with their specific tasks at certain time intervals. It is down to the administrator or implementing partner to construct the workflow and – to make this easier – templates can be created first. The use of a template when constructing Workflow Profiles means that any updates on input types can be cascaded to many profiles in one go.

The construction of the workflow starts with the cube root, where the Workflow Profiles are added. There are base, parent, and review Workflow Profiles with input types of Import, data entry Forms, and Journal Adjustments. It might be advisable to first sketch out the workflow hierarchy to understand how many of each are required.

Once the profiles have been created, their properties will require configuration for security, workflow names, any data source, and transformation rules. Other options may then be considered; for example, if data entry or adjustments are required as a task, then the profile will select the Form or Journal profiles. Or if intercompany transactions are required to be done, then matching will be enabled.

For data quality and data integrity confirmation rules and certification, questions are applied to the Workflow Profile, which is usually used by the reviewer. They do so to complete the final workflow steps and certify their business area for corporate to then consolidate the values.

8

Reporting Part 1
– Show Me The Data!

Report Types

As mentioned at the start of the book, the OneStream platform is well-equipped to cater for various levels of reporting across an organization. At Top Training, the analysts work with data to turn it into meaningful information, which the operational team can then use for day-to-day tasks, and the executives for decision-making.

This chapter, and the next, aims to capture an overview of basic reports and dashboards, be a good springboard to further learning, and a good segue to the *OneStream Advance Reporting and Dashboards Handbook*.

Here is this chapter's learning journey:

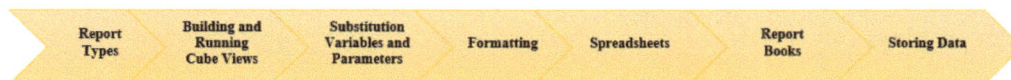

Report Types	Building and Running Cube Views	Substitution Variables and Parameters	Formatting	Spreadsheets	Report Books	Storing Data

Figure 8.1

As a reminder of what has been covered already, we have discussed OneStream's report types when presenting data. These are:

- **Forms:** An easy-to-create data entry and presentation output, constructed by using either a Cube View, spreadsheet, or dashboard. Functionality, such as parameters (discussed later), can be used to aid user interaction.

- **Report Books:** Report books allow a combination of report types and files to be brought together in a single report or zip file.

- **Extensible Documents:** Word, Excel, and PowerPoint documents that have embedded dynamic links and parameters to data and metadata within the application. These act as placeholders showing the latest values every time the report runs.

- **Dashboards:** A graphical user interface with multiple formatting capabilities for data grids, charts, and key performance indicator cards, with user interactivity available.

- **Spreadsheet / Excel Add-in:** A spreadsheet-based output for getting the data from the OneStream database, analyzing or amending it, and producing formatted reports

Most of the report types above have a common theme of using Cube Views as a foundation for accessing the data; therefore, Cube Views provide a good starting point when discussing reporting.

Cube Views

A Cube View is a multidimensional set-up (two or more dimensions) comprised of a flexible grid-based view. The data can be viewed by running the Cube View from the Data Explorer icon as shown in Figure 8.2 , or by simply clicking the Cube View from the OnePlace tab (access to the Cube View has to be granted to be in this tab), or from the Excel Add-In. Additional options then allow the Cube View to be run in a report format from the Report Viewer icon or exported to other formats, such as PDF or Excel.

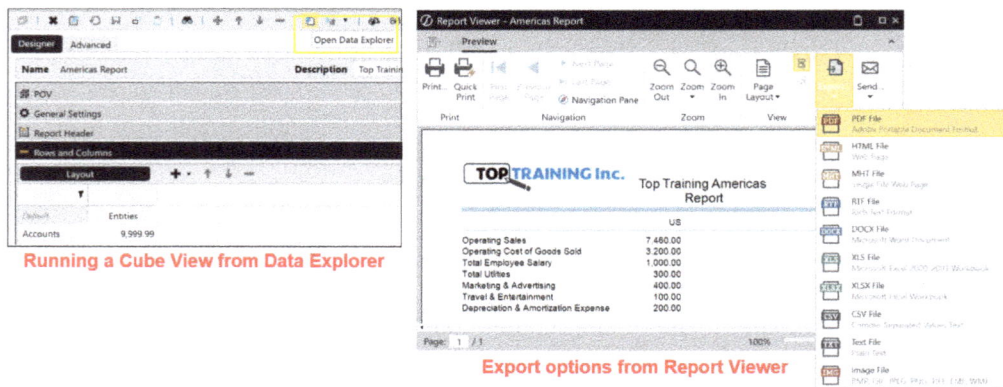

Running a Cube View from Data Explorer

Export options from Report Viewer

Figure 8.2

Cube Views are considered the main building blocks of reports and are used by the other report types mentioned above. As cubes themselves do not show data in OneStream, Cube Views are used to query and display the cube data. They are simple to create, versatile, and used for analyzing data, inputting data, running calculations, translations and consolidations.

Cube Views can be built and maintained in the Application tab under Cube Views, or built in Workspaces, if the Cube View needs to be used in a dashboard.

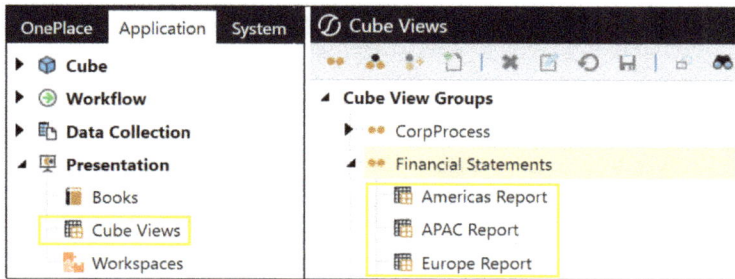

Created from the Cube Views menu

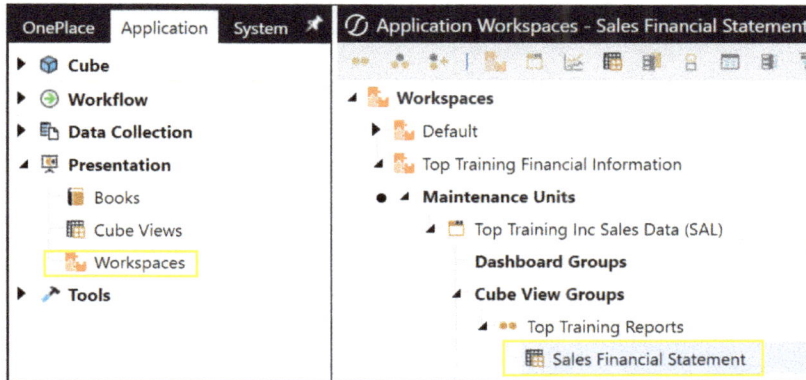

Created from the Workspaces menu

Figure 8.3

For the user to access Cube Views (depending on how the administrator has set this up, as well as security factors), the OnePlace tab in the Navigation pane is the usual go-to (or Excel Add-In if that's the only user access set-up). The Cube View slider will contain the Cube Views that can be run (just click on each one).

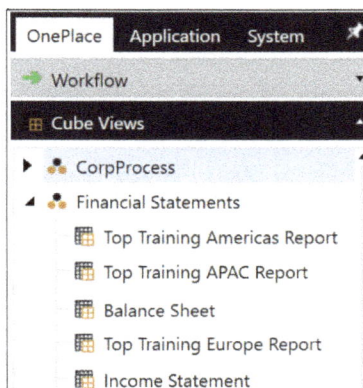

Cube Views accessed from OnePlace

Figure 8.4

Other Cube Views will be in the workflow task, such as a form or the workflow analysis section; they present users with the reports required as they perform their workflow tasks.

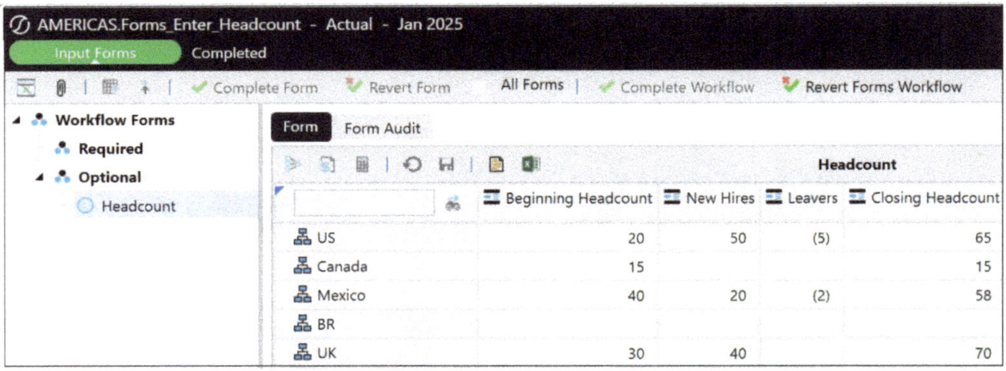

Cube View accessed from Workflow task

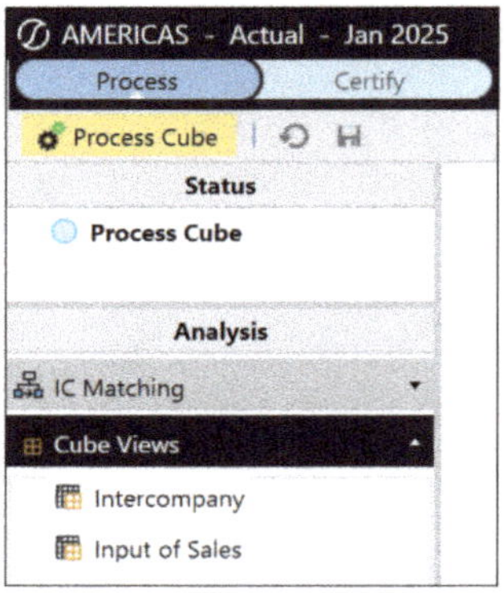

Cube Views accessed from Workflow Analysis

Figure 8.5

Cube Views can also be found within dashboards or within a Spreadsheet (created from the Cube View Connection).

Building a Cube View for Top Training Inc.

An easy rule to follow when building a Cube View is to have the user in mind; specifically, what are *their* Cube View requirements? Let's build an example for Top Training for the Americas region. The initial discussion when building the Cube View will take the form of:

- Is the report for analyzing data?

- For presenting key performance indicators?

- Used by the operational team and therefore requiring detail?

- Used by executives who only require high-level information?

- Which entities, accounts, and user defined members are required in the report?

Once the framework around the requirements has been drafted, Cube View creation is straightforward.

We start by creating a **Cube View Group** which will be assigned to a Cube View Profile. The concept of profiles (mentioned earlier in the book) determines where the Cube View can be accessed in the application.

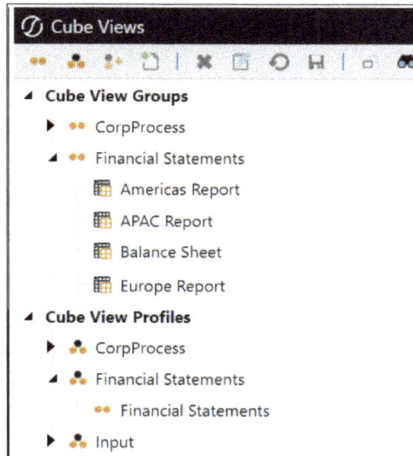

Figure 8.6

Within the Cube View Group, we select Create Cube View and name the Cube View (this can always be renamed if required, but with caution if linked to other components as the renaming does not follow through and may require manual updates within these artifacts). The Description can be used to create a user-friendly name if required. This will be displayed in selected parts of the application where the user accesses the Cube View.

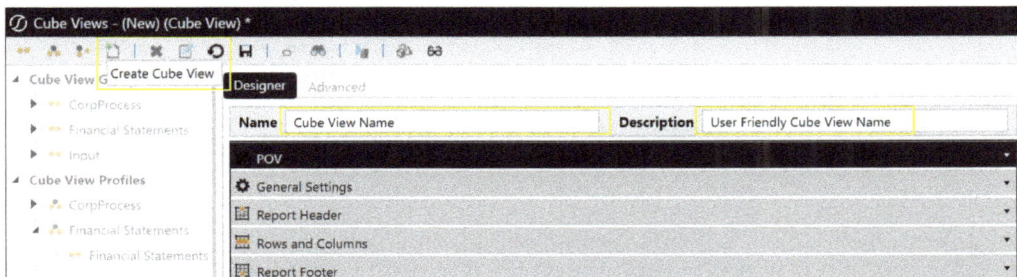

Figure 8.7

Various sliders are available in the Designer tab of the Cube View, with the Advanced tab having the same content, just laid out differently.

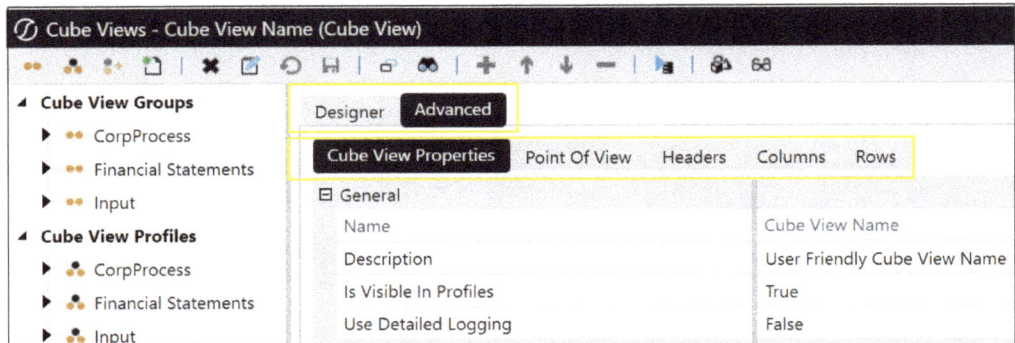

Figure 8.8

POV Slider

The first configuration required is in the POV (Point of View) slider. But, as a reminder, we have already discussed that if this is left untouched (and all the fields remain blank), the Cube View will use the parameters from the Cube POV, and the Cube View will still be able to run.

The configuration starts with selecting a cube (this is where the Cube View will be showing the data from) and then working through the member selection of the 18 dimensions. Where members are going to be defined in the rows and columns, then these can be left blank in the POV.

A neat trick is to drag and drop (or copy and paste) the Cube POV into the Cube View POV, which acts as a starting point. This is useful if only a few members need to be changed for the Cube View's requirements.

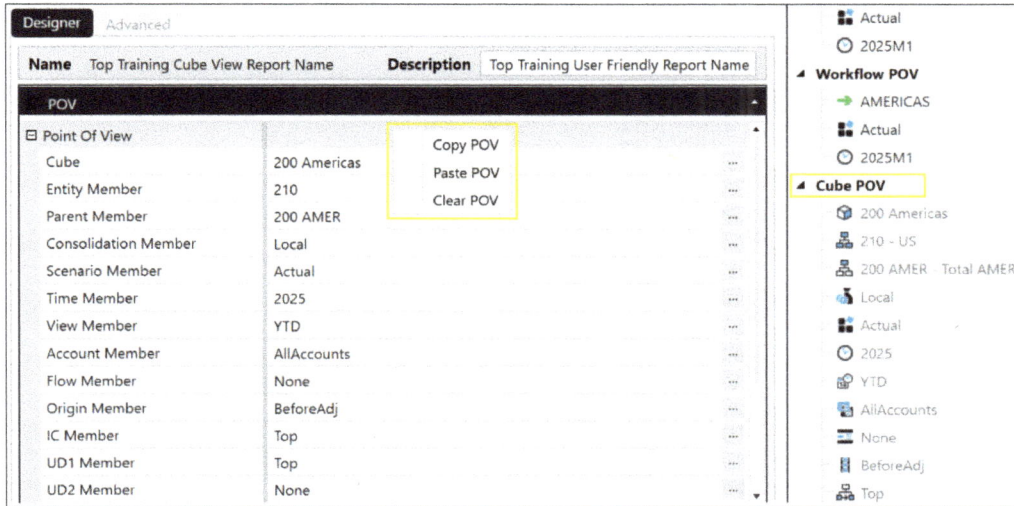

Figure 8.9

General Settings Slider

The General Settings slider offers various column or row template sharing settings. Sharing is a way of using other Cube View structures for their row or column settings, which helps jumpstart our Cube View creation.

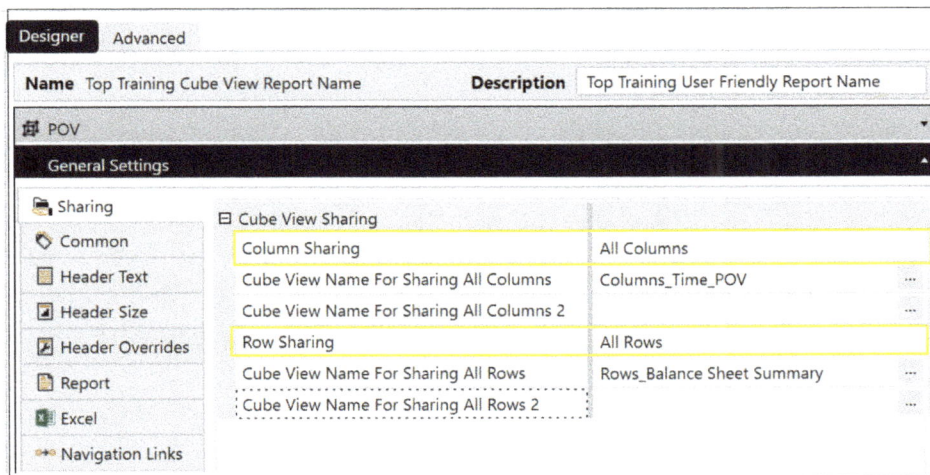

Figure 8.10

Other configurations found in General Settings are the header text and size, plus the navigation link option provides a feature to set up interactivity between Cube Views where a selection change in one Cube View updates another; very useful in dashboards.

Report Header

Here, you can enter header information that will be displayed in the header area when the Cube View is run from the Report Viewer icon or as a PDF.

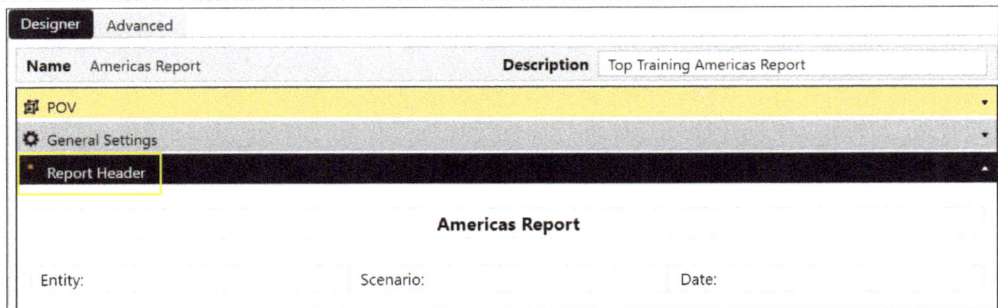

Figure 8.11

Rows and Columns Slider

These define the intersections that will be queried by the cube, as well as adding members to the rows and columns where the Member Filter can be used to assist. The Member Filter is where dimension members, variables, expansions, and expressions can be selected. Various formatting and data settings can be applied to rows and columns, too.

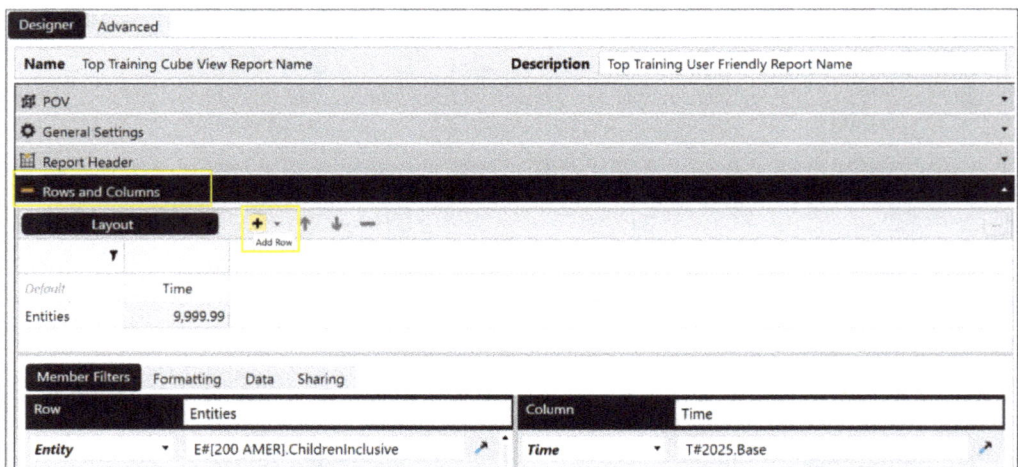

Figure 8.12

The information in a Cube View is determined by its rows (horizontal data cells) and columns (the vertical data cells), which together form a grid. Additional rows or columns can be added by using the + icon and are able to be renamed. Each row has four nested levels available and each column has two. For each level used, a dimension must be selected from the drop down.

The Member Filter can now be applied. This starts off with a **dimension token** (for example, Entity is E#) and then the corresponding member with an additional filter command if required. The Member Filter, as mentioned, provides the opportunity to expand members in the Cube View, target the current workflow entities, and use functions, variables or expressions. In a nutshell, they are very helpful!

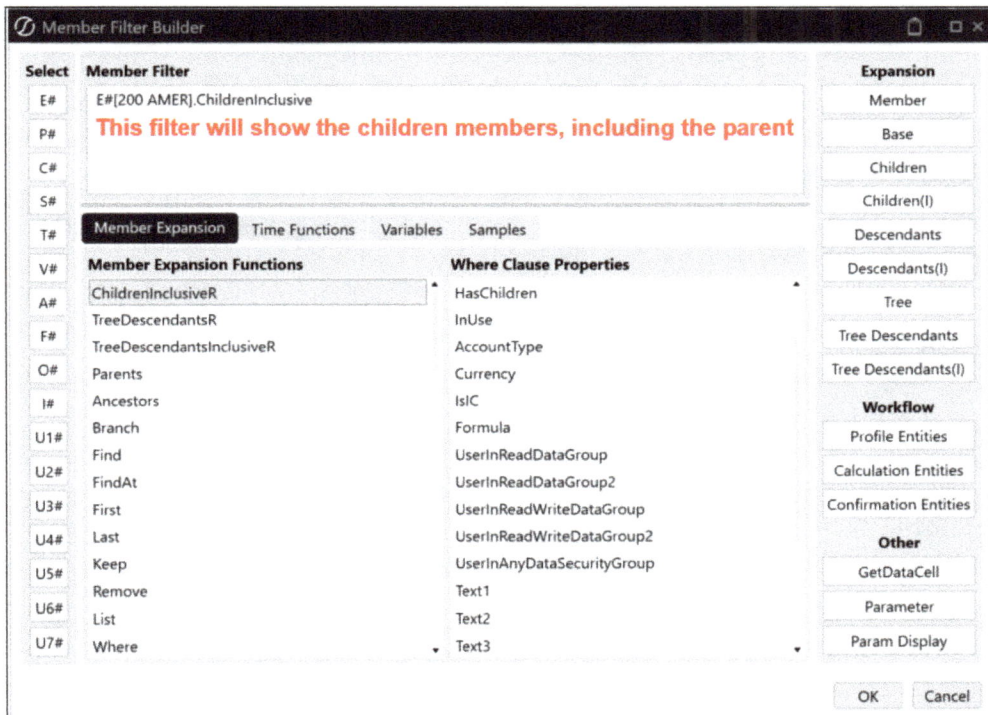

Figure 8.13

Overrides

A feature available both in the rows and columns is overrides, accessed from the tab as shown in Figure 8.14 . This provides the required setting for both Member Filter calculations and formatting. Ordinarily, if there is, for example, a dynamic calculation working in both the rows and columns, the row formula will take precedence. But using **Row Overrides** in the column can change this and the column formulas will be used instead.

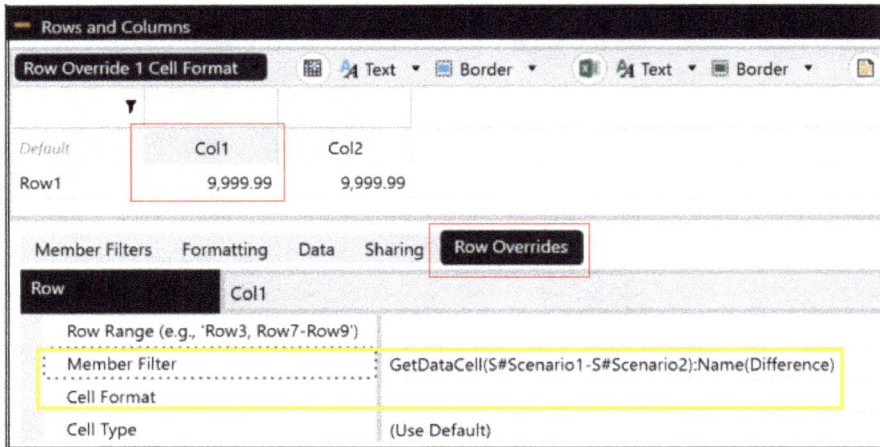

Figure 8.14

Report Footer

Footer information, such as author name and date of report, will be displayed in the footer area when the Cube View is run as a report or PDF.

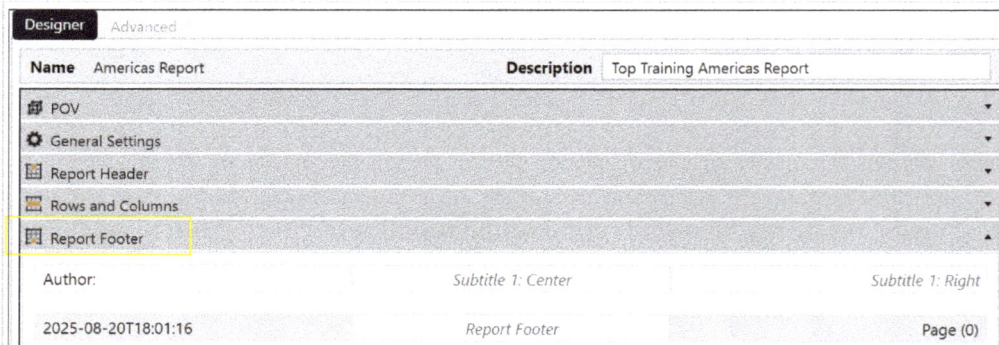

Figure 8.15

Copying a Cube View

In addition to creating a Cube View from scratch, a faster way can be to copy an existing Cube View from a Cube View Group. The Cube View can be pasted into the same Cube View Group or a separate one. The copied version will have a suffix of _Copy and needs renaming as two Cube Views cannot have the same name. Then, the settings – POV, General Settings, and rows and columns – can be changed to form a unique Cube View.

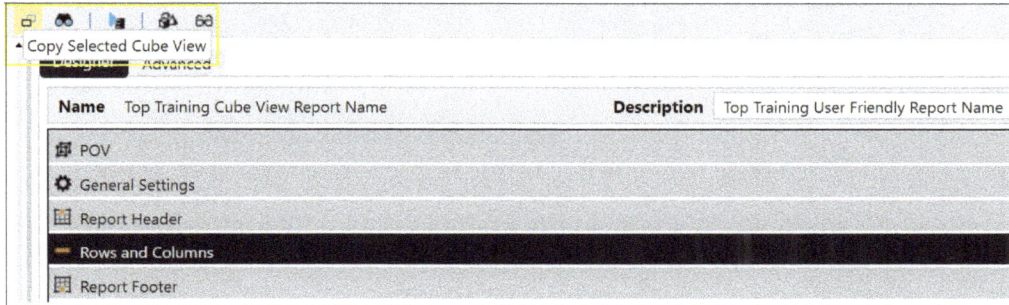

Figure 8.16

Running The Cube View

The Cube View is run in what is known as **Data Explorer** mode. In this mode, the data is presented in its grid view, but there are further options that allow the user to see the data as a report in the Report Viewer (which has further options for exporting to various formats).

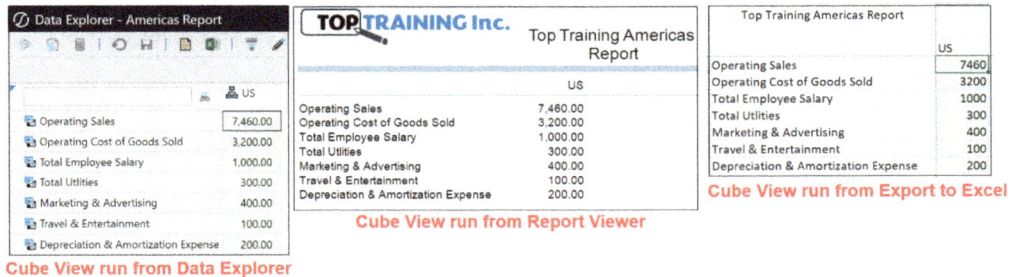

Figure 8.17

To change the data points of the grid, and if a parameter (explained later) has been used within the Cube View, a parameter icon is available to change the members, as shown in Figure 8.18.

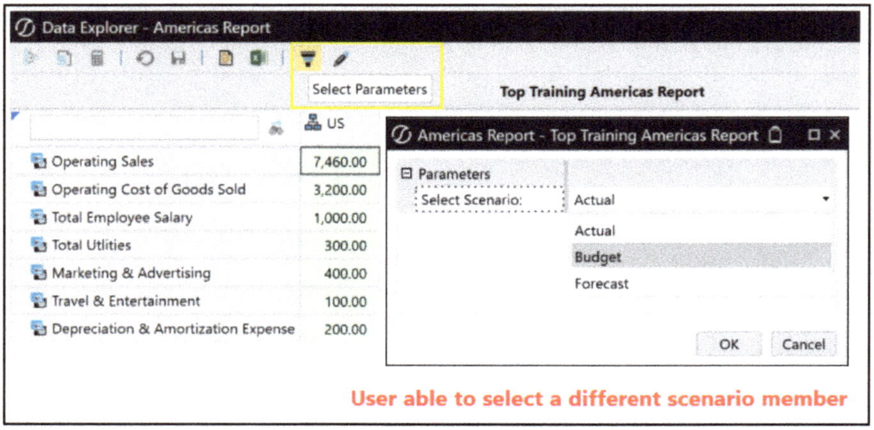

Figure 8.18

The cell has options to drill down further (if applicable) or ascertain each member that makes up the value by using the Cell POV Information feature. This feature has member scripts and formula syntax that can be utilized to see the member names that the cell value in the Cube View is made up of (using the **Cb syntax**). It can also be used to copy the XFGetCell script to retrieve specific data in a spreadsheet, or the XFCell script that is used in extensible documents or text files.

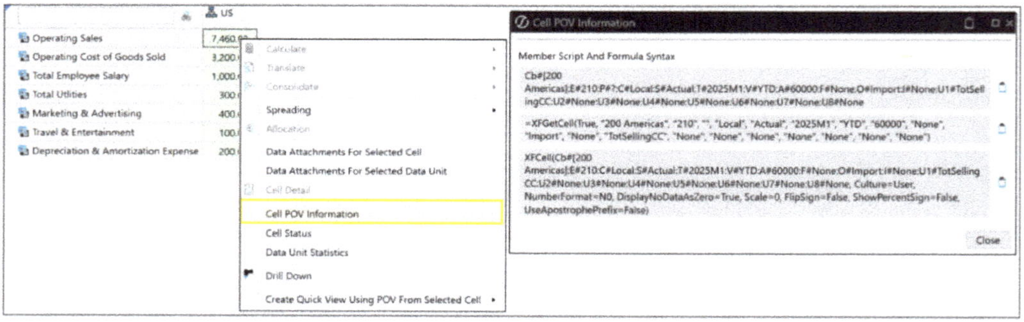

Figure 8.19

Data Cell Values

Cube Views display their values in cells. These can be colored and the colors are configurable. A typical Cube View cell color setting can be:

A green cell is a read-only cell. This displays a valid POV selection, where at least one of the dimensions has a selected member that is not at the lowest level, or the cell data has come about through a calculation, which always displays as read-only (this does depend on the Allow Input setting, but in the context of using CV math, the cell will be read-only).

A white cell will indicate a writable cell and all the selected members are at the lowest level of their hierarchy, which indicates data input. This is only available if the user has write access and the Cube View has been modified in the General Settings as Can Modify Data to True, (the setting can also be applied to individual rows, columns or simultaneously to both).

Figure 8.20 has Price and Volume as white input cells with Revenue as a calculated cell (therefore showing green read-only cells).

	Price	Volume	Revenue
Software Courses	2,000.00	400.00	800,000.00
Professional Development Courses	1,500.00	80.00	120,000.00
Management Training Courses	900.00	500.00	450,000.00
Sales and Customer Service Courses	1,200.00	200.00	240,000.00
Financial Training Courses	3,000.00	100.00	300,000.00
Project Management Courses	800.00	80.00	64,000.00

Price and Volume are writable cells
Revenue are read-only cells

Figure 8.20

In Figure 8.21, a pink cell has come about due to some invalid selection of the POV members. For example, a particular account member does not work with a Flow member selection. Or the members displayed in the report are outside the Cube View's permitted selection.

Net Revenue	
Cost Of Goods Sold	99,121,875.00
Cost of Goods Sold	
Total Operating Expenses before Allocations	36,257,844.25
Operating Expenses	
Gross Profit	
Net Income Before Interest and Taxes	33,878,282.37

Figure 8.21

Calculations In Cube Views

Calculations for Cube Views have been discussed in the previous chapter on Figuring Out Calculations. We established that calculations in Cube Views are dynamic and not stored in the database. The calculated cells are derived when the Cube View is executed, and these usually represent key performance indicators (KPIs), variances, or what-if scenarios.

Also, to clarify, it is the data that we load from an import workflow task, or manually enter in a writable cell, that is being used by the Cube View to perform calculations.

With data now seen in the Cube View, it can be used to create calculations in additional cells either through **Cube View Math** or **Cube View Expressions**. The Member Filter Builder can assist in creating these calculations. The calculated values will be presented as green cells (if not color configured) that are read-only, as a user cannot overwrite a calculation for **Cube View Math**.

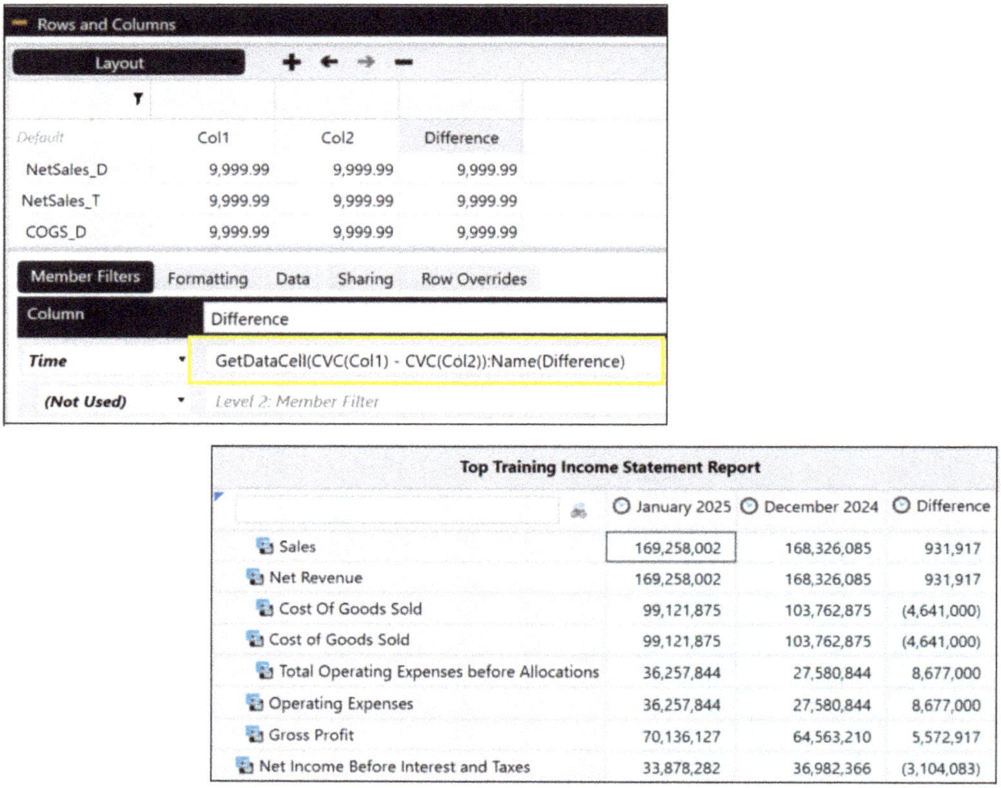

Cube View Math calculating the difference between two columns

Figure 8.22

Another way data is added to the Cube View (that is then stored in the cube that the Cube View is representing) is by manually entering the values into white writable cells, which can be assisted by the data spreading tool.

Data Spreading Options

As established, a white cell is writable. As well as being able to enter data in each individual cell, the spreading tool can be used to help populate data in many cells.

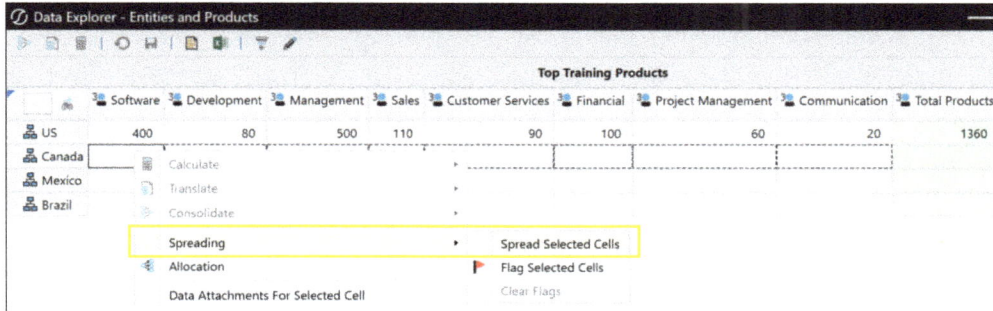

Figure 8.23

Any flagged cells can be set to retain the existing data (in the cells) and not get written over by the spreading tool.

The main **Spreading Types** are:

Even Distribution

The amount is distributed evenly across the selected cells.

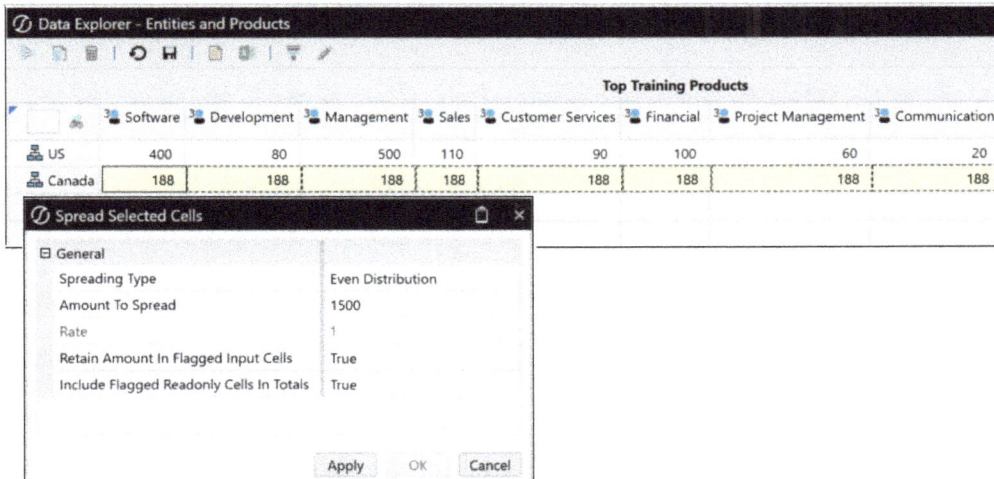

Figure 8.24

169

Fill

The same value is used to populate each of the selected cells.

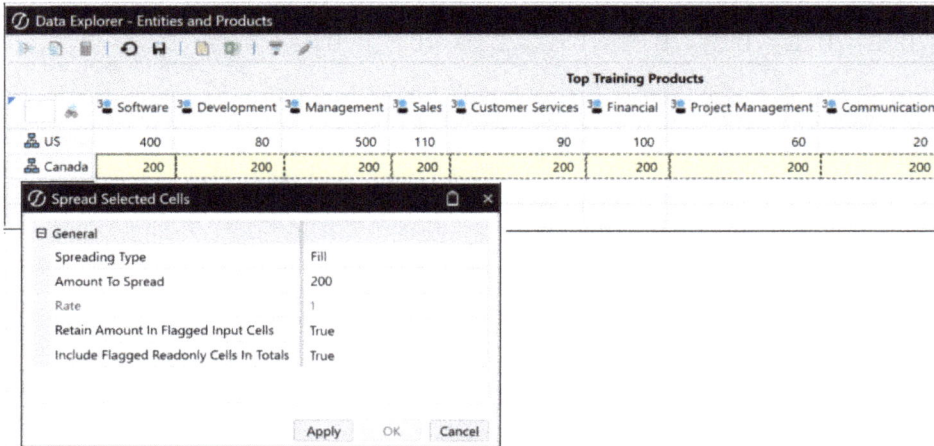

Figure 8.25

445 or 454 or 544 Distribution

The amount is distributed according to the selected number weighting. For example, 445 will distribute the Amount To Spread with the weight of 4 in the first two selected cells and then 5 in the third.

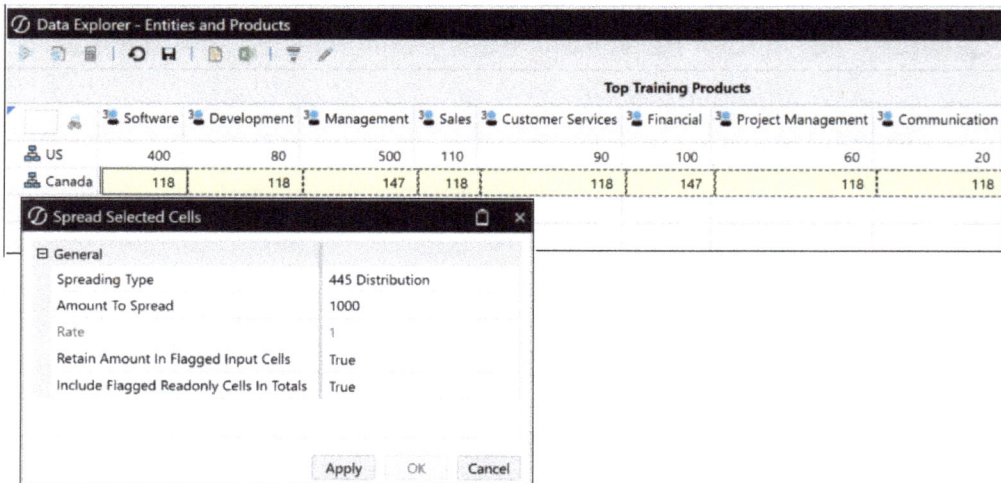

Figure 8.26

Factor

This will multiply all cells by the specified rate.

Accumulate

The rate specified is multiplied by the Rate amount, with the result in the first selected cell. The rate is then multiplied by the new value in the first cell to put a result in the second cell, and so on.

For example, the four cells (in Figure 8.27) below will use the rate of 2.5 with the starting amount of 40.

- Cell 1 will then be: 40 * 2.5 = 100
- Cell 2 will then be: 100 * 2.5 = 250
- Cell 3 will then be: 250 * 2.5 = 625
- Cell 4 will be: 1,563

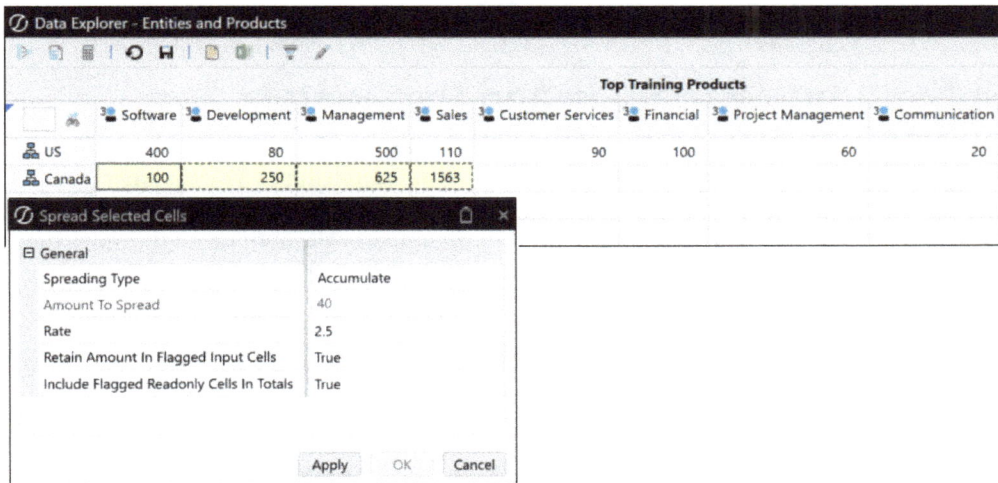

Figure 8.27

Proportional Distribution

This will take the selected cells' existing values and apportion the Amount To Spread according to the same proportions. Figure 8.28 shows a newly distributed value from the original proportion.

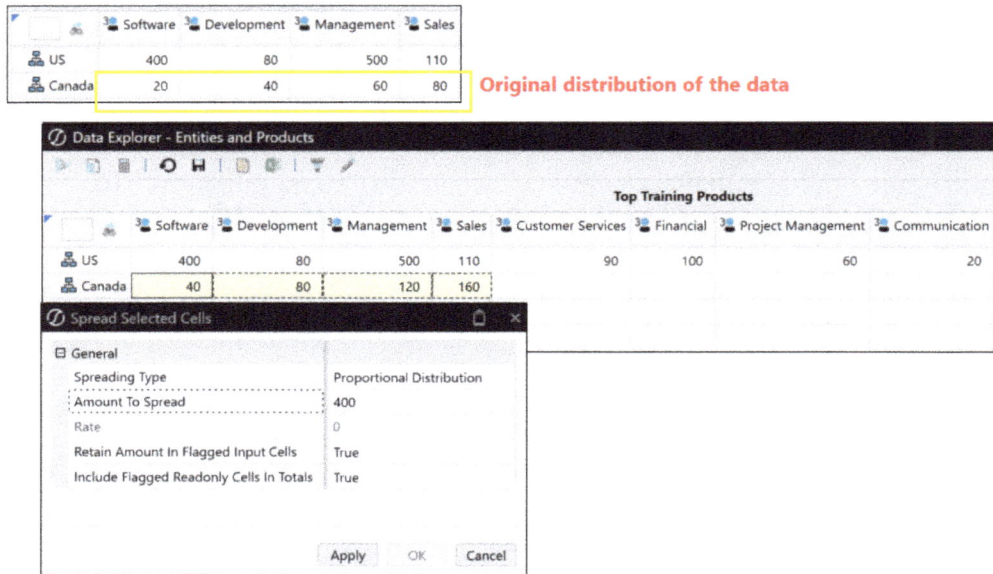

Figure 8.28

Substitution Variables and Parameters

With a Cube View, we have established that the data we are analyzing is a combination of member selections from each of the dimensions. The members are selected logically from, firstly, the row overrides (in the column), then column overrides (in the row), then row, then column, then Cube View POV, and finally the Cube POV.

The logic also extends to dimensions being set once; for example, once an Account dimension is found, say in the row definition, it will not be continued to look for in the column, Cube View POV, or Cube POV.

The selected members have been hard-coded, so to speak, which means any changes would require the reselection of members. While this is an option, another way is to apply *dynamic* selection members. These can be in the form of a prompt at runtime that ultimately leads to fewer manual changes in the actual Cube View itself.

In the OneStream platform, the two types of dynamic member selections are **Substitution Variables** and **Parameters**.

Substitution Variables

Substitution variables do not prompt the user but instead display the data for the referenced member when the Cube View is run. They can be used to create dynamic headers, footers, or page captions in the Cube View. Further to this substitution, variables can be embedded in Member Formulas. They take the form of a pipe character on either side of the substitution variable name (as per the examples in Figure 8.29).

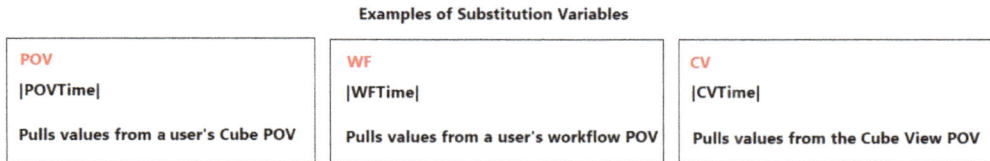

Figure 8.29

OneStream's substitution variables are all predefined, non-customizable, and no additional ones can be added to the platform by the administrator or end-user. A good use case for using substitution variables in a Cube View is when a common header is used in a Cube View across reports, and these relate to the Cube View name |CVName|.

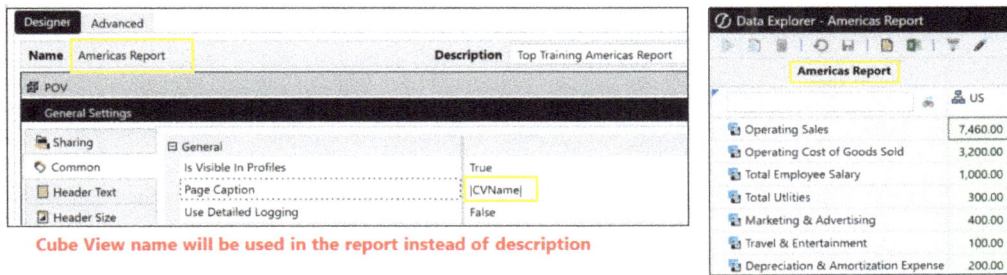

Figure 8.30

Parameters

Parameters are created in the platform and are super flexible. They can be used in a variety of objects and set up to prompt a user to do something at runtime. Most of the time, parameters take the form of pipe and exclamation point characters on either side of the parameter name, for example, |!prm_Scenario_Select!|.

When the parameter is being used, the selections are cached by the user (with literal parameters being the exception). This then does not impact other users.

Types of Parameters are:

Member List

Creates a drop-down list of members.

A good use case for using a member list parameter in a Cube View is when a Cube View must prompt users to select specific Entity, Time, and possible Scenario members.

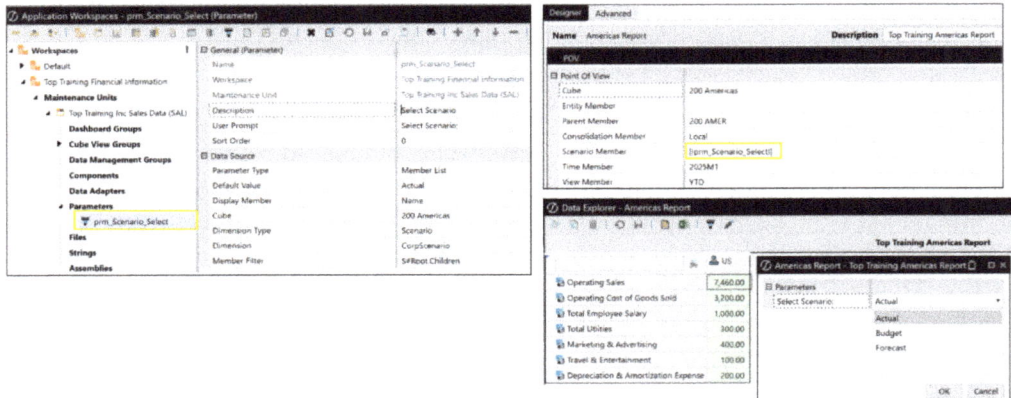

Figure 8.31

Member Dialog

Creates a pop-up member selection screen.

Delimited List

Produces a list of members created by the user.

Input Value

Prompts the user with an empty field to type an input value.

Literal Value

This parameter ensures consistent settings, such as report formatting standards by Top Training, across all reports. Unlike parameters that require user selection, the literal parameter applies conditions automatically during runtime.

Bound List

Displays a list of members created using a SQL expression (Structured Query Language takes the form of detailed commands to interact with databases) or a method query (SQL scripts predefined in OneStream).

Formatting The Cube View

Formatting can take place in many parts of the Cube View. Therefore, to prevent a clash in the view for certain configurations – such as a color selected for a cell in the column setting with another color selected for the same cell in the row setting – the Cube View has a built-in order of operation. In this example, the row setting color will take priority.

Figure 8.32 shows any row setting formats applied, otherwise the search continues downwards, applying the Application Properties settings if specific format options are not found in the column or Cube View settings.

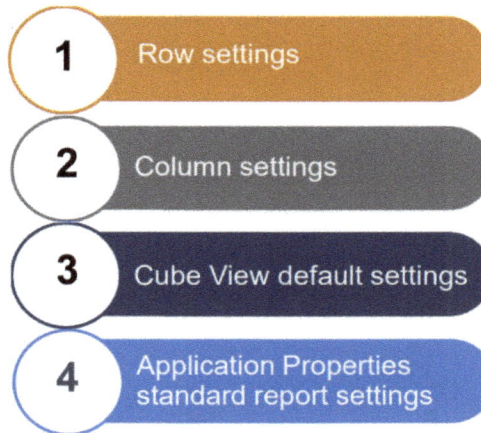

Figure 8.32

There are more intricate forms of formatting, such as **Column** or **Row Overrides**, that would be considered the final configuration from the above order. These are discussed in detail in the *OneStream Advanced Reporting and Dashboards Handbook.*

The standard report settings are found in Application Properties and used to set default formatting on the PDF export or the Cube View. The key settings relate to an organization's logo, margins, and font sizes, which will then be applied consistently across all Cube Views unless (as mentioned) a particular Cube View setting overrides the standard report setting.

Moving on from standard report settings, formatting options can be targeted to specific outputs of the Cube View. Formatting can be applied individually to the Data Explorer, the Report Viewer, the Excel output, or all three at the same time.

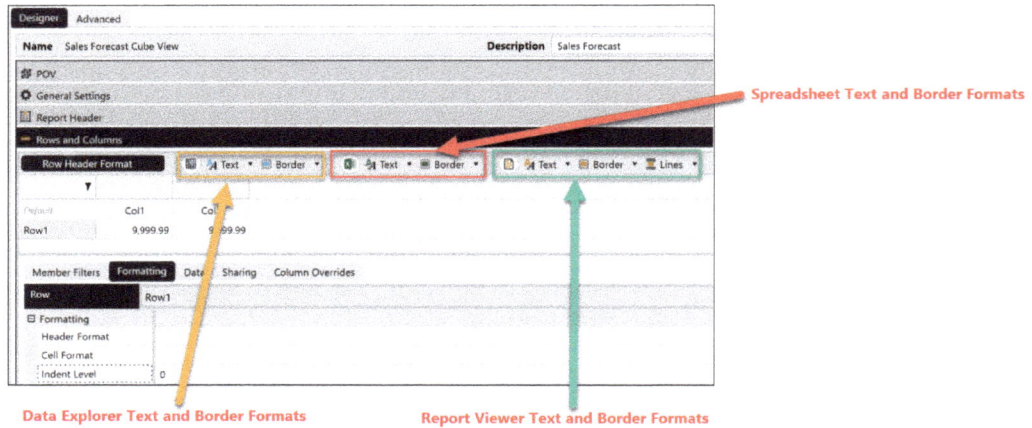

Spreadsheet Text and Border Formats

Data Explorer Text and Border Formats

Report Viewer Text and Border Formats

Figure 8.33

Within an individual Cube View, **blanket cell formatting** can be applied by selecting the default intersection. Alternatively, each row or column or header or cell can have a unique format setting. The data itself can have scaling applied to the original value, converting numbers to represent thousands or millions, with a further option to display a currency code in the cell (for example, USD or GBP).

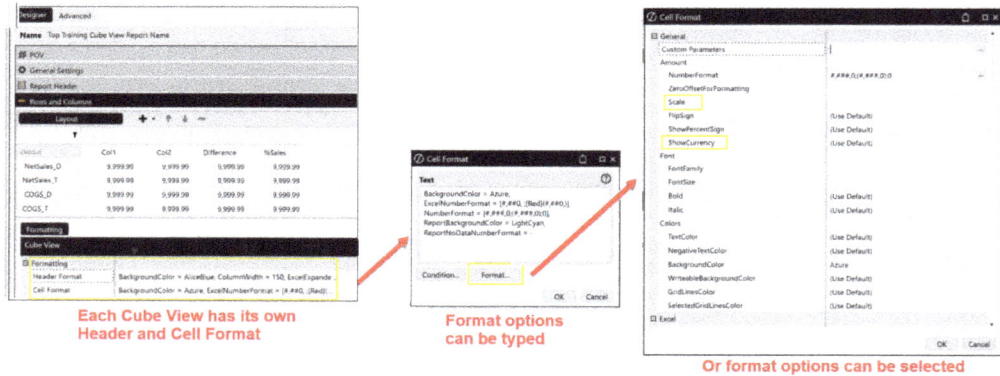

Each Cube View has its own Header and Cell Format

Format options can be typed

Or format options can be selected

Figure 8.34

Indentations can be applied to make the layout of the report easier for the end-user to read. This can be targeted on a row-by-row basis using an indent setting of, for example, 0, 1, or 2 (potentially up to 20 indent levels).

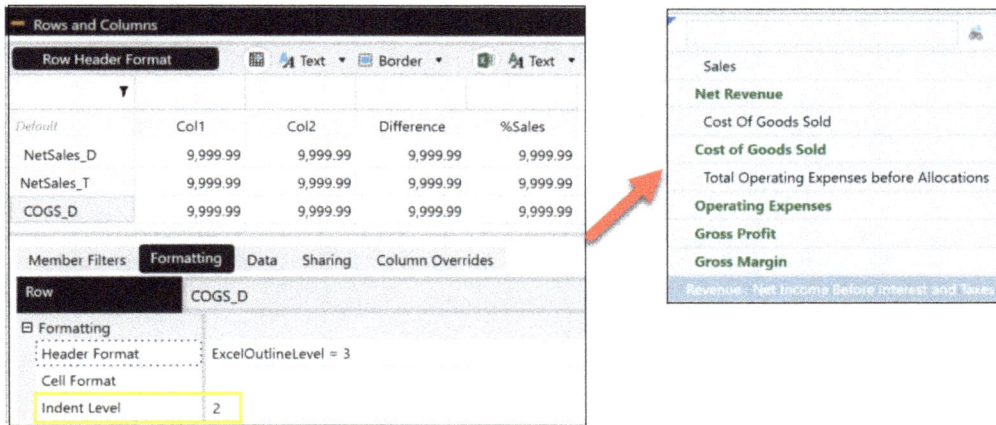

Figure 8.35

Formatting Using a Literal Parameter

Parameters have been discussed, particularly how useful they are when it comes to having dynamic selections or to provide the ability to apply consistent settings across many artifacts, such as Cube Views.

When it comes to Cube View formatting, literal parameters can aid an organization's need for reports to have a consistent look and feel by having, for example, the color, fonts, margin, and settings embedded within the parameters. Then, it is just a case of populating the parameter name in each Cube View formatting field, with the result having the format setting applied at runtime.

This will provide an easy update approach and save maintenance time. By changing any format configurations in the literal parameter, this will cascade throughout all the reports using it.

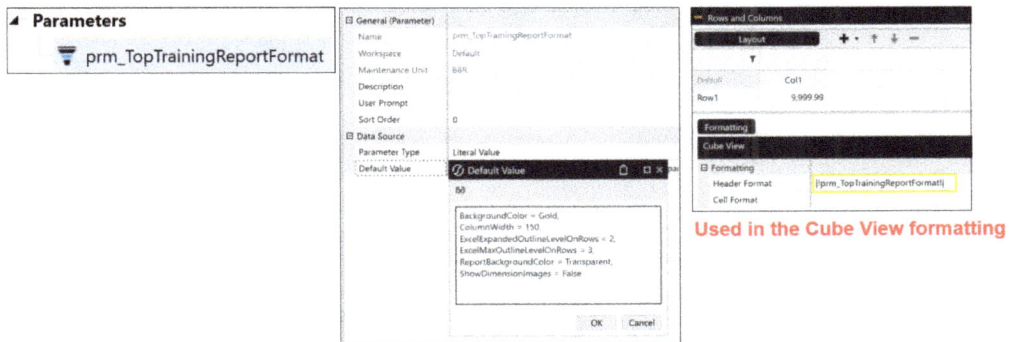

Literal Value Parameter with the format settings defined

Figure 8.36

Chapter 8

Conditional Formatting

This can be used to format headers or cells that are driven by a defined criterion. The result can highlight a specific cell or range of cells. A **Conditional Formatting Wizard** can be found in the Cube View's cell formatting field that can guide the user on targeted cells.

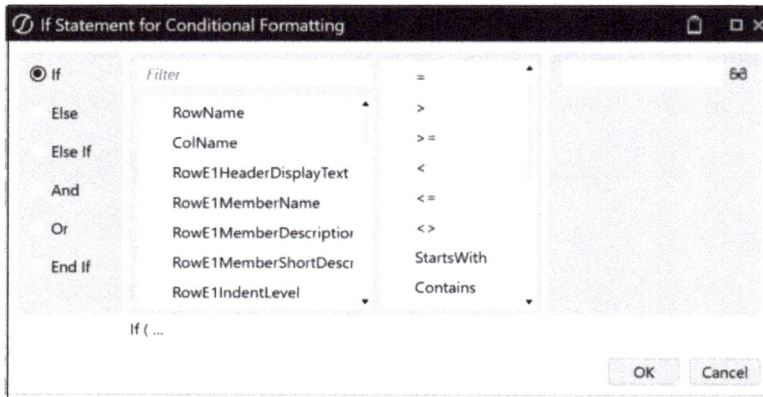

Wizard assists with creating the conditional statement

Figure 8.37

The conditional statement is then formed…

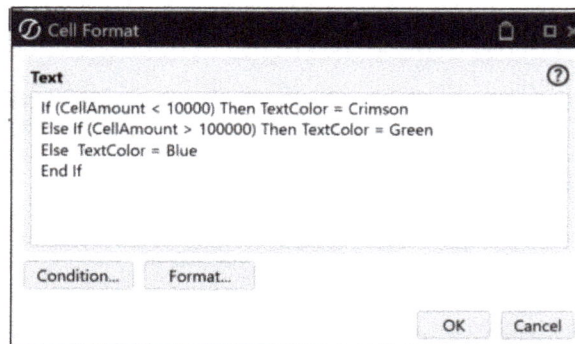

Conditional statement

Figure 8.38

…with the result in the Cube View.

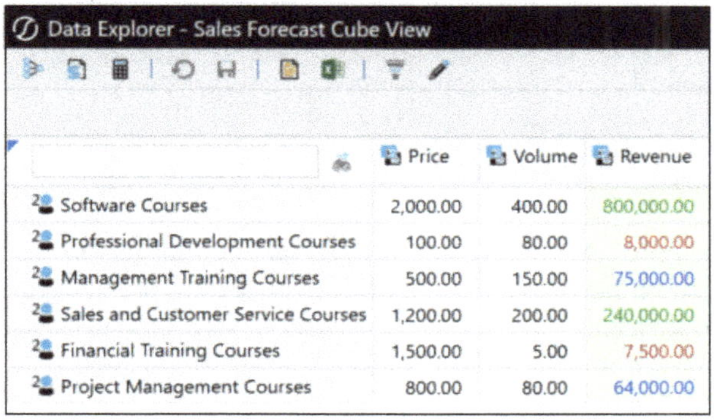

Result of the conditional statement in the Revenue column

Figure 8.39

Suppression Formatting

When a Cube View is run, the data may not be populated in every cell. This is a consequence of the combination of members selected in, for example, the Cube View's rows and columns, which are then displayed in the report but which have not been part of a data load or manual data entry requirement. The cells can be suppressed and not displayed at runtime for these situations. This is commonly used in larger reports, so they become more manageable for the user.

Suppression settings can be found in the Rows and Columns data tab, providing options to turn on suppression for invalid rows (a result of an incorrect combination of members), cells with no data, or zero data.

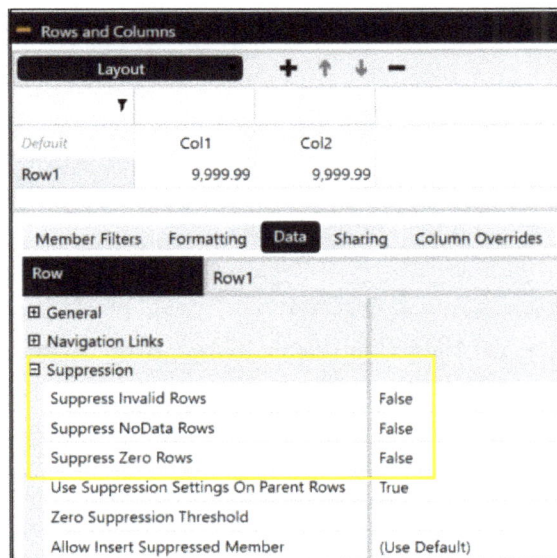

Figure 8.40

Other more detailed forms of suppression are available within the General Settings, which are applied to individual columns meeting a certain suppression criterion (such as having a zero threshold), resulting in rows being suppressed.

Spreadsheet

The reports presented in spreadsheet format can be accessed from the Application tab and Excel Add-In. In the OneStream ribbon, an additional tab will appear in the Spreadsheet, which is made up of various sections, each providing the user with reporting features.

The Excel Add-In takes on all of Excel's features. OneStream's Spreadsheet tool (accessed from the Application tab) will provide most, but not all, of Excel's features.

Let's take a look at the OneStream tab on the Spreadsheet.

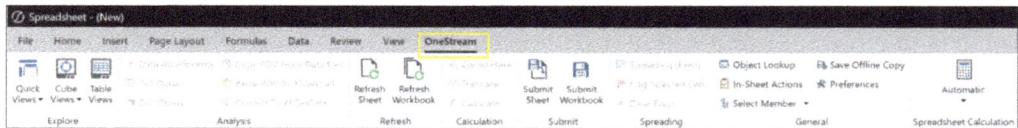

Figure 8.41

OneStream Login

Allows the user to login if accessed from the Excel Add-In.

Refresh and Submit Sections

Refreshes the data displayed, as well as submits the data back to the OneStream platform.

Calculation Section

Able to perform calculation, translation, and consolidation processes if granted permission.

Explore and Analysis Sections

Creates Quick Views, Cube Views, and Table Views, with capabilities to drill down and attach documents to the cells.

Spreading

Offers the data spreading options discussed earlier.

Quick Views In Spreadsheets

As the name suggests, a Quick View takes up less set-up time by displaying an ad-hoc grid.

Once the members have been typed in the rows and columns – within a highlighted area on the Spreadsheet, and the Quick View option selected from the Explore section – a Quick View POV is created (this overrides the Cube POV).

The Quick View POV is where the cube and members are selected, with the option to pivot the rows and columns. The data is displayed in the Spreadsheet but can be changed by reselecting members, as well as using the toolbar features that manage, update, change, and refresh the data.

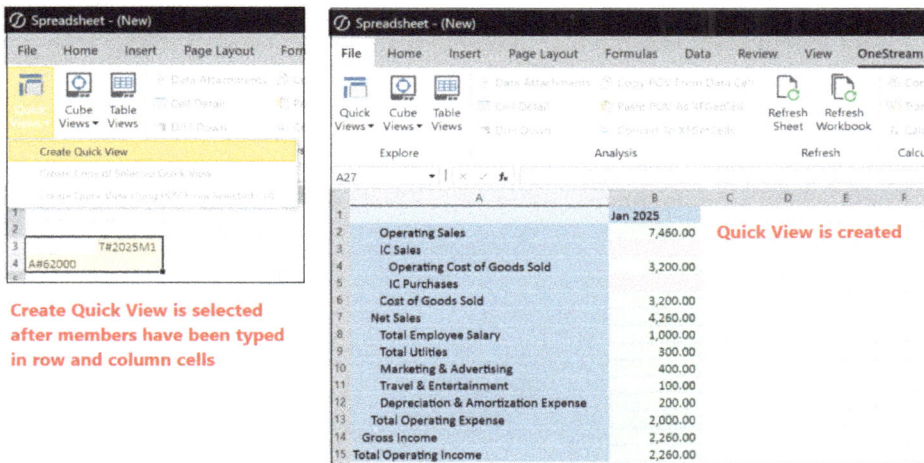

Create Quick View is selected after members have been typed in row and column cells

Quick View is created

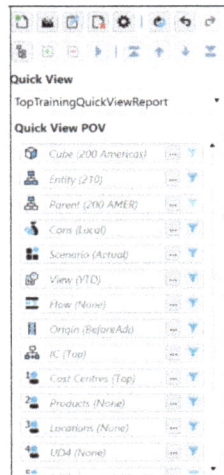

Quick View POV used to update member selection

Figure 8.42

A Quick View can also be converted to what is known as a **Spreadsheet Retrieve**. This provides the ability to see all dimension members in the formula bar for each cell. The combination of these members retrieves the data using the XFGetCell function, as per Figure 8.43. The opposite can apply, and data can be sent back to the OneStream platform using the XFSetCell function.

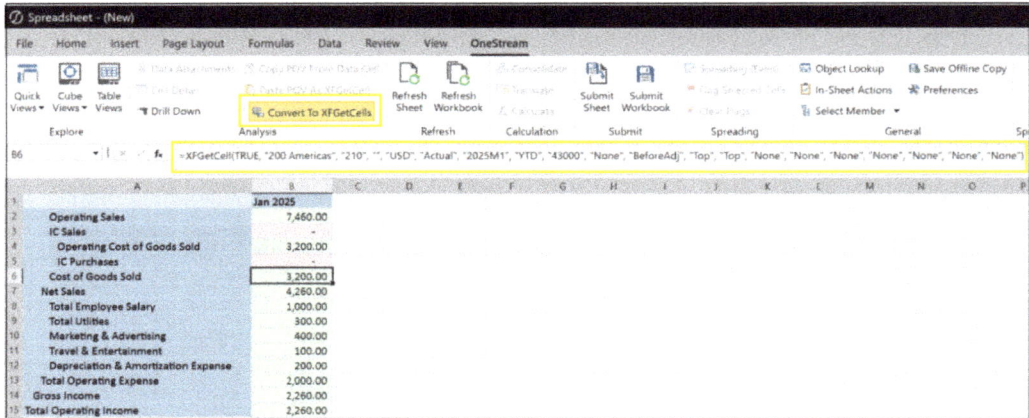

Figure 8.43

Cube Views In Spreadsheets

Another neat way the Spreadsheet tool and Excel Add-in can be utilized is to display the Cube View from the platform into a sheet. With permission to access the Cube View, and the Cube View Profile having the appropriate visibility set (that includes Excel), a Cube View connection can be established. This is a live connection to the database with any Cube View updates flowing through to the Spreadsheet (as opposed to a Cube View export to Excel which will be static data).

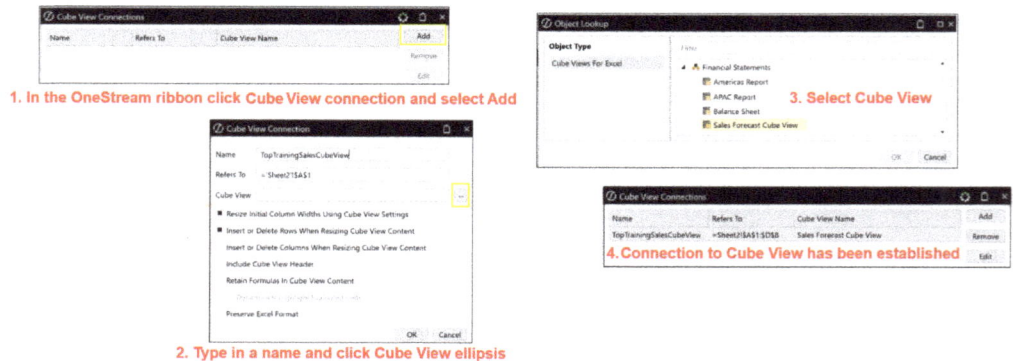

Figure 8.44

Once the connection has been made and the Cube View displays, each cell has access to the OneStream menu, providing similar options to the Cube View within the platform. These are the Cell POV Information, Drill Down, and Spreading.

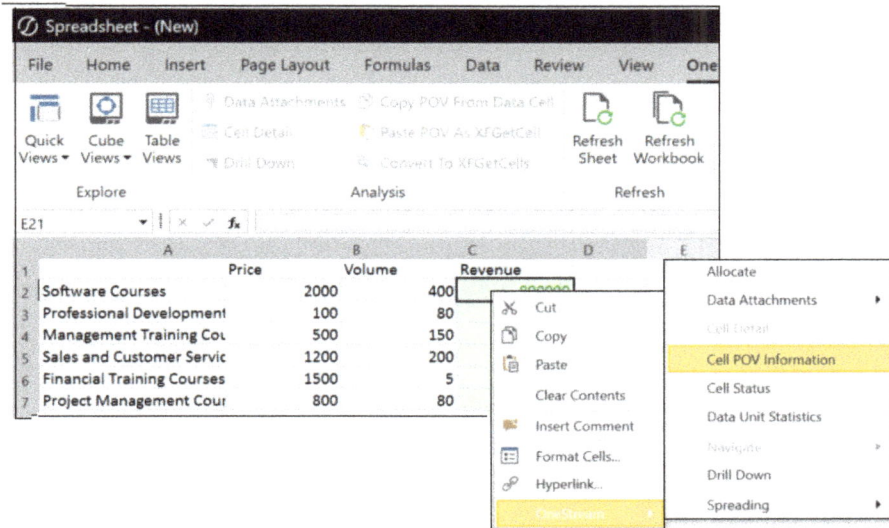

Figure 8.45

Formatting can be applied to the Cube View. To avoid losing any formatting upon a refresh, a more robust solution is **Selection Styles**. This feature allows for named areas to have formatting applied that can also be similar to the Excel styles palette, resulting in changes to entire rows, columns, or specific cells. Selection Styles formatting then has the capability to be disabled, enabled, or deleted from the area.

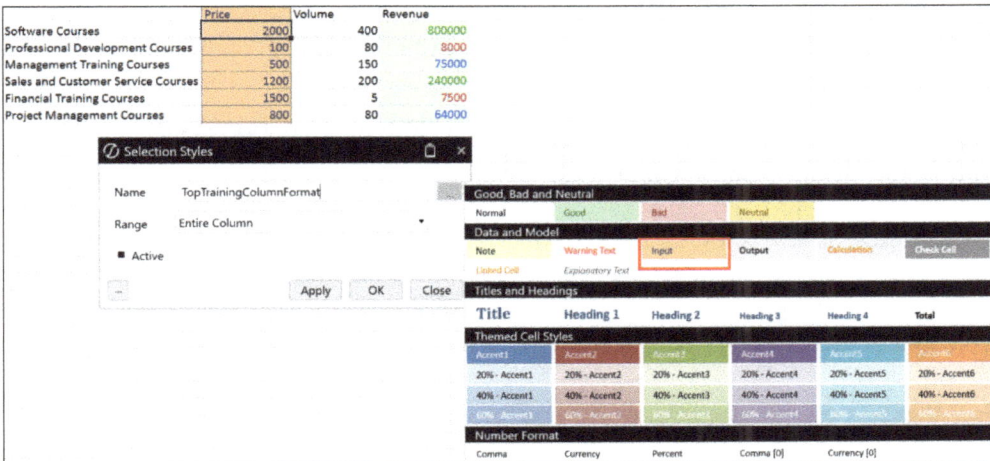

Figure 8.46

Which Spreadsheet Option To Use?

While all spreadsheet options are suitable for reporting, each has distinct attributes that make it better suited for specific tasks.

Spreadsheet Cube Views are ideal for standardized, centrally managed reports. They offer extensive formatting capabilities, support links to other Cube Views and dashboards, and enable drill-down for deeper analysis. Cube View connections remain live and data can therefore be refreshed and submitted. Additionally, Spreadsheet Cube Views support dynamic prompts and parameter selection, making reports interactive and adaptable. They do, however, require security settings, and Spreadsheet Cube Views may not be the best option for quick, ad-hoc analysis.

Quick Views are ideal for rapid, ad-hoc analysis, easily created by end-users as needed. They enable on-the-fly data exploration, with new members appearing automatically to minimize ongoing maintenance.

Formatting options are limited compared to Spreadsheet Cube Views and users do need an understanding of the data model to build effective Quick Views.

Spreadsheet Retrieve is ideal for creating highly tailored reports, allowing full customization of calculations within Excel. However, it does not maintain a live connection to the data source – manual refreshing is required to update values. Features such as drill-down and dynamic prompts are not supported, and maintaining reports can become challenging if the underlying data model changes.

Report Books

A report book has the capability to display a variety of report types, including Cube Views, dashboards, dashboard charts, Spreadsheet, and extensible documents. Once set up, the results of these reports can be previewed as individual documents page by page, or combined as a single document. The output can be a PDF document or a multi-tab Excel file, which can be zipped as a package if required. Report books are ideal for reviewing the results of a workflow that can easily be distributed to all the stakeholders who are part of the financial close (monitoring the status and health of the business), as well as executives for decision-making.

The report package can be simply emailed out, but for a more robust distribution method, the **OneStream Parcel Service** solution (from the Solution Exchange) sets up a more efficient process.

The creation of report books is straightforward. Within the Application tab, the Books page is selected. The Report Designer is seen where an existing Report Book can be opened or by using the Create New Book icon followed by the + icon in the toolbar to select the item we need to add to our Report Book. The options to select from are a File, Excel Export Item, Report, Loop, conditional statements, or Item to Change Parameters.

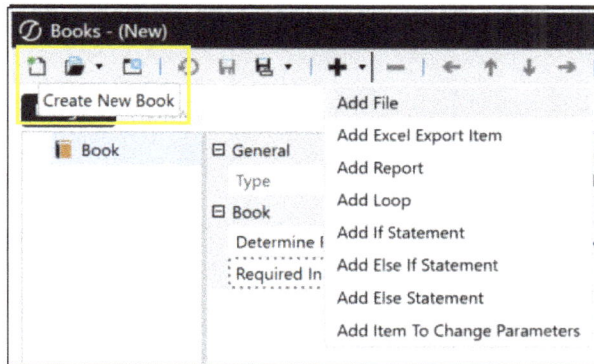

Figure 8.47

If the Add Report was selected, for example, this is where a report type – such as a Cube View or dashboard – can be embedded, as shown in Figure 8.48

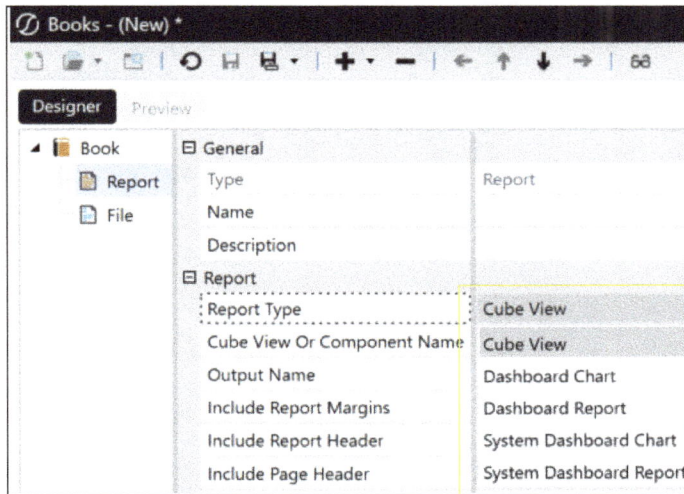

Figure 8.48

One of the key points to take away on the use of report books is the ability to loop through a range of members instantly, displaying a report for each of those members. For example, in Top Training, Americas has four Entities: US, Canada, Mexico, and Brazil, and a loop can be set up in the report book with a filter that displays Americas and its children. This will then run a process multiple times, displaying a report for all the entities.

Item To Change Parameters allows you to turn off parameters that are embedded in the reports used. For example, if a parameter is for an entity selection, this will be ignored to instead work with the loop.

Further to creating loops, conditional statements that embed certain criteria can also be applied. When this event happens, the report book then adds an additional report. For example, Top Training has a pop-up training center in Miami that is used from time to time (defined in the User Defined dimension). Our report book can contain an If statement to check if Miami has data; if so, the report book then adds the Miami report to the output.

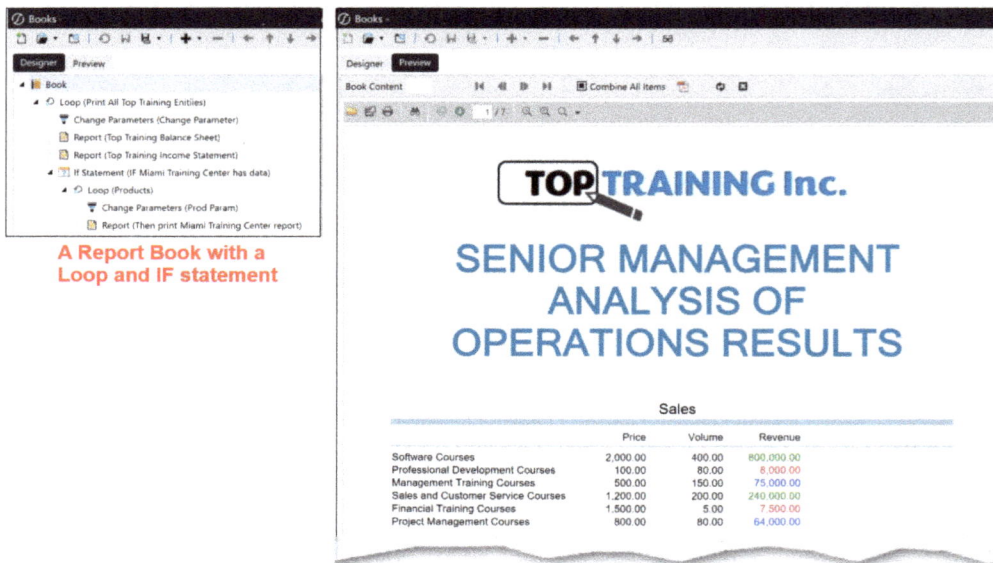

Figure 8.49

When using If / Else statements and Loops, more advanced criteria can also use business rules that allow you to add reports (as per our Miami example in Figure 8.49) or completely omit a report if it has no data.

Further indepth discussions on report books are covered in the *OneStream Advanced Reporting and Dashboards Handbook*

Best Place To Store Data For Reporting

When reporting in OneStream, the cube is the key place to retrieve data from. But this may not always be the case as reports can also depend on the granularity or detail of the information required.

When we require large amounts of data or transient data – which change regularly – this may have been placed outside of the cube for efficiency, or to avoid the cube holding large infrequently-used data such as names, invoice numbers, and addresses.

Apart from the cube, data can be stored in external tables or databases. Examples such as BI Blend tables and Table Data Manager are optimized for reporting on large data sets.

BI Blend Table is a read-only modeling solution designed to combine multidimensional analysis with transactional data, making it ideal for operational data that changes frequently.

Data is stored in relational tables, enabling the use of existing cube dimensions and hierarchies while supporting real-time, responsive reporting and rapid aggregation. Calculation capabilities are limited – there is no support for complex consolidation logic or translations.

Although BI Blend Table does not connect directly to source systems, it leverages the same integration tools as the OneStream platform.

Table Data Manager (downloaded from Solution Exchange) assists with creating customized tables and views within a database. Business rules can be written to automate data loads and access to Table Data Manager can be restricted.

Once created, these tables can be used in dashboards, workflows, and reports, enabling advanced analytics and operational reporting beyond the cube.

The staging area in the OneStream platform is another place where data can be stored, which is a lot more granular than the cube.

This area is considered the holding ground to validate data against transformation rules and check the intersection between the source items and target members. It has the capability to use **Label Source Dimensions** that hold descriptions such as trial balance narrative, or bank statement transaction information.

Attribute Dimensions and **Attribute Value Dimensions** are also available and can hold, for example, invoice descriptions and invoice values respectively. These will not be loaded to the cube, but can be queried by a report writer to obtain the data directly from the staging area if required.

Non-cube data that is stored in external tables, databases or OneStreams staging area can be queried into reports, dashboards and spreadsheets.

Conclusion

From this chapter, we can see how Cube Views play an important role in the OneStream platform. Cube Views are versatile and easy to build, and they are the first place to view cube data. Other report types, such as dashboards and spreadsheets for reporting also use them.

When building a Cube View for reporting, it is important to keep 'the end in mind', and work with the user on requirements. Cube Views start in the Cube View Group and end in the Cube View Profile, where access can then be provided to the user.

Construction of the Cube View takes the form of working through the sliders in the Design tab (or the Advanced tab), with the Cube View POV, or General Settings that include sharing, being able to modify the cell, being able to calculate, as well as other settings. Then, the various header and cell formatting menus.

The Cube View can be run from various places in the platform and – once executed – the data cells will be read-only or writable or a combination of both. If writable, data can be manually entered by the user, or the spreading tool can assist in populating a range of cells at once, using a number of spreading methods.

The members used for Cube View data can be handpicked, but with the ease of having substitution variables prebuilt into the platform (as well as parameters that can be created) member selection can be made dynamic.

For the avid spreadsheet user, the Spreadsheet tool provides most of the Excel features with the Excel Add-In option having the full complement. In either option, Quick Views can be constructed, bringing in data and the ability to format. A direct Cube View connection is also available, presenting the Cube View in spreadsheet fashion with spreading and formatting features.

The report book feature in the presentation section of the Application tab is to work with the many finished report types, for ease of presentation and distribution.

This chapter has delved into a lot of the reporting aspects of OneStream, but a certain reporting report type has stayed out of the limelight so far. It makes a grand entrance next!

9

Reporting Part 2 – Show Me Even More Data!

Dashboards

If you were wondering why we covered so little on dashboards in the previous chapter, it's because they deserve a whole chapter to themselves!

Dedicating an entire chapter to dashboards will give time to discuss the individual components that make them such an effective way to present information for many organizations. We shall explore a logical approach to building dashboards, one that can be carried forward should you have the chance to read the *OneStream Advanced Reporting and Dashboards Handbook*.

Here is this chapter's learning journey:

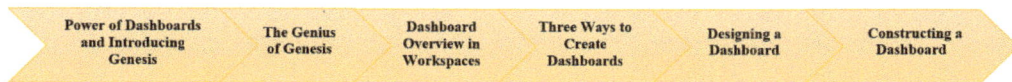

| Power of Dashboards and Introducing Genesis | The Genius of Genesis | Dashboard Overview in Workspaces | Three Ways to Create Dashboards | Designing a Dashboard | Constructing a Dashboard |

Figure 9.1

Dashboards are considered the most versatile reporting option in OneStream for both financial and non-financial information. Dashboards can be built to meet application design requirements and serve as the canvas for many solutions in the Solution Exchange.

The Power of Dashboards and Introducing Genesis

Going back to our Top Training example, executives use dashboards for timely, accurate information on Key Performance Indicators (KPIs) and their individual business-area metrics, which can be drilled into for further analysis. This information can support strategic decision-making.

Interactive users, meanwhile, use the dashboards for workflow tasks such as data entry, analysis, financial close, and the reporting of KPIs. With interactivity built in, dashboards can display real-time warnings, such as low product stock levels.

Administrators use dashboards to monitor the health of the OneStream application, providing a mechanism to govern platform changes, raise and monitor support tickets, perform consolidations, and help seed data for budgeting and forecasting.

With OneStream, users can rapidly create and deploy dashboards tailored to their business requirements. Starting with version 9.0, **Genesis** revolutionizes this process, offering administrators and users a powerful, intuitive solution for building dashboards.

Whilst learning dashboard creation, the author identified a few methods: either using the Genesis solution for a streamlined experience, or by assembling components within a Workspace menu and compiling the pieces of the required dashboard to integrate into a final deployment.

This chapter begins by highlighting Genesis – OneStream's game-changing, user-friendly dashboard-building interface. Then (for the inquisitive reader), we will transition to the Workspace menu, explaining how each part comes together to form a complete dashboard (what could now be described as 'behind the scenes').

The Genius of Genesis

As already mentioned, Genesis is a powerful tool designed to streamline solution development. While this chapter highlights its role in dashboard creation, Genesis extends far beyond that - enabling rapid configuration and deployment of solutions that support operational workflows, planning, analytics, and capabilities that extend into many other areas of OneStream, such as managing datasets or configuring API-based connections.

Its intuitive interface and flexible architecture allow seamless integration with existing environments and effortless scaling to support new business needs.

When focusing on its reporting and analytics capabilities, Genesis enhances administrative efficiency by simplifying configuration for the delivery of dashboards to consumers, supporting Cube Views, pivot grids, spreadsheets, charts, key performance indicators, and more.

Installing Genesis Could Not Be Easier

The Genesis solution can be set up in each OneStream application that requires its use. Download it from the Solution Exchange and then load it into the OneStream application via the Application tab's Load/Extract menu.

The solution takes the form of a Workspace called Genesis. This could be the one and only instance, but – as discussed later – further instances of Genesis can be created with additional unique Workspace names.

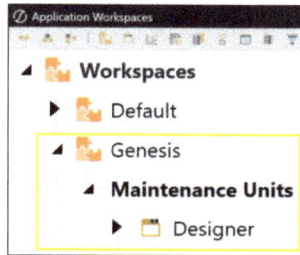

**Genesis Workspace in the
OneStream Windows App**

Figure 9.2

The Genesis Framework

Genesis is accessible through the **Modern Browser Experience (MBE)**, which will serve as the primary login for all users. While a desktop client app with Genesis is available for any remaining on-premise clients, the Software-as-a-Service (SaaS) platform is the standard moving forward. Upon logging in, users interact with two interfaces: **Genesis Designer**, intended for administrators and power users, and **Genesis Navigation**, designed for end users.

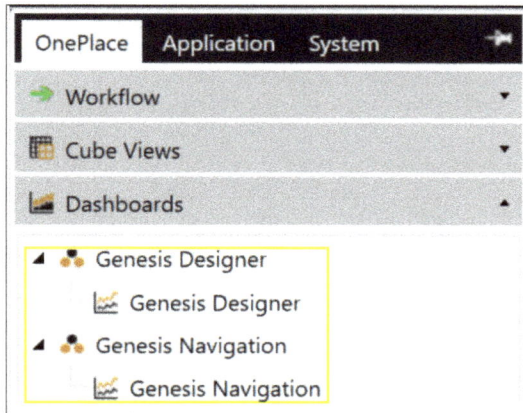

**The two interfaces for Genesis in the
OnePlace tab for the OneStream App**

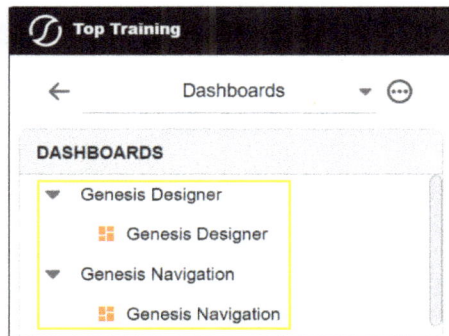

**The two interfaces for Genesis in
the Modern Browser Experience**

Figure 9.3

Genesis Designer enables administrators and power-users to create the structural hierarchy needed to configure interfaces that are customized for specific business requirements. The core completed frame, as shown in Figure 9.4, comprises Application Groups, Navigation Groups, Pages, and Content Blocks (outlined in red), which provide a modular framework that enables flexible organization of these components and an efficient set-up of functionality.

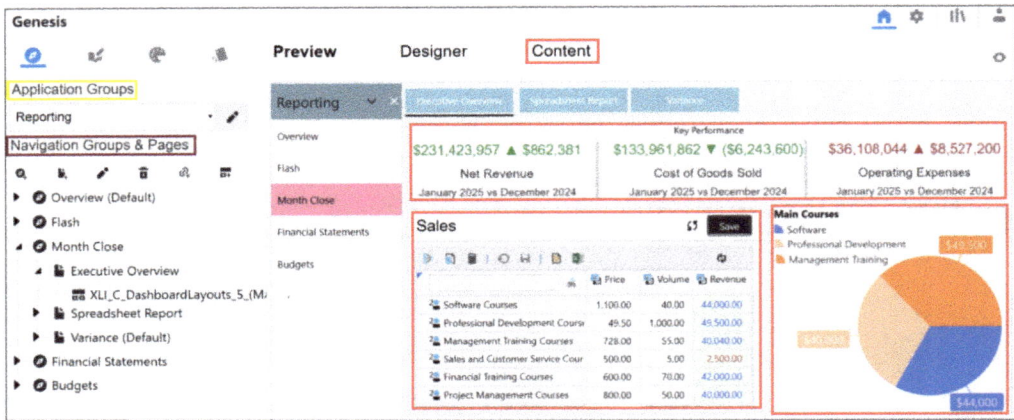

Figure 9.4

Application Groups

Application Groups are fixed, editable containers for organizing content according to business needs. Genesis provides four pre-named Application Groups, which can be renamed or hidden, but additional groups cannot be created. Instead, as mentioned above, additional instances of Genesis can be created from the Instance Management menu, which provides four more Application groups for each instance of Genesis.

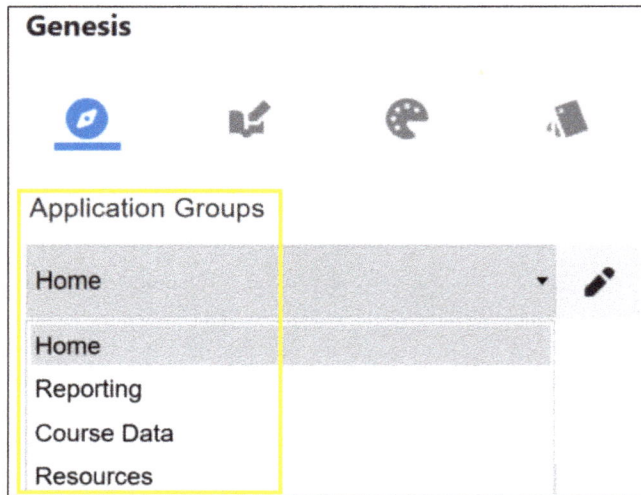

Figure 9.5

Navigation Groups

Navigation Groups are flexible subgroups within Application Groups, designed to organize and present content (once Pages and Content Blocks are added) according to specific business needs.

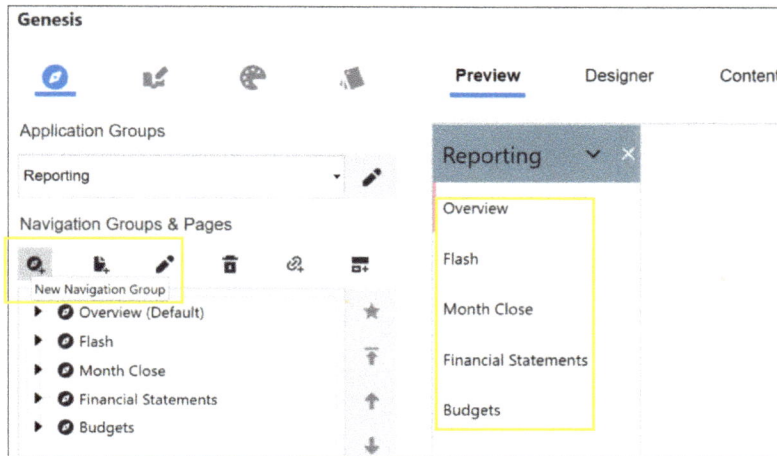

Figure 9.6

Pages

Within Navigation Groups, Pages serve as customizable screens that showcase reports, dashboards, and other outputs, either using Content Blocks or by linking to an existing item from a shared Workspace (to be able to share other Workspaces in the Genesis environment, the Workspaces must have Is Shareable Workspace set to True). Currently, Pages take a tabular layout across the top of the screen.

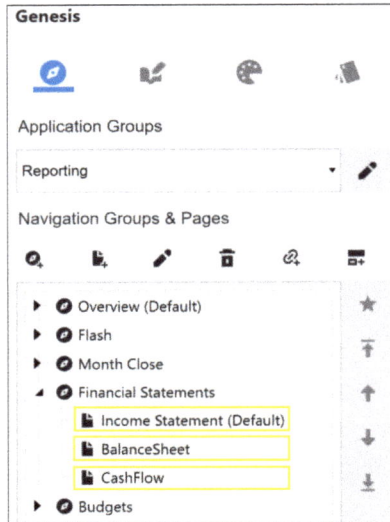

Figure 9.7

Content Blocks

Content Blocks are configurable elements injected within a Page to display dynamic content. Blocks are continuously being added to Solution Exchange. At the time of writing, there are over 40 Content Blocks available (see Figure 9.9 for some examples), and these are effortlessly imported into your instance of Genesis for the on-premise OneStream Application (relevant for any current remaining on-premise customers). For cloud users, there is an option to upload automatically once the Content Block has been released to Solution Exchange.

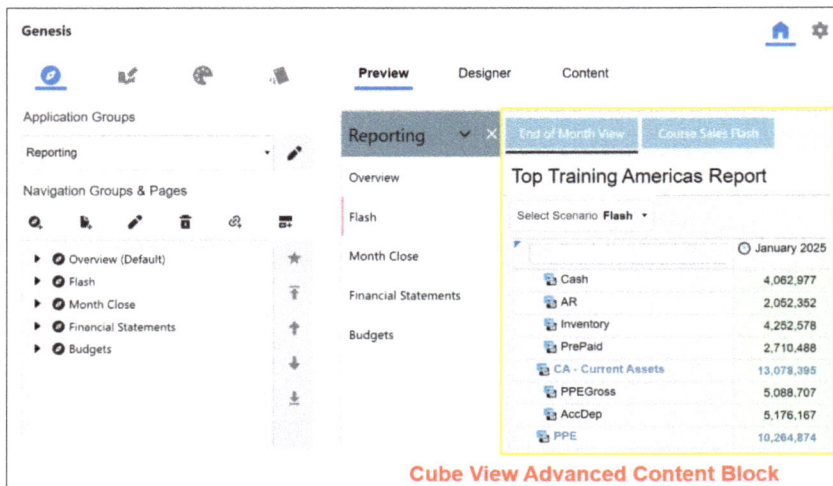

Figure 9.8

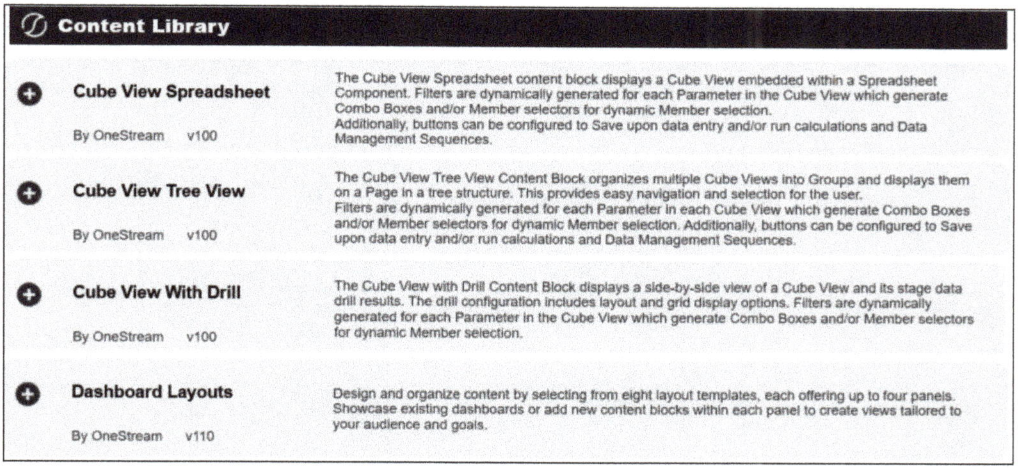

Content Library

Cube View Spreadsheet

By OneStream   v100

The Cube View Spreadsheet content block displays a Cube View embedded within a Spreadsheet Component. Filters are dynamically generated for each Parameter in the Cube View which generate Combo Boxes and/or Member selectors for dynamic Member selection.
Additionally, buttons can be configured to Save upon data entry and/or run calculations and Data Management Sequences.

Cube View Tree View

By OneStream   v100

The Cube View Tree View Content Block organizes multiple Cube Views into Groups and displays them on a Page in a tree structure. This provides easy navigation and selection for the user.
Filters are dynamically generated for each Parameter in each Cube View which generate Combo Boxes and/or Member selectors for dynamic Member selection. Additionally, buttons can be configured to Save upon data entry and/or run calculations and Data Management Sequences.

Cube View With Drill

By OneStream   v100

The Cube View with Drill Content Block displays a side-by-side view of a Cube View and its stage data drill results. The drill configuration includes layout and grid display options. Filters are dynamically generated for each Parameter in the Cube View which generate Combo Boxes and/or Member selectors for dynamic Member selection.

Dashboard Layouts

By OneStream   v110

Design and organize content by selecting from eight layout templates, each offering up to four panels. Showcase existing dashboards or add new content blocks within each panel to create views tailored to your audience and goals.

Some examples of Content Blocks in the Content Library

Figure 9.9

Showcasing Genesis

Businesses often have diverse requirements for dashboard development. While this section does not cover every scenario, it offers an overview of selected Genesis output examples and possibilities.

In each example, the Application Group includes multiple Navigation Groups. Within each Navigation Group, dedicated Pages are created to host (a term known as **injected**) specific Content Blocks tailored to business needs or linked directly to an object from a Workspace (for example, an existing dashboard).

Figure 9.10 shows some of the icons used in Genesis to create the hierarchy structure.

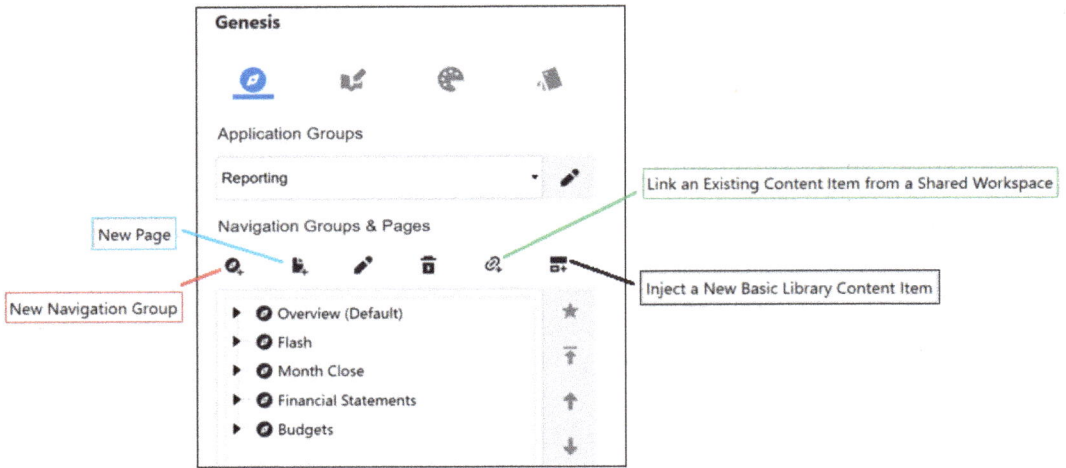

Figure 9.10

Home Page

The Home Page block is injected into the Page, where you can use the Designer tab to customize its appearance and content. You can select images from the library or upload your own, enter announcement text, adjust colors, and edit buttons to suit any business requirements.

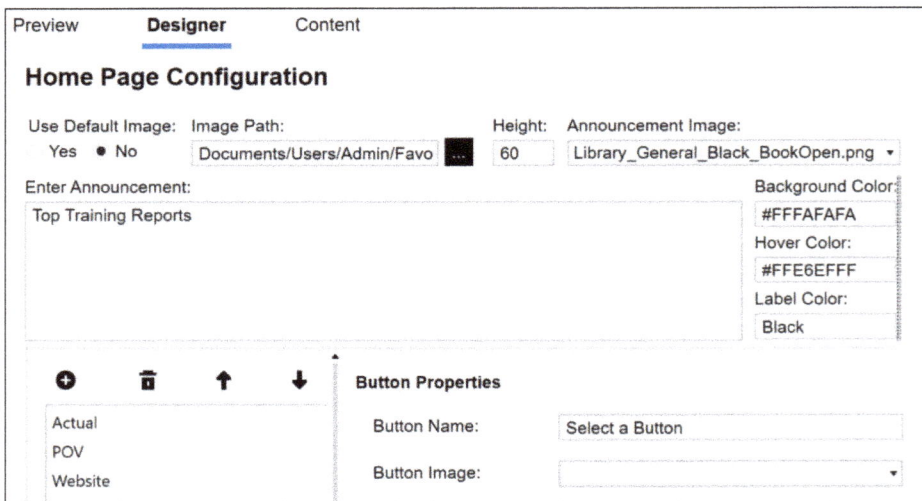

Figure 9.11

Figure 9.12 shows the output in Genesis Navigation.

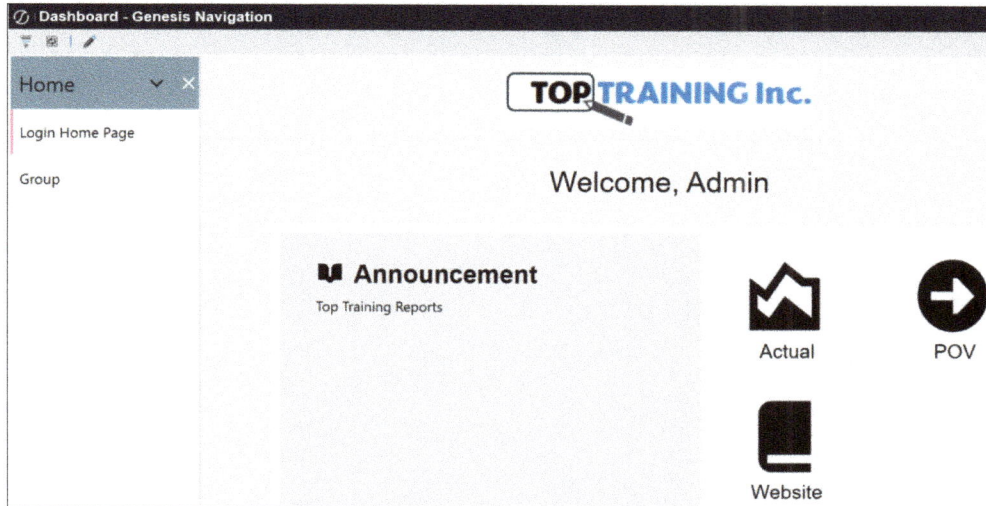

Figure 9.12

Cube View Advanced

This Content Block offers additional configuration options on parameters if embedded in the Cube View. The system automatically generates drop-down lists (referred to as combo boxes in OneStream), which can be customized in both description and display format (e.g., member lists or dialogue boxes).

Buttons can be enabled or disabled as needed, and the calculation button can trigger business rules, data management sequences, or pre-defined actions such as calculation, translation, and consolidation.

The Content tab confirms that the Cube View renders correctly with the Preview tab displaying what the user will see (as shown in Figure 9.13).

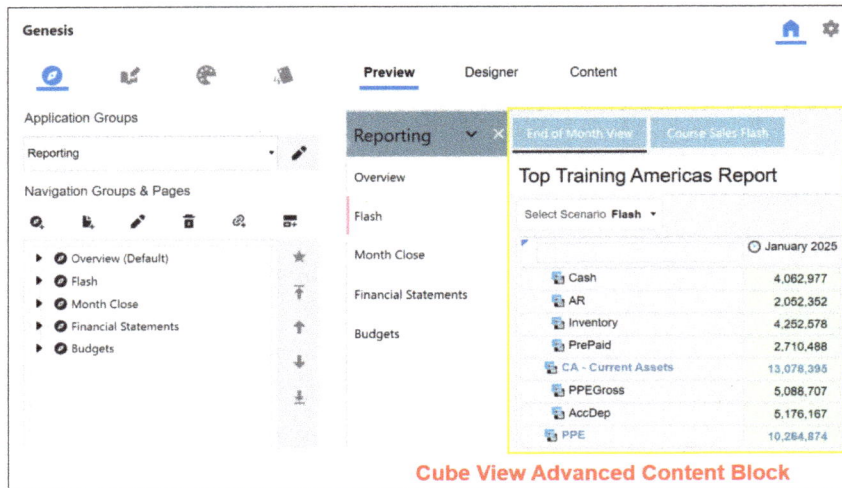

Figure 9.13

Cube View Charts

The Content Block can display charts, including pie, line, waterfall, and bar, by either selecting an existing Cube View from a Workspace or using the Cube Query option. With Cube Query, you specify the point of view, column, and row members, and the resulting data is used to generate the chart.

Configuration options range from changing point labels and the number format to modifying legends and color schemes.

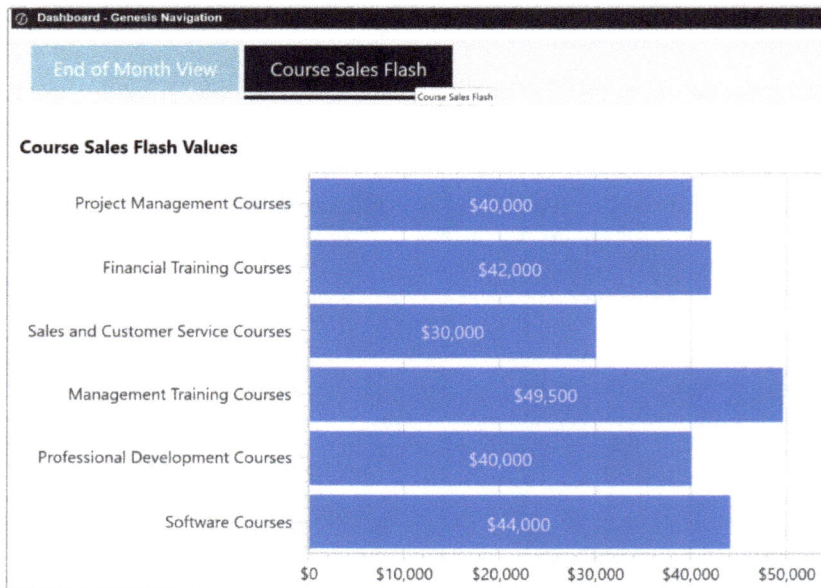

Figure 9.14

Cube View Spreadsheet

Within this block, the Spreadsheet is generated from a Cube View connection, with any parameters automatically converted into drop-down lists inside the sheet. You can customize both the parameter descriptions and drop-down display format. Buttons are also configurable as needed. Note that the sheet is saved within the block itself, not in File Explorer.

	Jan 2025	Feb 2025	Mar 2025	Apr 2025	May 20
Income Statement					
Revenues	9,267,833.43	9,168,302.30	10,562,782.35	10,728,308.91	11,702
Cost of goods sold	2,646,560.14	2,910,418.95	3,381,944.77	3,495,619.74	4,046
Gross income	**6,621,273.29**	**6,257,883.35**	**7,180,837.58**	**7,232,689.17**	**7,655**
Compensation	2,732,919.61	3,048,034.42	3,140,520.68	2,895,367.56	3,285
Research & development	80,282.46	89,653.88	94,592.09	112,021.04	112
Marketing & advertising	652,438.94	716,271.13	946,859.01	957,368.66	953
Other operating expenses	716,596.66	884,222.58	905,298.06	916,740.48	938
Total operating expenses	**4,182,237.67**	**4,738,182.01**	**5,087,269.84**	**4,881,497.74**	**5,290**
Depreciation and amortization	366,109.80	366,109.80	366,109.80	366,109.80	366
Total operating income	**2,072,925.82**	**1,153,591.54**	**1,727,457.94**	**1,985,081.63**	**1,999**
Total other income (expense)					
Earnings before interest and taxes	**2,072,925.82**	**1,153,591.54**	**1,727,457.94**	**1,985,081.63**	**1,999**

Figure 9.15

Dashboard Layouts

This Content Block has several pre-defined layouts and allows you to inject additional Content Blocks into the selected layout or link to existing objects from a Workspace (for example, an existing dashboard).

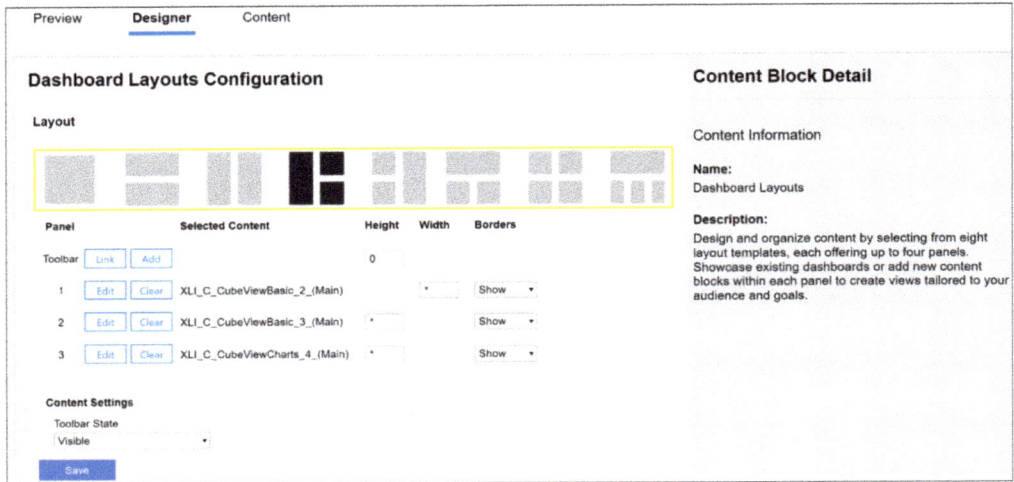

Figure 9.16

Figure 9.17 shows an example in Genesis Navigation with the selected layout containing two Cube Views and a chart.

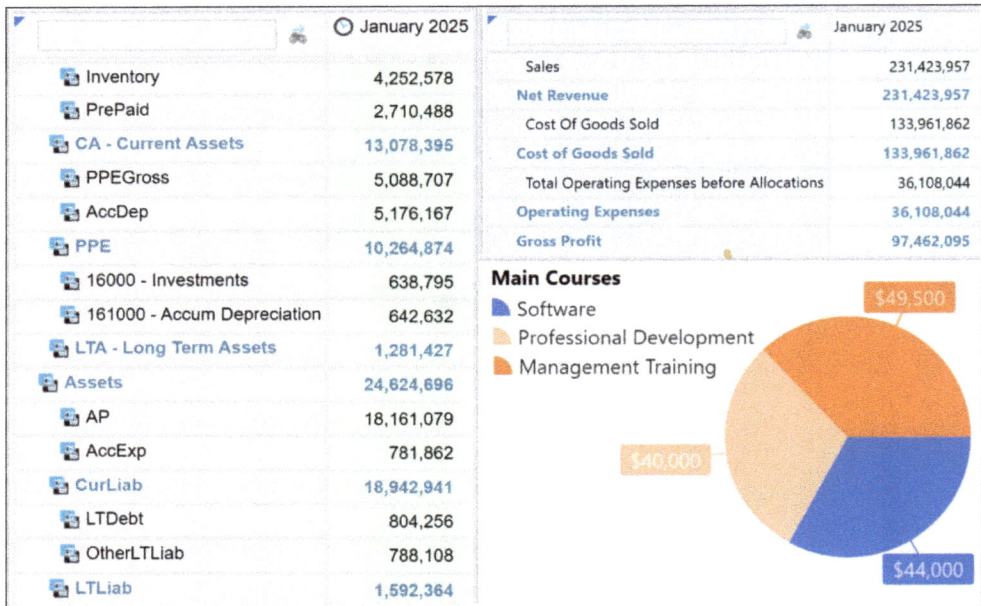

Figure 9.17

The Advanced Dashboard Layouts Content Block provides even more flexibility with the ability to have up to 12 rows, each containing up to 12 cards (where links to existing dashboards or further Content Blocks can be injected in each card). This will enable views to be further tailored to the business requirements.

KPI Tile

This Content Block displays a value after you add a Member Filter. (Tip: You can copy the Cell POV from a Cube View to set the initial members; there is no need for the Cb# or P# dimension tokens.) You can also add a description, select a Scenario, compare values against the previous year or period, and define the variance behavior (for example, whether something is better or worse).

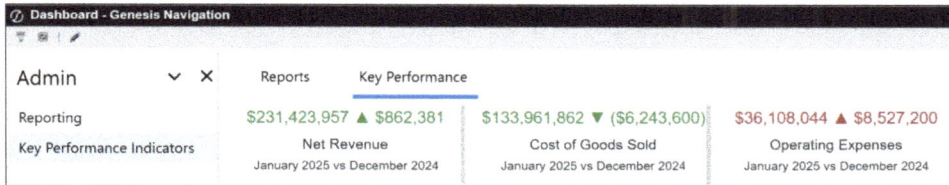

Figure 9.18

Pivot Grid

This Content Block enables users to efficiently analyze and filter large data sets. The underlying data source can be easily configured by selecting a Data Adapter from a Workspace. The user can drag and drop fields into columns, rows, filters, and data areas.

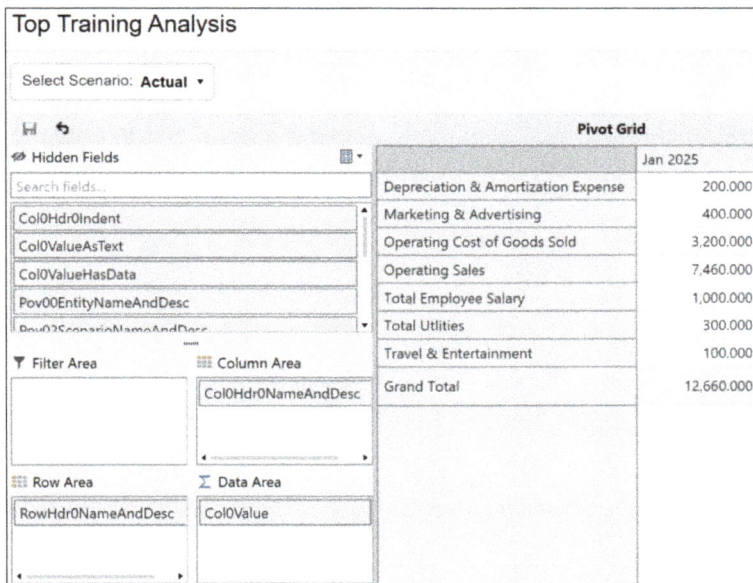

Figure 9.19

Spreadsheet Tree

This Content Block is designed specifically to display Excel files stored in the File Explorer. Users can browse a selected folder, and as they click through the hierarchy, each sheet is instantly available for viewing or editing.

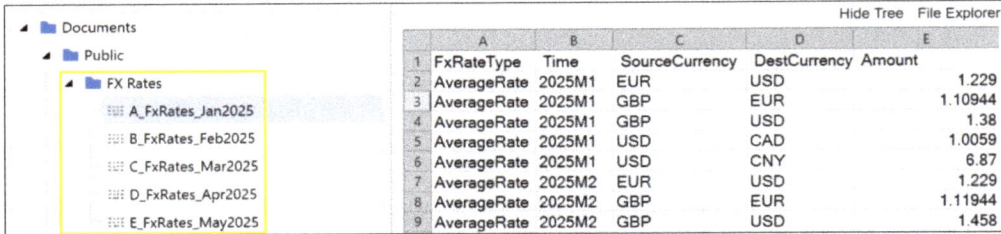

Figure 9.20

Link an Existing Content item from a Shared Workspace

This feature allows you to link existing dashboards and related artifacts from Workspaces directly into Genesis (refer to "Dashboard Overview in Workspaces" for details). As a result, there is no need to recreate dashboards within Genesis—users transitioning from traditional Workspace development to Genesis can seamlessly reuse all previously built dashboards.

Figure 9.21 illustrates how a dashboard from Top Training's Workspace is integrated within the Genesis Frame.

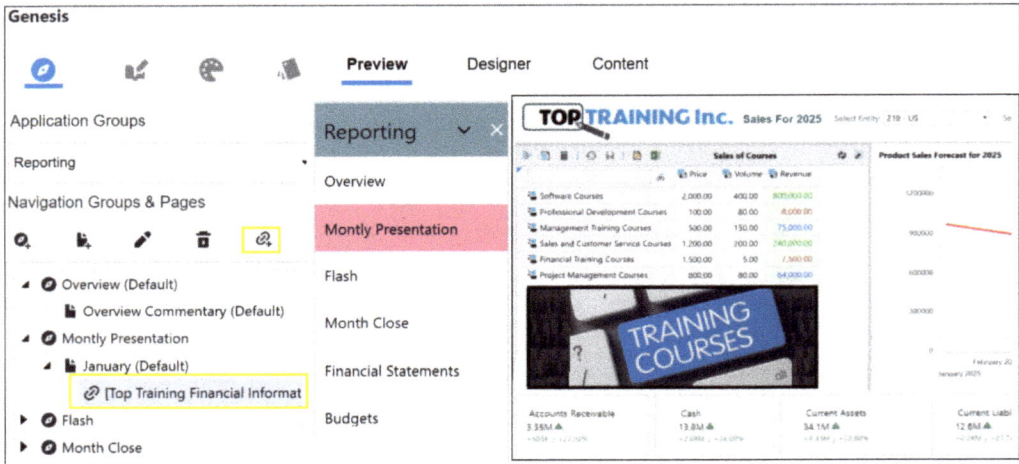

Figure 9.21

Colors and Styles

The color palette icon offers a range of built-in color and style options, which can be easily customized. Additionally, you have the flexibility to create your own custom setups. These color changes can be applied to different elements throughout the Genesis frame.

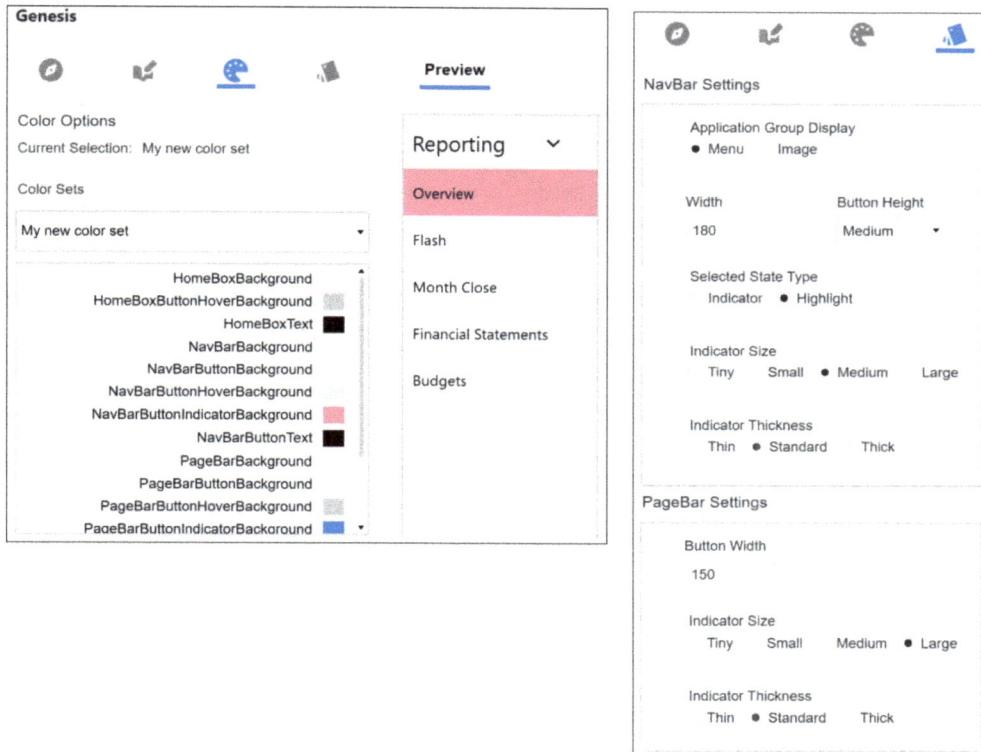

Figure 9.22

Genesis Can Make You a Star

Genesis is the future of dashboard creation, a solution that can transform administrators into finance or non-finance heroes. Having explored the framework and its practical examples, Genesis empowers administrators to rapidly configure, personalize, and deploy great dashboards. Users can seamlessly blend new and existing content, choose from a variety of layouts, styles, colors, and images, and easily adapt the dashboards to evolving business needs.

Dashboard Overview in Workspaces

Now that we have explored the power of Genesis as the go-to tool for dashboard creation, the remainder of this book will provide administrators and consultants with guidance on building dashboards directly within the Workspace. This approach will also help illustrate what Genesis automatically generates *behind the scenes* in Workspaces.

The jigsaw puzzle analogy used in this book previously is probably most appropriate for how dashboards can be constructed in OneStream Workspaces. Throughout this chapter, we will discuss various components and embedded dashboards, as well as source items, that are then pieced together in a final frame to present information intuitively.

To begin our learning, and continue with the jigsaw analogy, an overview is shown in Figure 9.23. Likened to the complete picture on the jigsaw puzzle box, we see a typical method of how a dashboard is assembled in OneStream. This consists of a dashboard named Frame, where header, content, and footer dashboards are combined.

Each of these dashboards has various components (that use source items) added to them.

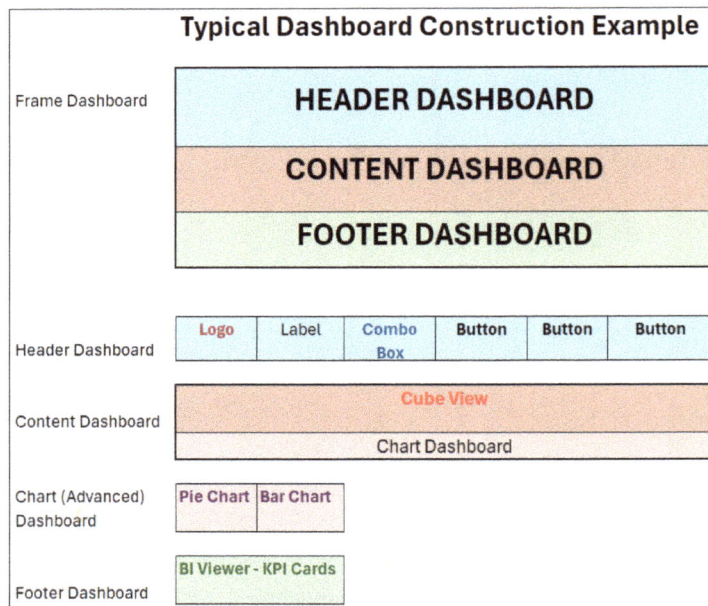

Figure 9.23

Here are the main pieces now laid out on the table

Logo

This is the organization's chosen logo component. It retrieves its source from the uploaded image in Application Properties. A recommended naming convention is to use the prefix `lgo_Name`.

Label

A component used for displaying text with various font color and size options, and a recommended naming convention that uses a prefix of `lbl_Name`. The typed text can be set against a substitution variable. For example, after typing the text Forecasting for, the substitution variable `|WFYear|` can be added. This will embed the year the user's workflow task has been set to – once the dashboard is run – as per Figure 9.24.

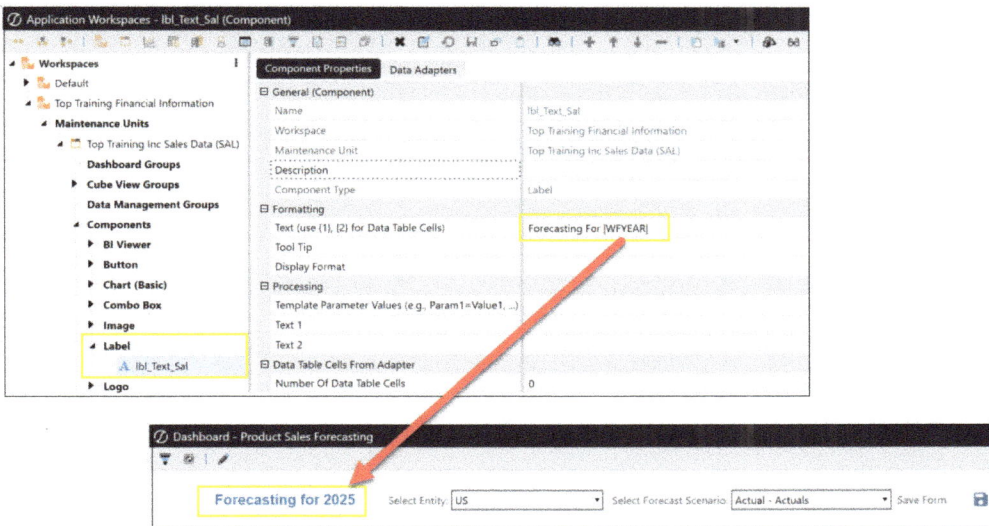

Figure 9.24

Combo Box

This provides the user with a drop-down list of members from which to select. The source of this list has come from a parameter (see previous chapter on parameters) that an administrator will create and embed in the combo box component. A recommended naming convention is using the prefix `cbx_Name`.

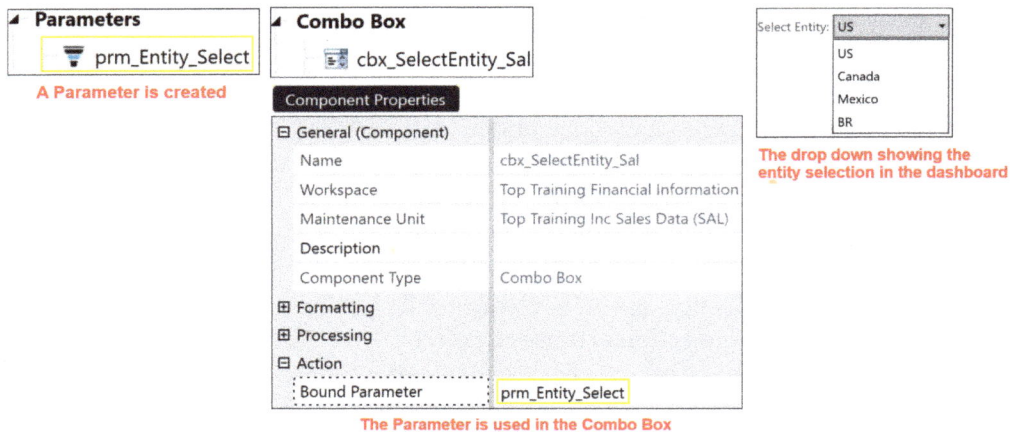

Figure 9.25

Button

This allows the user to click on an icon in the dashboard. The icon's image comes from a file the administrator will create and then connect to the button component. The button component will also have an action set that performs a task when the button is clicked. Tasks such as navigating to another dashboard, page or screen, running a calculation, updating items, or downloading a document. A recommended naming convention to use the prefix btn_Name.

Chart (Advanced)

Examples of charts that are created include pie, bar charts, and line charts. A recommended naming convention is using the prefix cht_Name.

BI Viewer

The built-in features within the BI Viewer component make it possible to create a complete standalone dashboard (as explained further in the section on Three Ways To Get To One Dashboard, below). This interactive business intelligence visualization of data has features that take the form of charts (used instead of the Chart (Advanced) component), grids, and KPI cards – sourced from a data adapter. Also compatible with existing dashboards, the BI Viewer is viewed by adding the component to a dashboard that is part of a larger frame dashboard. Refer back to Figure 9.23, which shows the BI Viewer as part of the Frame's footer.

The BI Viewer is simple to build with drag-and-drop building features. A recommended naming convention is using the prefix biv_Name.

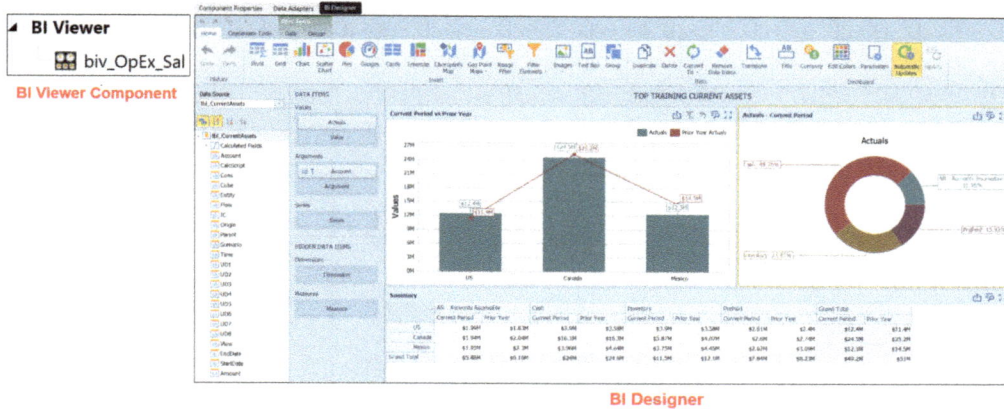

Figure 9.26

Image

Images are displayed on the dashboard and sourced from, for example, a file or URL link. A recommended naming convention is using the prefix img_Name

Data Adapter

Data adapters specify the data source types used in components. The key source items that can be used are a Cube View, a Structured Query Language (SQL) script that retrieves data from a database, or a **Method Query** (some method queries can be prebuilt SQL scripts in the platform). A recommended naming convention is using the prefix da_Name.

All the components have a separate named section, as shown in Figure 9.27.

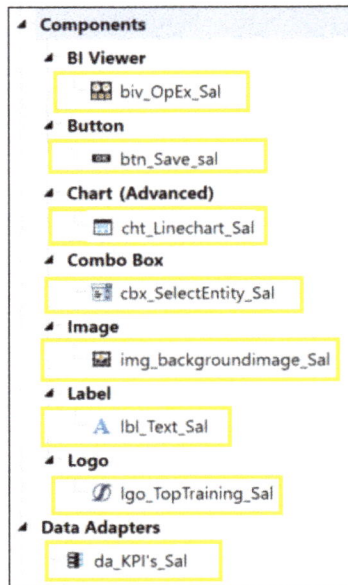

Figure 9.27

Three Ways To Get To One Dashboard

There are three ways to create a dashboard in OneStream. Using Genesis (as already seen above), or just the BI Viewer dashboard component (found under Components within a maintenance unit that's in a Workspace) is another way, and the grids, charts, and KPIs in this component all interact with each other. All the user has to do is click and view the results. A user accesses the BI Viewer (once it has been built by the administrator) by placing it in a dashboard frame.

The third way a dashboard can be created in OneStream is by conventionally constructing individual components – such as charts, grids, drop-downs, and buttons – and then implementing the interactivity between them. For a user to access these components, they are placed in individual dashboards, which are then assembled in one final dashboard frame.

Typically, there might be a hybrid construction of the latter two methods for more detailed dashboards. These could consist of the generic components being built and used within the sub-dashboards (that are then added to the final frame dashboard), as well as using a feature of the BI Viewer (such as the KPI cards) to complete the final part, which is also added to the Frame.

Designing A Dashboard

When you set out to create a brand-new dashboard (and just like we talked about in the previous chapter), thinking about the end in mind is key. It is important to understand what the dashboard will be used for and then sketch out a wireframe or template that includes the components being utilized and how they are laid out. Excel is a handy sketching tool, as pixel sizes can be comparable to OneStream component sizes.

Top Training would like a dashboard to show sales of their courses and various key performance indicators and to utilize a logo, text, a drop-down to pick a training centre, and charts. Finally, some key performance indicators targeting specific accounts should be included.

Here's the wireframe.

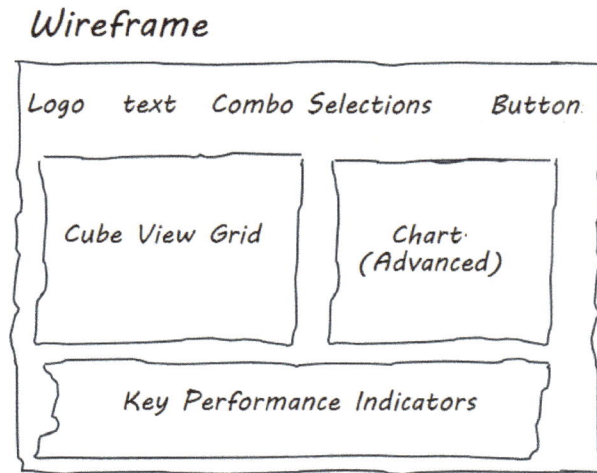

Figure 9.28

Dashboard Layout

A dashboard can present components in a user-friendly format for the end-user. This is done by the administrator selecting the most appropriate layout type in the Dashboard Properties tab. The key layout types used are:

Grid

This organizes components into a fixed grid of rows and columns. These are used when embedding dashboards within dashboards. The grid layout also provides the option to create line separators or movable splitters, which users can drag to resize components.

Tabs

This layout type will slot each component into its own tab. When the dashboard is run, the user will be faced with a series of tabs in the dashboard to work through, with the highlighted tab being the current view.

Uniform

This layout transforms itself to automatically distribute space equally among all dashboard components, either vertically or horizontally.

Horizontal Stack Panel

This layout will horizontally align the components. These are good for horizontal header or footer requirements and used for linear component arrangements, enhancing the user readability from left to right. Examples commonly used are an organisation's logo, text information, and buttons to other dashboards.

Vertical Stack Panel

This layout will vertically align the components. These are useful when the administrator would like to assign buttons in a vertical set-up for the end user. A vertical stack panel facilitates a top-down approach to viewing components and is suitable for step-by-step processes. Examples commonly used are workflow steps (guiding the user from top to bottom) or a toolbox in the form of various buttons on the left-hand side.

Constructing A Dashboard

When creating a dashboard, the convention is to use a logical approach with each part named effectively (to make maintenance easier and allow a successor to follow the build). Top Training's approach is to take its requirements and work through the stages of the build. We start in the Application tab and select the Workspaces menu option.

Workspaces

With our requirements to hand, the dashboard requires a Workspace to be created (or an existing Workspace can be used). This is an area set up for individuals or a team to build all the parts for one or more dashboards. Each Workspace can be isolated or shared with other Workspaces. The naming convention should consist of a relevant and meaningful name with spaces if necessary.

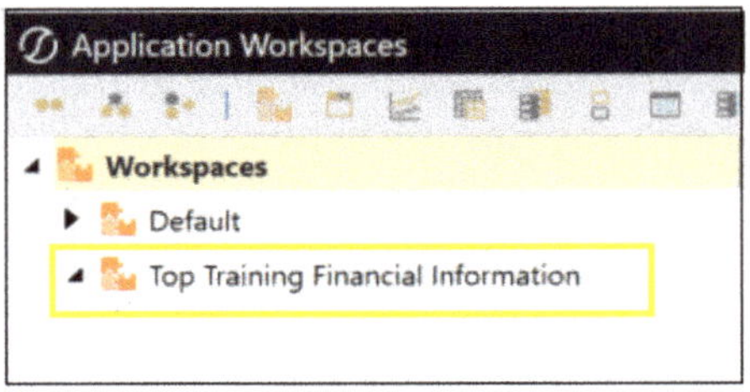

Figure 9.29

Maintenance Unit

Under the Workspace, we can divide up the construction of various dashboards (creating separate projects so to speak) through **Maintenance Units**. Each maintenance unit will automatically present itself with the menu options required for the build; for example, dashboard and Cube View groups, components, data adapters, and parameters.

The naming convention can take the form of a prefix to order the maintenance units and a suffix, which is considered a unique code related to the dashboard construction area.

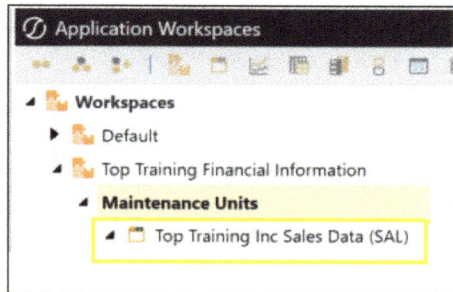

Figure 9.30

From Figure 9.30 above, we can see that to work on the Top Training dashboard, under the Maintenance Unit called Top Training Inc Sales Data (SAL), we require the build of:

- A dashboard group that will contain the dashboards required

- A Cube View group that will have the Cube View for the grid and chart

- Components such as logo, label, images, combo box, chart(Advanced), and KPI cards

- A data adapter for the source data, which will be from our Cube View

- Parameters to assist us with the drop-down list in the combo box component

Dashboard Groups

The dashboards to create are:

- 0_Frame_SalesDashboard. This will use the grid layout type, and all the other completed dashboards will be finally added to this one.

- **1_SalesDashboard_Header**. This will have a horizontal stack layout type to align the components next to each other.

- **2_SalesDashboard_Content**. This will have a grid layout as it will – eventually – present two components and might require a movable splitter.

- **2a_SalesDashboard_Chart**. This will have a uniform layout as, currently, only one component is used. This may change to a grid if further charts are added.

- **3_SalesDashboard_Footer**. This will be a horizontal layout.

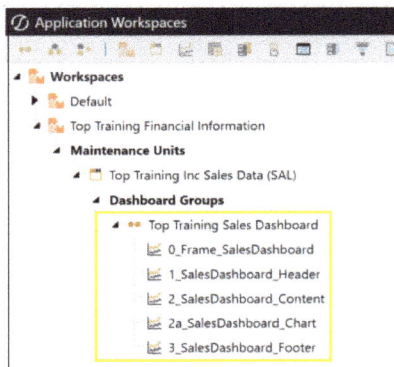

Figure 9.31

Workspaces, maintenance units, and dashboard groups can be built and organized as needed. Commonly, this will end up per stream, per dashboard type, or simply in areas for developing and testing. Ideally, they provide an isolated environment where the same-name items can exist separately.

Dashboard groups organize dashboards in the same way Cube View groups are used to organize Cube Views. They are then able to be deployed to end-users from dashboard profiles.

Cube View Groups

The Cube Views placed here will be the source for the Cube View component and the data adapter.

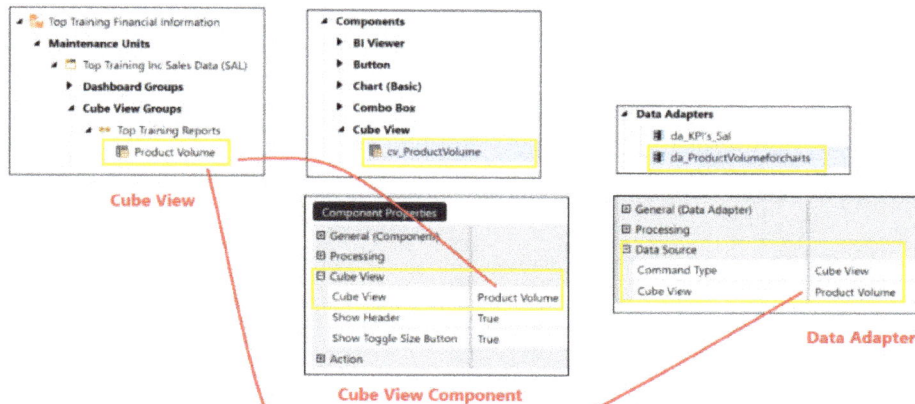

Figure 9.32

Components

For our dashboard, we will use the following components:

- BI Viewer with KPI cards using a data adapter which has a Cube View embedded for its source

- A button representing a Save Icon, using an image from a file

- A chart (advanced) that uses a data adapter that has a Cube View embedded for its source

- A combo box using a parameter to supply the drop-down members

- A Cube View displayed in the dashboard, with the data sourced from the Cube View group

- An image component using an image from a file

- A label with the text typed and formatting applied

- A logo that gets its image from the application properties

Data Adapters

Our data adapter will use a Cube View for the grid, the Chart, and the BI Viewer.

Parameters

Our parameter uses a member list for the drop-down in the combo box (as was shown in Figure 9.25 earlier).

Piecing It All Together

With all the work done on the individual parts, the next step is attaching the components to the best-fit dashboards and then the dashboards to the final Frame. Work with me on this one:

The Logo, Label, Combo Boxes, and Button will be added to the 1_SalesDashboard_Header.

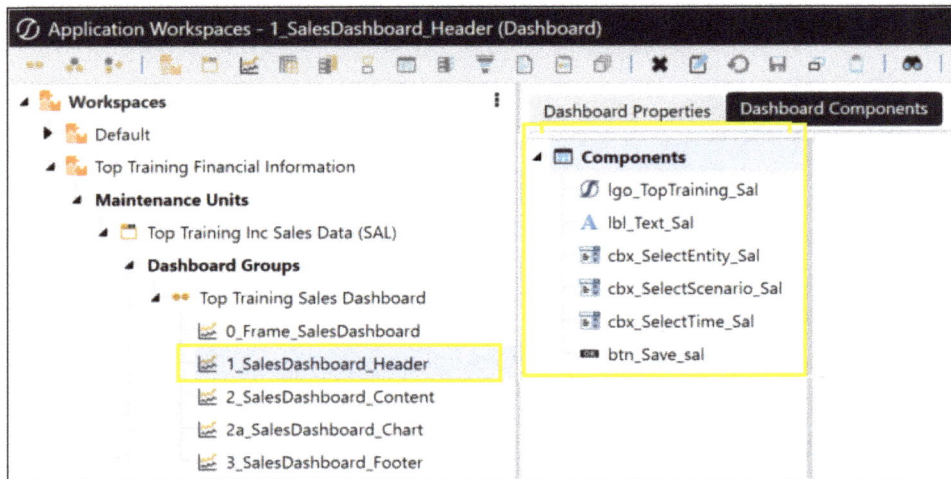

Figure 9.33

The Cube View and image component will be added to the 2_SalesDashboard_Content

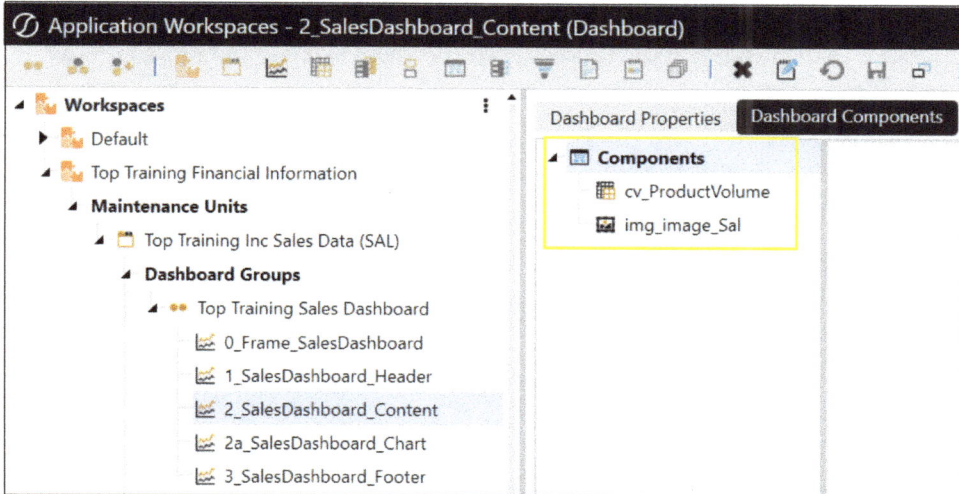

Figure 9.34

The Chart will be added to the 2a_SalesDashboard_Chart.

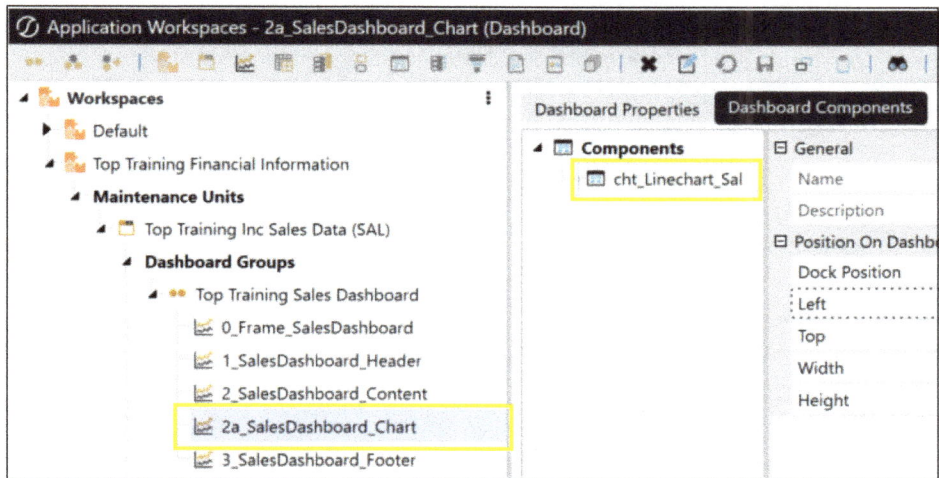

Figure 9.35

The BI Viewer KPI cards will be added to the 3_SalesDashboard_Footer.

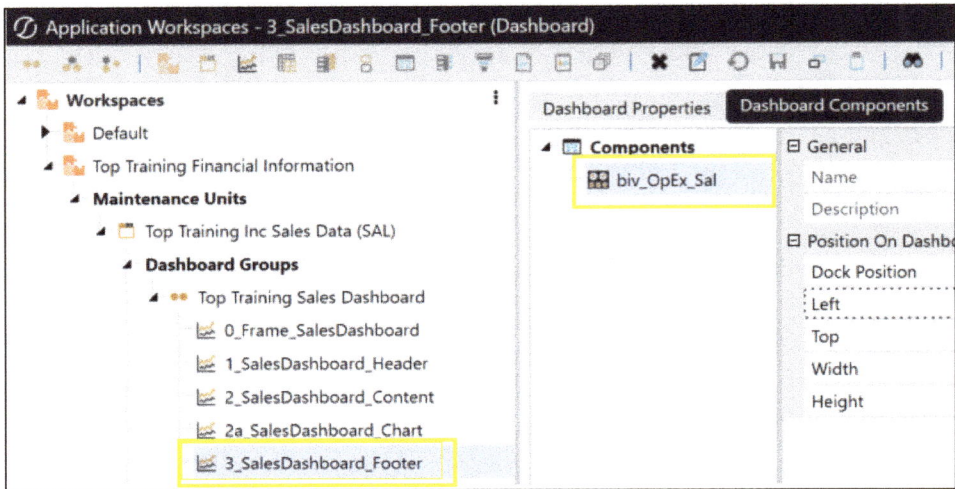

Figure 9.36

The 2a_SalesDashboard_Chart can then be added to the 2_SalesDashboard_Content dashboard.

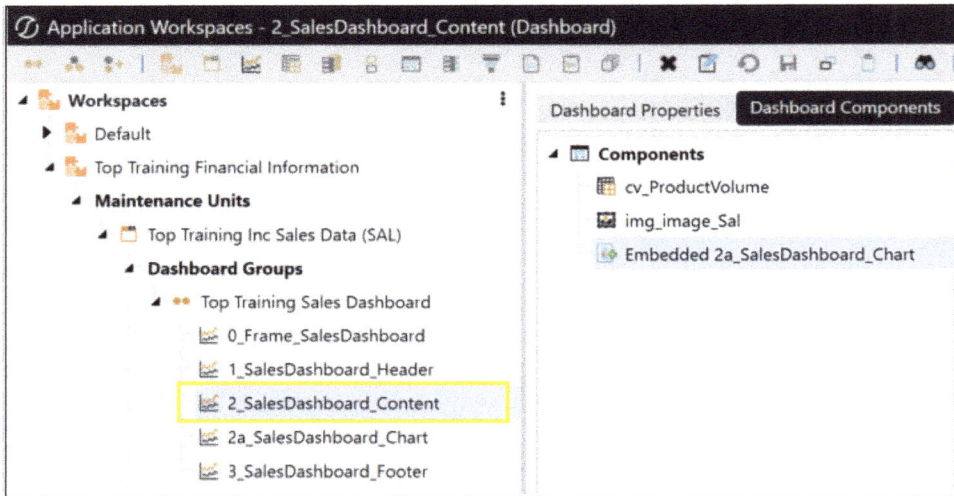

Figure 9.37

Finally, the 1_SalesDashboard_Header, 2_SalesDashboard_Content, and 3_SalesDashboard_Footer can all be added to the 0_Frame_SalesDashboard for the completed dashboard.

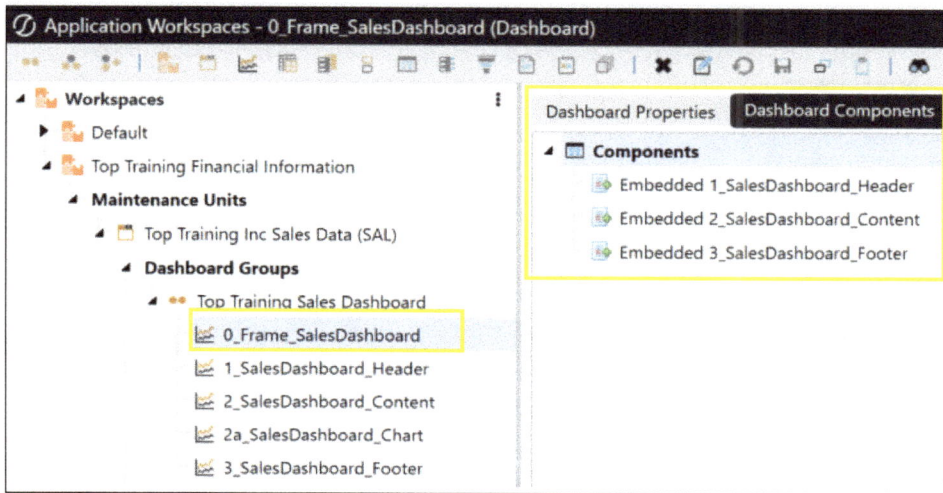

Figure 9.38

Figure 9.39 shows the completed 0_Frame_Salesdashboard once run.

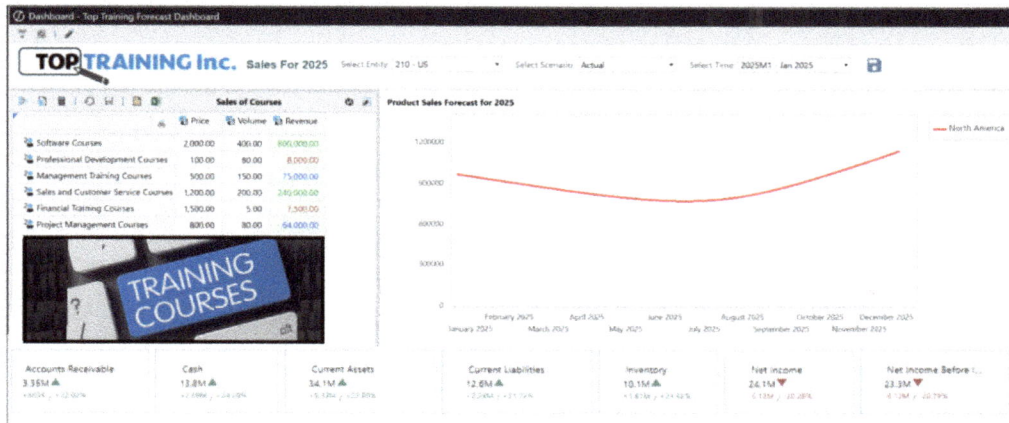

Figure 9.39

The final dashboard can be a landing page (the dashboard the user will see immediately as they log into the platform). This can be done by individuals using the OneStream icon once the dashboard shows and selecting Set Current Page As Home Page, or for a group using the Home Page Manager in Administrator Solution Tools, which sets the dashboard as the home page.

A neat design is to make the landing page a front-end portal for the user. This consists of an interactive experience by providing buttons to various other dashboards and back again. This would also be a good medium to communicate any OneStream news from the Centre of Excellence team.

Other items, such as links to non-OneStream areas (like Top Training's intranet page), may then make the portal an easy-to-use one-stop shop.

Conclusion

Creating dashboards is an art, and – with practice – it soon becomes clear that they can cater to a very broad range of requirements in an organization. They are consumed by many roles for various reasons and are considered a living report… one that can evolve easily.

There are three ways to create dashboards in the platform – Genesis, BI Viewer, or the more traditional use of each component. Using the latter two for a single dashboard is also an option.

Dashboards are evolving in OneStream, heading towards being built around the framework we now know as Genesis. This low-code, plug-and-play architecture with enhanced capabilities, provides a means to fast dashboard creation. Genesis will aid non-technical users to design, build and deploy visually pleasing and dynamic user-friendly interfaces within their teams.

Financial and operational dashboards will also be able to incorporate AI narrative summarization for planning, operational analytics and key performance indicators.

When designing a dashboard – whether using Genesis or building directly within the Workspace – always begin with the end in mind. Sketch out where each component will appear to guide your layout and structure. Familiarizing yourself with the available components will help you determine exactly which elements are needed for your project. By following a logical approach, including consistent naming conventions and thoughtful embedding of individual dashboards, you can create an effective and visually appealing final Frame dashboard.

10

OneStream in The Real World and Troubleshooting

OneStream Project Implementation

Every OneStream implementation is unique, but a common methodology can be adopted where the project team completes a number of phases, leading to a successful go-live and beyond.

This chapter aims to provide a high-level understanding of how a software consultant utilizes a structured approach to software implementation and the Software Development Life Cycle (SDLC) for those new to the field. This introductory read also serves as a good segue to the *OneStream Foundation Handbook*, specifically the chapter on 'Methodology and the Project', as well as the ongoing maintenance.

Here is this chapter's learning journey:

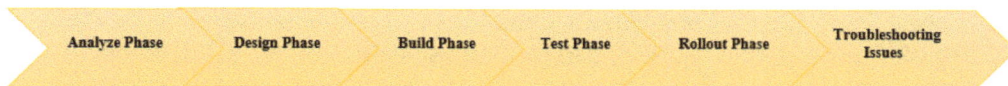

Figure 10.1

At the start of the book, when discussing OneStream artifacts, I listed the SDLC phases under the headings of Analyze, Design, Build, Test, and Rollout. Each phase is a collaborative team effort, ensuring efficient working practices day-to-day throughout the project's timeline, while also helping to minimize any risk factors.

Top Training adopted these phases as their methodology, working with a project team comprised of an administrator, OneStream consultant, Top Training subject matter expert(s), and an engagement or project manager.

Analyze

The initial scoping session with the consulting team and Top Training project stakeholders would have been a discussion of their current processes, pain points, and what is expected of future processes. After this, a requirement-gathering workshop would have taken place.

The workshop introduces the team members and discusses the project's objectives and expectations. For Top Training, this involves transforming their existing planning, consolidation, and reporting to OneStream.

The analyses drill down to the operational requirements, which include the entities, chart of accounts, and possible cost center / profit center, products, plus regions that may need to be incorporated as part of the platform's metadata setup.

The Analyze phase seeks to explore Top Training's current ecosystem and establish data integration in terms of the various data sources and how the data load can be streamlined into a workflow task.

For the preparation of planning and/or consolidation reporting, questions might include: Will this entail reporting in both a legal and management structure? Will there be additional reporting requirements (for example, by customer or product or both)? Also, which key performance indicators and variance analyses are required.

Before the workshop, the Top Training team would have provided a sample of their data sources, the existing chart of accounts, a list of users who interact with the platform, and documentation (including existing report formats, formula definitions, and calculated values) for the consulting team to have analysed then and discuss now.

For the consulting team, the goal will be to collect information from Top Training's subject matter experts to drive the next stage, which is the Design phase. This can be captured by category, priority, and in-scope requirements descriptions.

Design

This phase leverages the knowledge acquired in the Analyze phase to inform the design of Top Training's data integration, dimensionality, cubes, calculations, workflow structures, security, and reports. The design will incorporate thoughts on performance, user experience, and ease of system administration, with consultants trying to balance these and seeking to future-proof the application.

Various design areas are worked on by the OneStream team. This will be presented in a design document to Top Training's subject matter experts, who will also provide input and feedback until the document has been agreed and signed off.

Areas such as data integration can be worked on to understand the different sources and target areas. For example, whether the data load is coming directly from other systems or from files, which of the source transactions are targeting cubes, and which will reside in the staging table.

Other areas – such as workflow design – require knowledge of whether the setup will be centralized (with corporate performing the data load), or decentralized (relying on operational staff to load the data). Once loaded, is the data going to be validated or certified, and how many users are involved before the workflow gets signed off and consolidation can take place?

This is also a good opportunity to showcase what the platform is expected to do once live.

Build

When the application build in OneStream begins, it is not just a case of lifting the old and putting it into the new. With the requirements matrix and design documentation completed from the previous phases, the project team should use OneStream's exceptional features to enhance or streamline (if possible) the processes.

The correct building of the metadata (the most important part of the design and build phase) – *from the start* – provides a good foundation for all other artifacts. Metadata is built upon the structures required to support Top Training's various reporting formats.

The use of OneStream's **Extensibility** feature (as discussed in chapter 4 on Cubes), should be part of the design and build, allowing the financial model to span multiple business areas and scenarios within the same application. This entails putting a lot of thought into the design of Top Training locations, which can be a separate Entity dimension for each region or business area and then connected as one group hierarchy for corporate. This will, in turn, provide the capability to have individual business area cubes connect to the top corporate cube.

The chart of accounts built in OneStream helps collate all of the group's values. The creation of robust data sources and transformation rules, therefore, provides an easy-to-follow audit trail back to the transaction's origin.

During the data integration and data load build, consider how far back the transactional values need to be. Too much historical data may be an unnecessary overload, with the risk that it will either not be used or cannot be explained. Historical data should be within the bounds of comparison to prior years or used for future seeding. As data is validated by the client in OneStream, too many years may delay the go-live date.

Following the build of dimensions, cubes, and data integration, other artifacts can be worked on, including the tasks that make up the workflow, formulas that make up the calculated values, and reports.

The reports that will have a common, consistent build, can be used as templates for the administrator to take forward when creating further reports.

Security can be applied in the application by user, role, and group matrix – all of which would have been started in the design document. The key to security is not to overcomplicate, and to keep the setup maintainable by starting with a basic security model and then continuing to refine and enhance as the app matures.

Test

Thorough testing and build sign-off make for an easy post-rollout period. The goal is to avoid any major showstoppers once the application goes live. Key goals of testing are for end-users to try out the new system, validate functionality, and compare OneStream reports with their existing reports.

Broadly speaking, testing should ensure the application is performing as expected and that users accept the operations of their new system. But with so much relying on a smooth transition from the legacy way, to what is expected to be a new streamlined, efficient, and faster way of working, testing can be broken down into further categories, each focusing on a different aspect of the platform.

As mentioned at the outset, the *OneStream Administrator Handbook* offers a detailed examination of testing and its various types, connecting them in a comprehensive manner. Here are some key testing headlines.

Unit and Integration Testing

This entails testing each of the artifacts (or a series of artifacts as a group) to verify that the outcome is as intended. A unit test could, for example, involve checking the output of a business rule. Alternatively, an import workflow task has been built, and an integration test is applied to verify that the data source and transformation rules are functioning correctly with the data being loaded, moved into the staging area, and then loaded into the cube.

Data Integrity and Data Validation Testing

Data integrity ensures that data is accurate from import to reporting, with any necessary calculations and adjustments applied in-between, resulting in the correct final value. Data validation provides an additional layer of data integrity, ensuring that the correct number in OneStream matches the one in the legacy system (this typically occurs when a parallel run has been executed). It is recommended – during this testing phase – to do at least one parallel testing cycle with the existing planning and reporting system against OneStream.

User Acceptance Testing (UAT)

After an initial training session with the testers (who will then be the core end-users), test scripts are produced that outline the steps required for a desired result. The training session demonstrates login and navigation around the platform, providing examples of how to pass or fail a test script. The hand-picked testers play a key part in the overall sign-off because, in addition to testing the new platform before rollout, they possess the expertise and business knowledge to accept or reject the outcome.

Performance Testing

This type of testing requires a coordinated effort to almost break the system with data loads and mimics many users logged in simultaneously. Ultimately, it provides the reassurance to Top Training that the design and configuration are 'beyond sufficient' to support the end-user experience.

Rollout

After testing has been signed off, the system will be ready to go live. The Rollout phase would have been planned by the Top Training project team months in advance for a smooth transition from their legacy system. This would have initially involved migrating from the old to the new system, training groups of users, and ensuring support was in place.

The key to a smooth transition is to assess the size of the rollout. If centralized (e.g., located solely at Top Training's corporate headquarters), then the project team should be situated in one place. If decentralized, both training and support teams will either travel to regional Top Training locations, or virtual coordinated efforts may have to take place. Another option for a decentralized approach is to phase the rollout, with each country having its own completion milestone before the rollout of the next country begins.

The training of the platform can be documented and saved within OneStream's File Explorer (inside the platform, where the training documentation can be uploaded into a public folder) or within dashboard files.

End-user support can take the form of straightforward IT support or – as in Top Training's case – there is a dedicated administrator from day one who has been appropriately trained and who knows the application; they are a subject matter expert in Top Training's business.

Eventually, the support mechanism may grow into its own function, evolving to a center of excellence (CoE) setup. This will involve a team of individuals dedicated to supporting the OneStream Application. The team is represented by members who have a direct impact on OneStream (i.e., systems, finance, and audit functions).

The points to consider for a dedicated and successful center of excellence model:

Roles and Responsibilities

Roles and responsibilities are defined, with the main administrator of the application providing the leadership to sub-administrators and power users, as well as subject matter experts around Top Training.

The CoE should have access on a global scale to individual expertise across the various functions that have a direct connection with the platform.

Governance

Decision-making processes and sign-off from various reporting lines are implemented to deliver effective and efficient changes to the application as needed.

To ensure the CoE stays aligned with organizational goals and strategies, the CoE team works closely with internal stakeholders who provide support where needed, alongside buy-in from a member of the executive leadership team. This will help with securing necessary resources, including funding and personnel.

Additionally, a steering committee can be formed to provide guidance and oversight. This can be made up of individuals from various departments with specialized knowledge, and seniors with decision-making powers.

Central Repository

A go-to repository set up for project documentation, best practices, and naming conventions that have been adopted, plus tools and training resources available for users.

Improvement and Innovation

Improvement can come from continuous feedback on the platform, in terms of agreed-upon KPIs (including performance), or agreed-upon reporting cycle targets. Innovation can take the form of identifying other areas in Top Training that will benefit from Solution Exchange use cases.

Troubleshooting – You've Got This!

After the Rollout phase, and the application is in full use, a good training program will aid users with the knowledge of what to do in a given situation (e.g., a file will not load, or data entry in a cell is not possible when it should be, or reports will not render correctly). Where the solution lies beyond an end-user's platform access, the administrator (and ultimately the Center of Excellence team) will provide a permanent fix by updating a design or configuration feature. This part of the chapter will cover some examples of this.

Roll-up of Data

Account dimension settings apply financial intelligence to the roll-up of data. An example of an issue here might be if the values in the parent do not aggregate correctly, for example, Net Sales incorrectly sums up the child, Operating Sales and Operating Cost of Goods Sold (the child of Operating Sales) when it should be the difference.

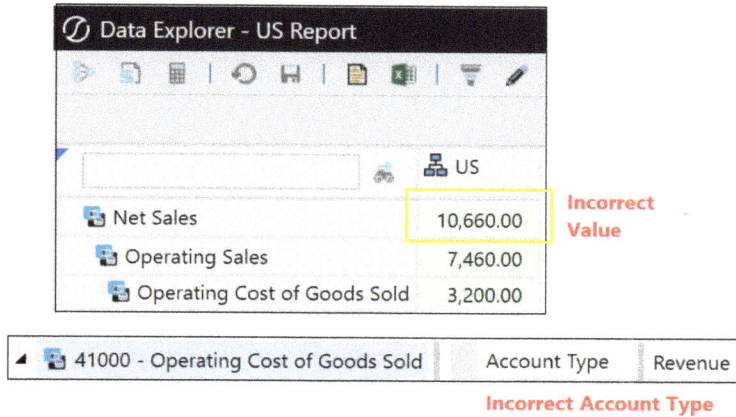

Figure 10.2

Here, the Account Type needs to be amended (from the default Revenue Account Type) so that the Operating Cost of Goods Sold is an Expense Account Type.

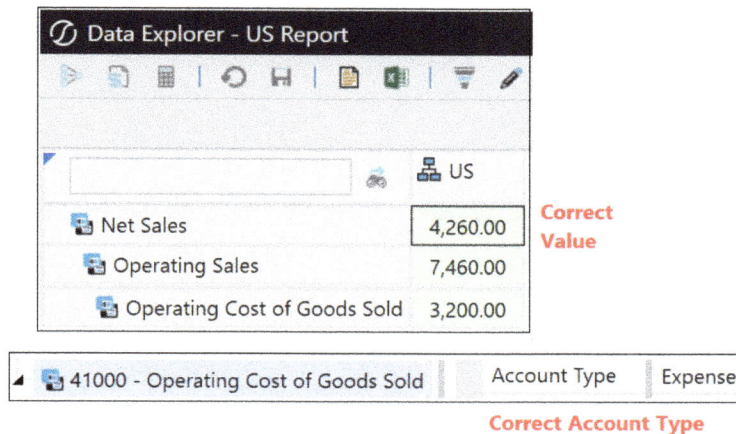

Figure 10.3

Aggregation Weight

Another reason for an incorrect roll-up in an Account member can be due to an incorrect Aggregation Weight setting (default is 1) in the Relationship Properties tab.

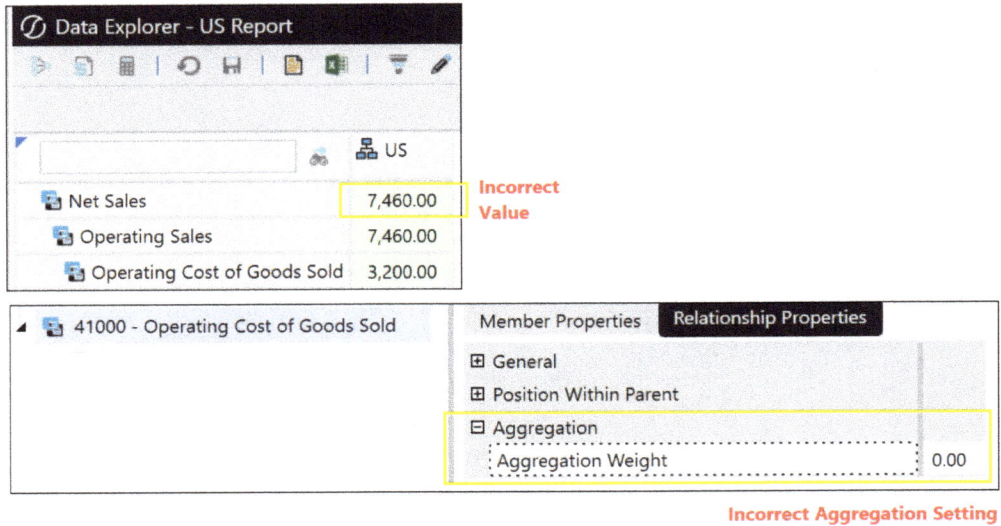

Figure 10.4

Amend the Aggregation Weight for the Operating Cost of Goods Sold. Here, we have changed the Aggregation Weight to 1.00, which means the whole amount is now rolled up to Net Sales (as the Operating Cost of Goods Sold Account Type is set to Expense, the amount is deducted from Operating Sales).

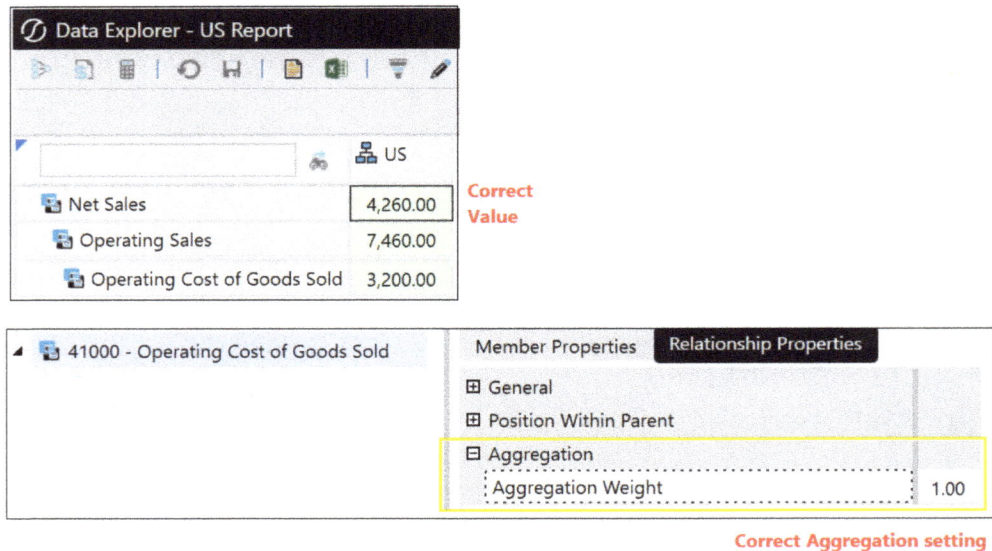

Figure 10.5

Aggregation Property Configuration

The Aggregation configuration property in the **Account Dimension Type** provides the option *not* to roll up data if it doesn't need to be reported on, or if the base members have unique values (so that rolling up does not make sense). An example might be the 'unit price' of each product.

If data is not rolling up to the parent in the Cube View but should be, then check that the account's Aggregation property is set to True (which is the default setting). This applies to all the other dimension types, too.

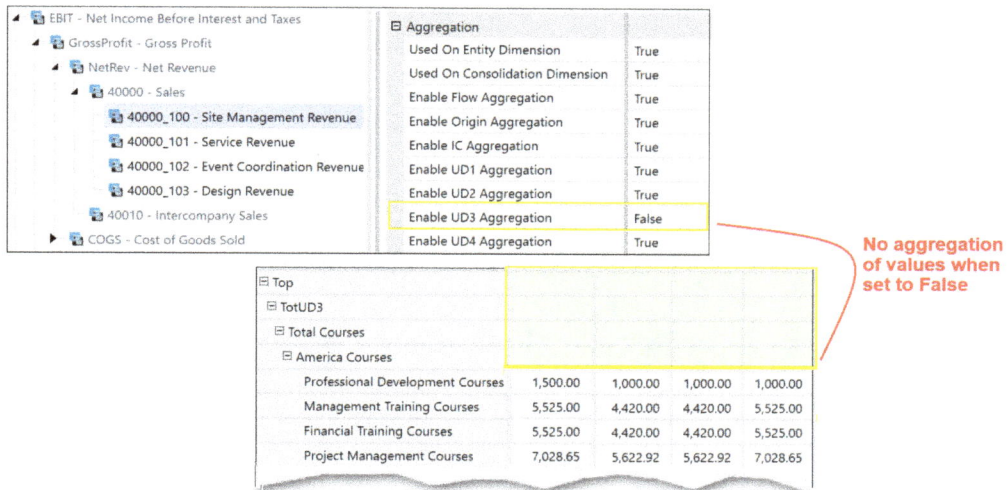

Figure 10.6

Changing the configuration will then roll up the values.

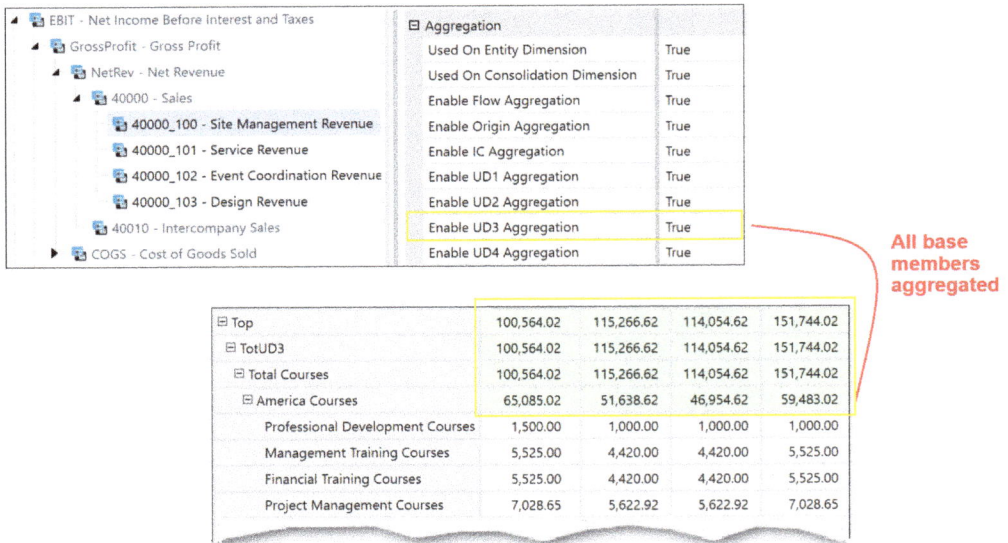

Figure 10.7

Account Dimension Type – Allow Input configuration

If data in the Cube View cell is read-only green, but should be writable white, check that the Account dimension member's Allow Input has been correctly selected as True.

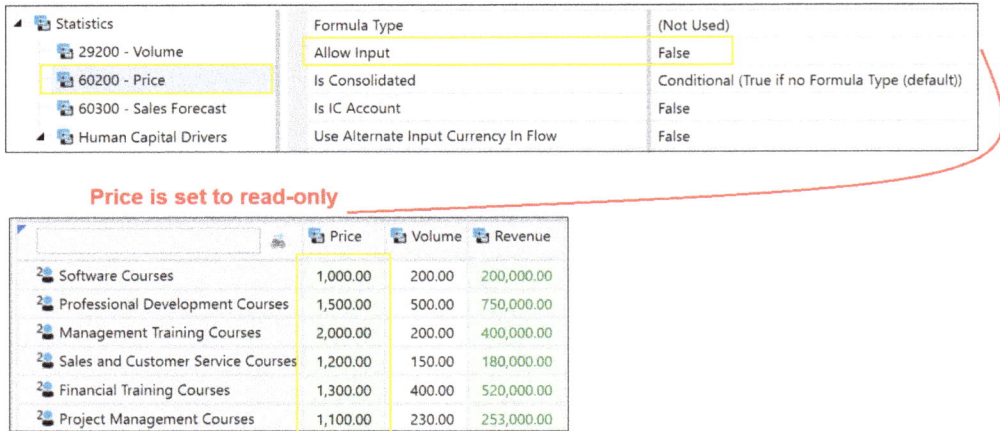

Figure 10.8

Changing the configuration to True will make cells writable as long as the Cube
View's Can Modify Data is set to True.

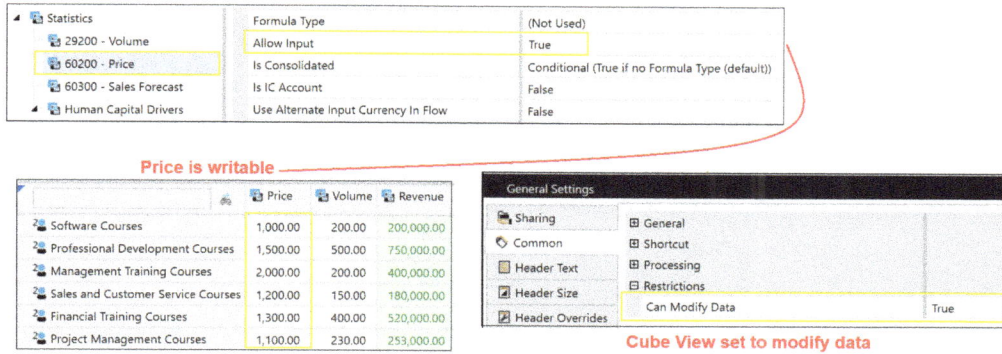

Figure 10.9

Missing Currency Code

If a currency code is missing when entering or importing currency rates, then there
will be a requirement to go to the Application Properties menu to select the Currency
Filter, and add the required **Currency Code.**

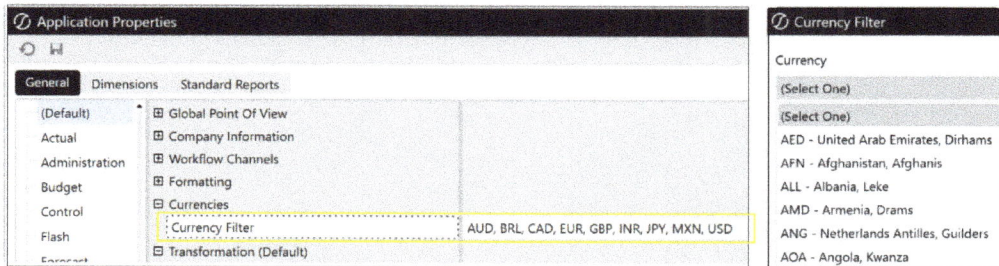

Figure 10.10

Preventing Import Errors

When setting application properties, Point Of View fields need to be populated for
both Global Scenario and Global Time. These settings gets overlooked if the Global
POV is not integrated into the client's processes. However, it only needs to be
completed once (but updated when required), and doing so will then prevent any
import errors related to missing POV settings.

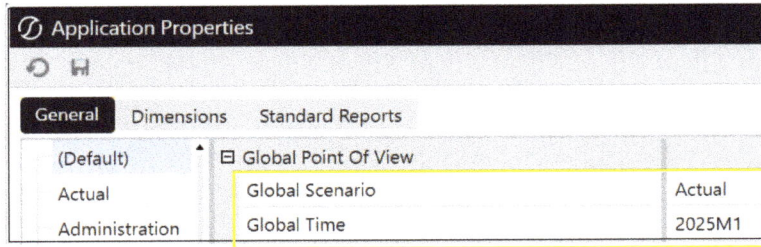

Figure 10.11

Source Dimension for Data Source

When creating the data source, if the source dimensions are missing or not required, you can use the Create Source Dimension or Delete Selected Item icons in the data sources, or revert to the Integration tab in the Cubes menu to either have the dimension in the data source menu or not.

Integration > Settings > Enabled set to True uses the dimension in the data source menu; False will prevent it from being available to map to the source file.

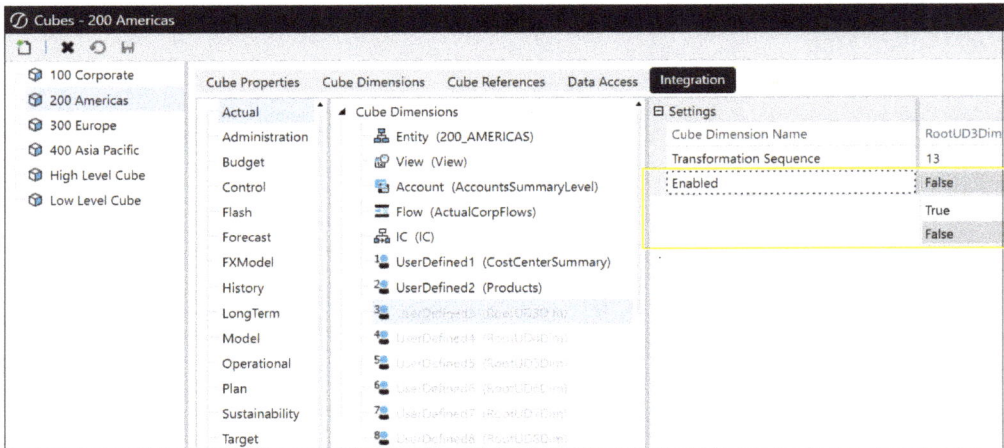

Figure 10.12

Data Load Errors

If errors occur when loading data and the Global Point of View in Application Properties has been set appropriately, then you should check the transformation rules. A mapping might not exist, or the **Transformation Rule Group** is not assigned to a **Transformation Rule Profile**.

Data will then need to be re-validated after the transformation rule error has been corrected.

If the transformation rules are now correct but a validation error is stopping the data load, then check for dimension members that do not exist or which are incorrectly mapped (for example, to a parent member). Data cannot be loaded to a parent member and will cause an intersection error. Alternatively, check that entities have not been missed out when being assigned to the workflow.

Cube View Errors

If a Cube View is not visible in certain places around the platform when it should be – for example in OnePlace, Spreadsheet, or forms – check the visibility option in the Cube View Profile that holds the Cube View group where the Cube View resides.

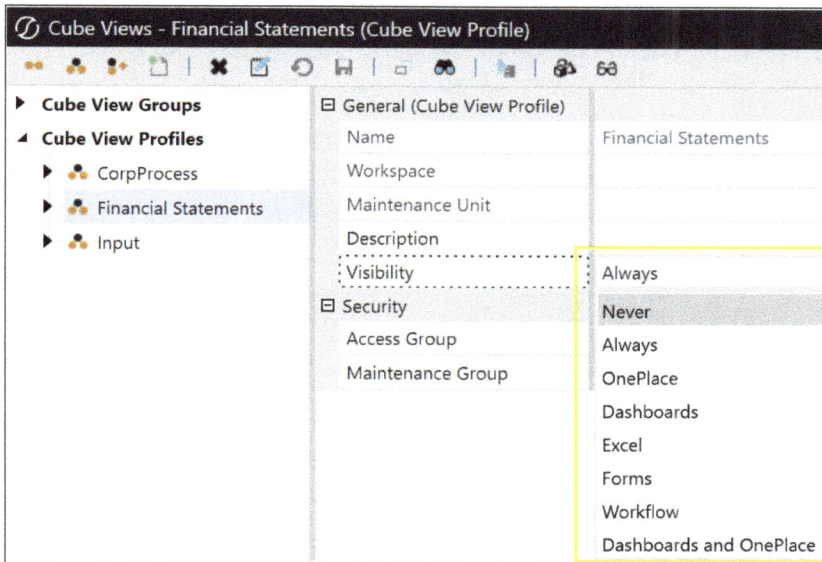

Figure 10.13

Cannot Modify Data

A Cube View has various settings in the General Settings slider menu. If the Cube View is read-only but requires data to be entered manually in a cell, check that Can Modify Data is set to True in the Common section.

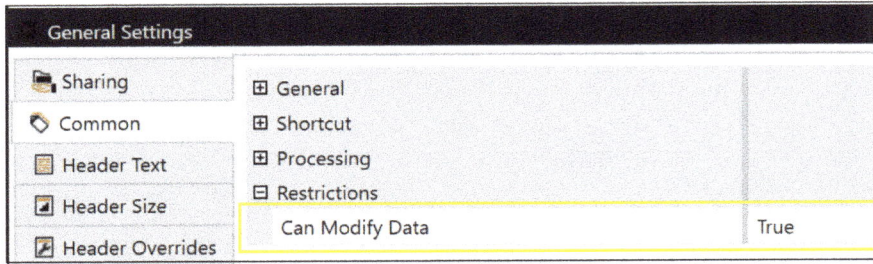

Cube View set to modify data

Figure 10.14

Other places to check Can Modify Data are in the rows and columns definitions.

Rows and Columns Dimension Type Selection Required

If you use a Member Filter to populate rows and columns, there will be an error when running the Cube View if the correct dimension is not selected against the dimension token in the Member Filter. This is solved by checking the Member Filter Dimension Type has been selected from the drop-down to the left of the Member Filter field before running the Cube View, as shown in Figure 10.15.

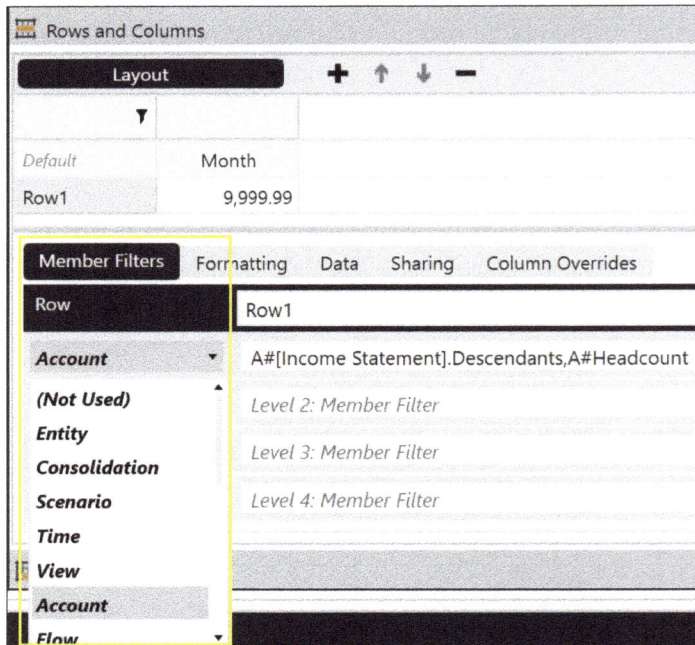

Figure 10.15

Cube View Cell POV

The Cell POV information can help troubleshoot an unexpected cell value. This is done by viewing each dimension member to then conclude if there is an incorrect selection of a member.

Member Script And Formula Syntax uses Cb# which represents the dimension tag for the cube, with the script providing the interections for Cube View troubleshooting, XFGetCell for Spreadsheet troubleshooting, and XFCell for extensible documents.

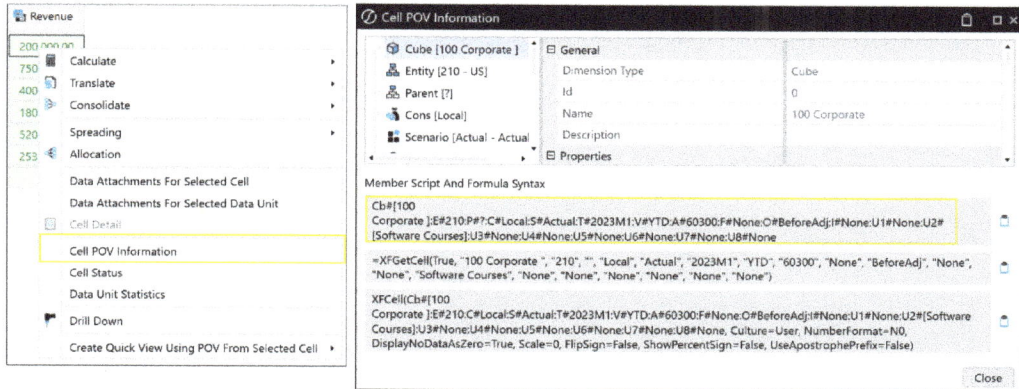

Figure 10.16

Drill Down

When investigating cell values, Drill Down is a useful tool. It is opened by right-clicking a cell and selecting Drill Down. When a new window opens, the amount in the cell, cube names, and all the dimension types with their selected members are shown.

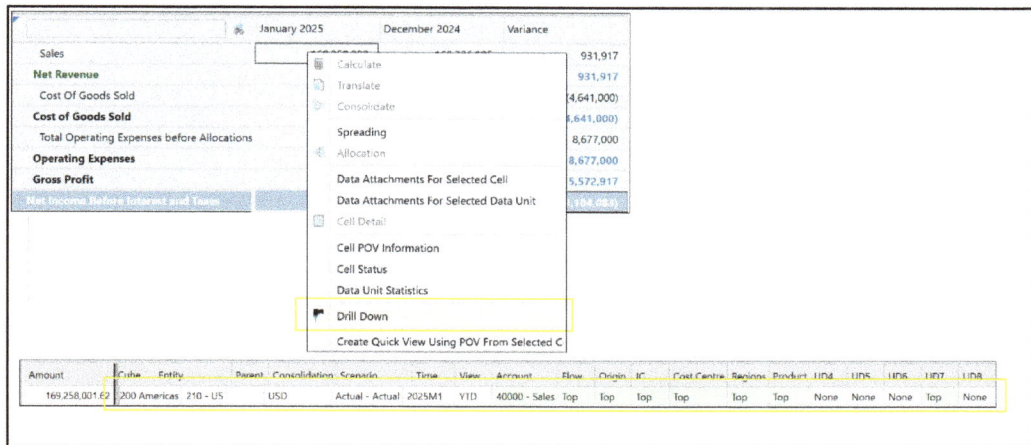

Figure 10.17

From the first drill down window of Figure 10.17, further analyses can be performed by drilling down on the members that have a green cell background, as shown in Figure 10.18.

ount	Cube	Entity	Parent	Consolidation	Scenario	Time	View	Account	Flow	Origin	IC
169,258,001.62	200 Americas	210 - US		USD	Actual - Actual	2025M1	YTD	40000 - Sales	Top	Top	Top	Top
169,258,001.62	200 Americas	210 - US		USD	Actual - Actual	2025M1	YTD	40000 - Sales	Top	Top	Top	Top

Results For Most Recent Drill Down

ount	Cube	Entity	Parent	Consolidation	Scenario	Time	View	Account	Flow	Origin	IC
4,152,276.00	200 Americas	210 - US		USD	Actual - Actual	2025M1	YTD	40000_101 - Service Revenue	None	Import	None
4,146,360.00	200 Americas	210 - US		USD	Actual - Actual	2025M1	YTD	40000_101 - Service Revenue	None	Import	None
4,363,310.00	200 Americas	210 - US		USD	Actual - Actual	2025M1	YTD	40000_101 - Service Revenue	None	Import	None
4,582,458.00	200 Americas	210 - US		USD	Actual - Actual	2025M1	YTD	40000_101 - Service Revenue	None	Import	None
4,575,449.00	200 Americas	210 - US		USD	Actual - Actual	2025M1	YTD	40000_101 - Service Revenue	None	Import	None

Figure 10.18

If the Origin dimension is showing the member O#Import, a right-click provides the ability to select Load Results for Imported Cell. The Navigate to Source Data button provides further options to drill down and revisit the original source document if required.

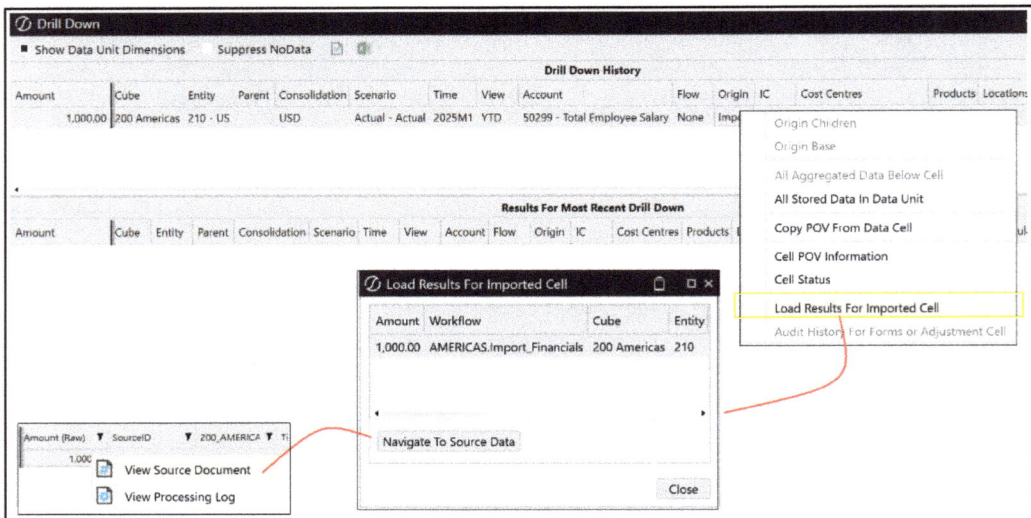

Figure 10.19

Audit History

Audit History For Forms or Adjustment Cell will be available for any base intersection Origin members that are showing O#Forms or O#AdjInput members in the initial drill down.

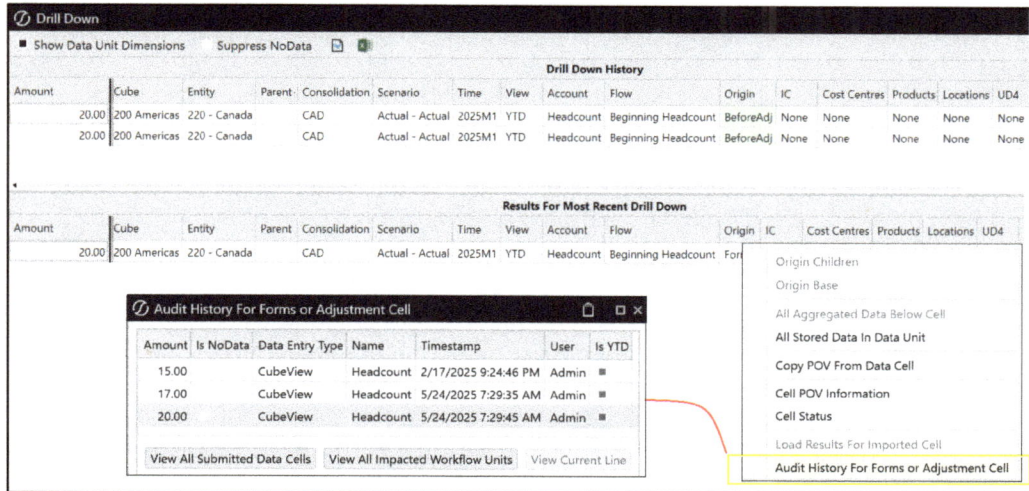

Figure 10.20

Workflow Profile

Check to see whether the Workflow Profile configuration includes the required artifacts (for example, Data Source, Transformation Rule Profile, Confirmation Rule Profile, Certification Questions, Form Profiles, Journal Profile).

When the Workflow Profile has been created with a task, but the end-user cannot see it, this can be due to security, where the user has not been assigned to the security group responsible for the task.

In turn, check that the Profile Active has been set to True for the Scenario Type the user is working on.

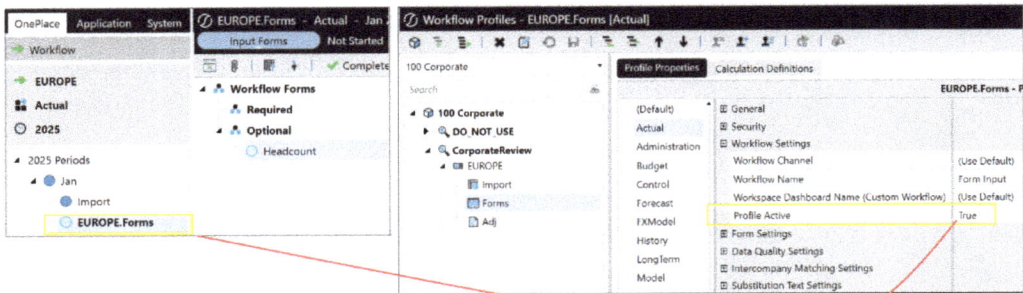

Figure 10.21

Task Activity and Processing Log

Task Activity can be used to review error messages to pinpoint where a process may have failed. The workflow has a configuration setting to initiate further detailed logging, which explains the various task types by description that can be drilled down further, along with the server's name and duration of the task. This feature is usually only turned on for a short while to avoid the log file filling up unnecessarily.

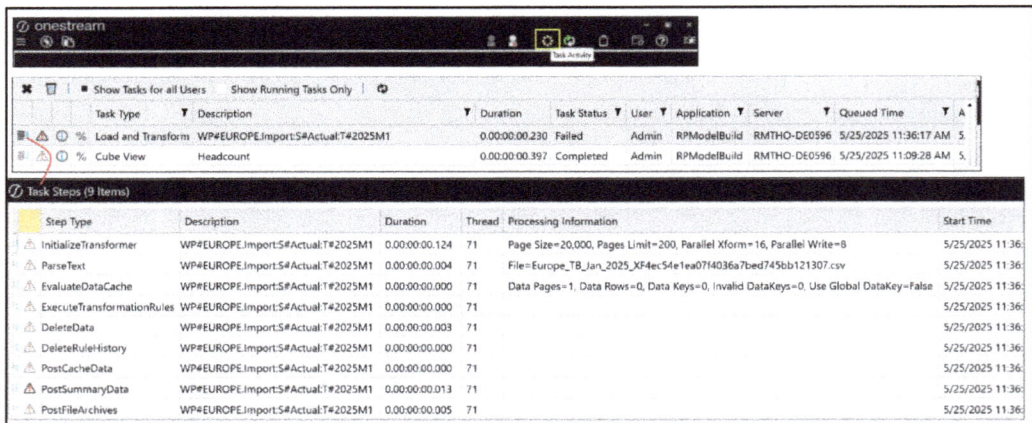

Figure 10.22

For detailed information, such as data source import errors (which may result from dimension types not being defined in the data source, or an incorrect file format), the processing log can be accessed by clicking the View Last Log File Processed For Current Workflow Profile button.

Once opened, the log codes can be used to determine the cause of the error.

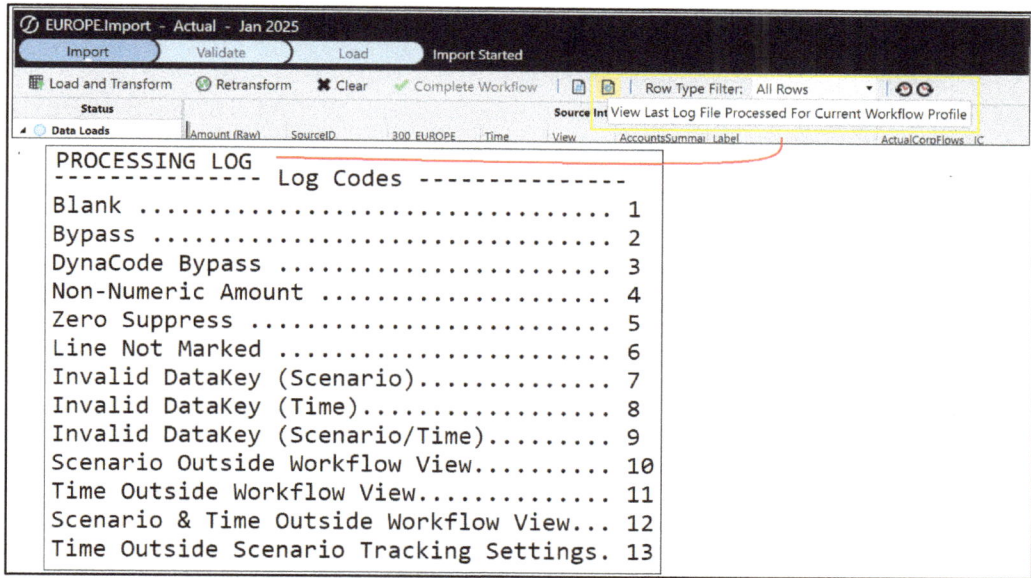

Figure 10.23

Dashboard Issues

As already pointed out, when building dashboards, a standard and *consistent* practice needs to be adopted. This is not only to have a neat and logical setup, but also to make troubleshooting issues faster and easier to locate. Certain issues – such as data adapters not being used by components, or buttons not being configured to have an action, or the combo box not showing a drop-down due to a missing parameter – can all be deduced by working backwards to locate the missing part.

Carry On Learning

With OneStream being a multifunctional platform that covers many use cases and constantly evolves, the learning doesn't just stop. This book aims to cover the fundamental aspects of the platform, which will serve as the basis for understanding and utilizing OneStream effectively.

With further features and best practices being introduced, the knowledge already obtained so far can be elevated by embracing additional OneStream book publications, Navigator, OneCommunity, and by attending various OneStream events.

Conclusion

In some ways, this chapter has brought us to the end of the book with the beginnings of how an organisation learns about OneStream projects. We can then circle back to the first chapter, where we introduced the platform.

A project can never be risk-free, but it can be minimized by adopting the structured phases and good practices discussed in this chapter. Collaborating with the client to form a project team, plus having a sponsor and buy-in from stakeholders, will help make a project a success. In turn, the design document will provide a template during the build and then become a resource for the administrator of the OneStream platform.

Above, we discussed how testing is an important phase in any project, but it is also an ongoing concern. When an administrator manages the platform to meet further business requirements, testing in the development environment will still take place before said addition or enhancement is migrated to production.

The administrator, often regarded as the knowledgeable expert on OneStream, works either independently or as part of a center of excellence team and possesses the skills to overcome business challenges within the platform. Business experience and a knowledge of the platform build enable the administrator to be well-equipped for troubleshooting eventualities. Knowing how to solve issues with minimal disruption to the business can only add kudos and recognition as a OneStream specialist.

Thank you for being part of the OneStream journey over the course of this book. Much has been learned, and you are now well-positioned to further discover the full potential of OneStream as part of your personal voyage. Go have fun with it!

Index

Access Group - 41, 137

Account Dimension - 9, 45, 56, 227, 228

Account Movements - 59

Account Reconciliations - 14

Account Type - 56, 120

Accounts, Supplemental - 2

Accumulate - 171

Actuals - 52

Administrator - 3, 6

Administrator Solution Tool - 129

Administrator, Application - 8

Administrator, System - 8

Aggregation Property Configuration - 227

Aggregation Weight - 56, 59, 120, 225

Alternate Hierarchies, Entity Business Areas - 50

Alternate Hierarchy - 24

Analysis - 63, 219

Ancestors - 23

api.data.calculate - 116

Append - 138

Application Administrator - 8

Application Artifacts - 71

Application Groups - 192

Application Properties and FX Rates - 37

Application Reports - 129, 148

Application Security Roles - 41

Application, Creating a New - 19

Artifacts - 8

Attribute Dimensions - 187

Audit History - 235

Base Input - 28

Base Input Profiles - 132

Base Level Tasks - 30

Base Member - 21, 22

BI Viewer - 206

Blanket Cell Formatting - 176

Bound List - 174

Browser UX (BUX) - 19

Build - 221

Business Rules - 112

Button - 206

Calculation Definitions - 148

Calculation Documentation Matrix - 128

Calculation Section, Spreadsheet - 180

Calculation Status - 122, 123

Calculations - 2, 109, 121, 123

Calculations, Cube Views - 167

Calculations, Dynamic - 111

Cannot Modify Data - 231

CB Syntax - 166

Cell Colors - 166

Cell POV Information - 166, 183

Central Import - 33

Central Repository - 224

Index

Certification Exams - 4

Certification Profile Name - 144

Certification Questions - 11

Certification Signoff Group - 137

Certify - 32

Chart (Advanced) - 206

Child - 21, 22

Clone Member - 68

Close - 2

Cloud Administration Tool - 20

Colors and Styles - 203

Colors, Cell - 166

Column Expressions - 117

Column Overrides - 175

Columns, Dimension Type Selection Required - 232

Columns, Slider - 162

Combo Box - 205

Components - 213

Composite Mapping - 103

Conditional Formatting - 178

Conditional Rule Type - 113

Configurable Dimensions - 48, 60

Confirm - 32

Confirmation Profile Name - 142

Confirmation Rules - 11

Connector Rule Type - 113

Connectors - 92

Consolidation - 2, 12, 46, 121

Consolidation Dimension - 10, 62

Consolidation Process, Entity - 50

Constraints, Member Property - 72

Content Blocks - 194

Corporate Only Workflow - 33

Corporate Performance Management - 1

Cube - 10, 110

Cube - 75

Cube Dimension - 25

Cube Point of View (POV) - 18, 26

Cube Properties - 24, 77

Cube References - 81

Cube Root Workflow Profile - 134

Cube Selection - 80

Cube View - 11, 34, 156

Cube View Advanced - 197

Cube View Calculations - 114

Cube View Cell POV - 233

Cube View Charts - 198

Cube View Errors - 231

Cube View Expressions - 168

Cube View Group - 159, 212

Cube View Icons - 124

Cube View Math - 168

Cube View Member Filter Builder - 116

Cube View Spreadsheet - 199

Cube View, Building - 158

Cube View, Calculations - 167

Cube View, Copying - 164

Cube View, Formatting - 175

Cube View, Running - 165

Cube View, Spreadsheets - 182

Cube, Building - 77

Cube, Dimensions - 24

Cube, Exclusive - 76

Cube, Existing, New - 88

Cube, Super, Detail - 76

Cubes, Monolithic, Specialty - 76

Currencies - 63

Currency Code, Missing - 229

Currency Filter - 37

Currency Setting - 51

Custom Calculation - 128

Dashboard Button - 127

Dashboard Groups - 211

Dashboard Issues - 237

Dashboard Layout - 199, 209

Dashboard Overview, Workspaces - 204

Dashboard, Constructing - 210

Dashboard, Designing - 208

Dashboards - 2, 11, 34, 156, 189

Data Access - 82

Data Adapters - 207, 213

Data Binding Type - 54

Data Buffer - 110

Data Cell Values - 166

Data Explorer - 156, 165

Data Import Preparation - 91

Data Integrity, Data Validation Testing - 222

Data Load Errors - 230

Data Load Methods - 138

Data Management Export Sequences - 92

Data Management Job - 125

Data Point - 24

Data Roll-Up - 224

Data Source Types - 92

Data Source, Creating - 93

Data Source, Source Dimension - 230

Data Source, Transformation Profile Name - 139

Data Source, Transformation Rule Process - 106

Data Spreading Options - 169

Data Unit - 84, 110

Data Unit Calculation Sequence - 128

Data Validation Testing, Data Integrity - 222

Data, Not Rolling Up - 227

DataQualityEventHandler - 149

Default Reporting Currency - 78

Delimited File Data Source, Creating - 93

Delimited Files - 92

Delimited List - 174

Descendants - 23

Design - 220

Design and Reference Guide - 8

Designer - 160

Developer - 5

Dimension Library - 45, 48

Dimension Token - 163

Dimension Type - 45

Dimension, Account - 9, 56, 227, 228

Dimension, Consolidation - 10, 62

Dimension, Cube - 25

Dimension, Entity - 9, 49

Index

Dimension, Flow - 10, 59

Dimension, Importing, Members - 71

Dimension, Intercompany - 60

Dimension, Origin - 10, 63

Dimension, Parent - 60

Dimension, Scenario - 9, 52

Dimension, Time - 10, 61

Dimension, User Defined - 10, 59

Dimension, View - 10, 64

Dimensions - 9, 20, 21

Dimensions and Members, Naming Conventions - 66

Dimensions, Building - 66

Dimensions, Configurable - 48, 60

Dimensions, Cube - 24

Dimensions, Designing - 45

Dimensions, Mapping To Source File - 94

Dimensions, System-Defined - 63

Direct Rule - 79

Distribution, 445, 454, 544 - 170

Distribution, Proportional - 171

Divide Function - 116

Do Not Use Structure - 136

Drill Down - 183, 233

Dynamic Calculations - 111

Dynamic Cash Flow - 15

Eliminations - 2, 121

Enterprise Performance Management - 1

Enterprise Resource Planning - 1

Enterprise Tax Reporting - 14

Entity - 45

Entity Assignment - 149

Entity Business Areas and Alternate Hierarchies - 50

Entity Dimension - 9, 49

Entity, Consolidation Process - 50

Even Distribution - 169

Even Level Hierarchy - 23

Eventhandler - 149

Exams, Certification - 4

Excel Add-in, Spreadsheet - 156

Excel Metadata Builder Tool - 71

Exclusive Cube - 76

Explore and Analysis, Spreadsheet - 180

Expressions - 112, 115

Extensibility - 13, 11, 35, 46, 85, 155, 221

Factor - 171

File Explorer - 18

Fill - 170

Finance Rule Type - 113

Financial Statements - 2

First Trap Method - 104

Fixed File Data Source, Creating - 99

Fixed Files - 92

Flow Dimension - 10, 46, 59

Form Templates - 140

Forms - 10, 30, 155

Formula List Report - 129

Formula Statistics Report - 129

Functions - 118

FX Currencies - 39

FX Rates - 10, 37, 39

General Settings Slider - 161

Genesis - 189

Genesis Designer - 191

Genesis Framework - 191

Genesis Navigation - 191

Genesis, Installation - 190

GetDataCell - 115

Global Point of View - 37

Governance - 223

Graphical User Interface - 18

Grid - 209

Grid View - 70

Grid View, Multiple Configurations - 70

Group - 40

Hierarchy, Alternate - 24, 50

Hierarchy, Even Level - 23

Hierarchy, Management - 51

Hierarchy, Ragged - 23

Hierarchy, Statutory - 51

Historic - 52

Home Page - 196

Horizontal Extensibility - 86, 88

Horizontal Stack Panel - 210

Image - 207

Import - 10, 30

Import Errors, Preventing - 229

Import, Central - 33

Improvement and Innovation - 224

Incentive Compensation Management - 14

Indentations - 176

Injected - 195

In-Memory - 111

Input Forms Profile Name - 140

Input Value - 174

Integration - 82

Integration Testing, Unit - 222

Intercompany - 10, 46, 58

Intercompany Dimension - 60

Intercompany Matching Settings - 146

Intercompany Trading - 51

Journal Input - 31

Journal Template - 31

Journal Template Group - 141

Journal Template Profile Name - 141

Journals - 11

KPI Tile - 201

Label - 205

Label Source Dimensions - 187

Learning Management System - 4

Lease Accounting - 15

List - 103

Literal Parameter, Formatting Using - 177

Literal Value - 174

Index

Load - 30

Lock After Certify - 37

Logo - 205

Lowest (Base) Level Tasks - 30

Maintenance Group - 41, 137

Maintenance Unit - 211

Management Hierarchy - 51

Management Structure - 51

Mask - 104

Matching - 146

Matrix Data Key - 100

Matrix Data Source - 100

Member Dialog - 174

Member Filter - 162

Member Filter Builder - 114

Member Filter Builder, Cube View - 116

Member Formula - 53

Member Formula Builder - 129

Member Formulas - 113

Member Hierarchies - 21

Member List - 174

Member Properties - 72

Member, Clone - 68

Member, Creation - 68

Members - 20

Members, None Member - 47

Metadata - 20

Method Query - 207

Micro Courses - 8

Missing Currency Code - 229

Modern Browser Experience - 19, 191

Monolithic Cubes - 76

Multi-Period Processing - 33

Naming Conventions, Creating Dimensions and Members - 66

Navigation Groups - 193

Navigator - 4

None Member - 47, 61

Object - 40, 41

Office of Finance - 2

OneStream Community - 4

OneStream Login, Spreadsheet - 180

OneStream Parcel Service - 184

OneStream Support Site - 8

One-To-One - 102

Origin Dimension - 10, 46, 63

Overrides - 163

Pages - 193

Parameters - 165, 173, 213

Parameters, Substitution Variables - 172

Parent - 10, 21, 46

Parent Dimension - 60

Parent Input - 28

Parent Input Profiles - 132

Parent Member - 22

Parser Rule Type - 113

Percent Consolidation - 50

Performance Testing - 222

Periodic Rule - 79

Pivot Grid - 201

Planning - 12

Plug Account - 58

Point Of View (POV) Settings - 18

POV Slider - 160

Pre-Process - 30

Process - 31

Processing Log, Task Activity - 236

Profile Active - 139

Profile Properties - 137

Project Implementation - 219

Project Manager - 5

Proportional Distribution - 171

Question Group - 145

Questions, Certification - 11

Quick Certify - 32, 145

Quick Views - 26

Quick Views, Spreadsheets - 181

Ragged Hierarchy - 23

Range - 103

Refresh and Submit, Spreadsheet - 180

Relationship, Selected Member - 50

Replace - 138

Report Books - 11, 37, 155, 184

Report Footer - 164

Report Header - 162

Report Types - 155

Report Viewer - 34, 156, 165

Report Writer - 7

Reporting - 2, 34, 189

Reporting Currency, Default - 78

Reporting, Store Data - 186

Review - 28

Review Profiles - 133

Role - 41, 223

Rollout - 223

Roll-Up, Data - 224

RootDim - 66

Row Expressions - 117

Row Overrides - 163, 175

Rows, Dimension Type Selection Required - 232

Rows, Slider - 162

Rule Types - 112

Scenario - 45

Scenario Dimension - 9, 52

Scenario Type - 25, 53

Security - 11, 40, 72, 137

Security Roles, Application - 41

Security Roles, System - 43

Selection Styles - 183

Siblings - 21, 22

Slice Security - 82

Slider, Rows, Columns - 162

Snippets - 118

Solution Exchange - 8

Source Dimension, Data Source - 230

Specialty Cubes - 76

Spreading - 183

Spreading, Spreadsheet - 180

Index

Spreading, Types - 169

Spreadsheet - 180

Spreadsheet Retrieve - 182

Spreadsheet Tree - 202

Spreadsheet, Calculation Section - 180

Spreadsheet, Excel Add-in - 156

Spreadsheet, Explore and Analysis - 180

Spreadsheet, OneStream Login - 180

Spreadsheet, Refresh and Submit - 180

Spreadsheets - 11, 34, 36

Spreadsheets, Cube Views - 182

Spreadsheets, Quick Views - 181

Stack Panels - 210

Standard Reports - 39

Standard Time - 61

Statutory Hierarchy - 51

Statutory Reports - 51

Store Data, Reporting - 186

Stored Calculations - 110

Styles and Colors - 203

Subject Matter Expert - 7

Substitution Variables - 172

Supplemental Accounts - 2

Suppression Formatting - 179

Syntax - 118

System Administrator - 8

System Security Roles - 43

System-Defined Dimensions - 63

Table Views - 37

Tabs - 209

Task Activity, Processing Log - 236

Task Manager (UTM) - 14

Test - 221

Time - 46

Time Dimension - 10, 61

Time Profile - 46

Top - 62

Training - 3

Transaction Matching - 14

Transformation Profile Name, Data Source - 139

Transformation Rule Group - 230

Transformation Rule Process, Data Source - 106

Transformation Rule Profile - 230

Transformation Rules - 11, 101, 102

Transformation Rules, Groups and Profiles - 104

Translations - 2, 121

Troubleshooting - 219, 224

Uniform - 210

Unit, Integration Testing - 222

User - 40

User Acceptance Testing - 222

User Defined (UD) Dimension - 10, 46, 59

Validate - 30

Variance Function - 116

VariancePercent Function - 116

Vertical Extensibility - 86

Vertical Stack Panel - 210

View - 46

View Dimension - 10, 64, 119

Workflow - 2, 11, 27, 131

Workflow Execution Group - 137

Workflow Name - 137

Workflow Point of View - 27

Workflow Profile - 235

Workflow Profile Types - 131

Workflow Profile, Cube Root - 134

Workflow Profiles - 127

Workflow Suffix - 150

Workflow Tasks - 30

Workflow Template - 151

Workflow, Constructing - 134

Workflow, Default - 135

Workspace - 32

Workspace, Shared, Link an Existing
Content Item - 202

Workspaces - 156, 210

Workspaces, Dashboard Overview - 204

XML files, Loading - 71

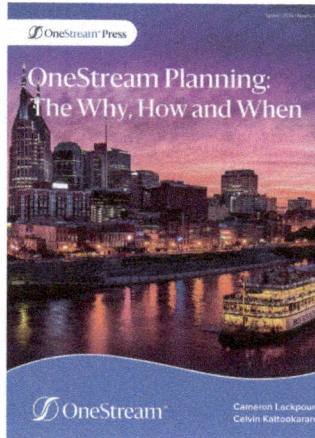

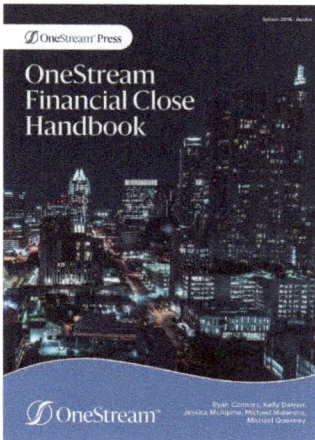

You can learn more about all
OneStream Press's books and PDFs at:

www.OneStreamPress.com

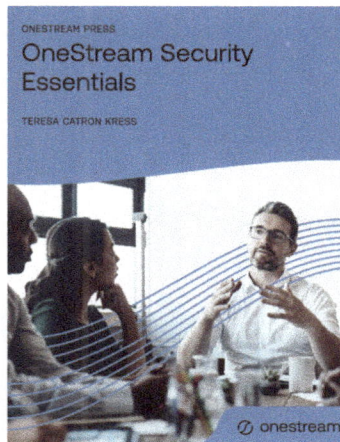

www.ingramcontent.com/pod-product-compliance
Lightning Source LLC
Chambersburg PA
CBHW050236220326
41598CB00044B/7412